SLIPPING AWAY

DISLOCATIONS

General Editors: August Carbonella, *Memorial University of Newfoundland,* Don Kalb, *University of Utrecht & Central European University,* Linda Green, *University of Arizona*

The immense dislocations and suffering caused by neoliberal globalization, the retreat of the welfare state in the last decades of the twentieth century, and the heightened military imperialism at the turn of the twenty-first century have raised urgent questions about the temporal and spatial dimensions of power. Through stimulating critical perspectives and new and cross-disciplinary frameworks that reflect recent innovations in the social and human sciences, this series provides a forum for politically engaged and theoretically imaginative responses to these important issues of late modernity.

Volume 1
Where Have All the Homeless Gone?: The Making and Unmaking of a Crisis
    Anthony Marcus

Volume 2
Blood and Oranges: European Markets and Immigrant Labor in Rural Greece
    Christopher M. Lawrence

Volume 3
Struggles for Home: Violence, Hope and the Movement of People
    Edited by Stef Jansen and Staffan Löfving

Volume 4
Slipping Away: Banana Politics and Fair Trade in the Eastern Caribbean
    Mark Moberg

SLIPPING AWAY

Banana Politics and Fair Trade
in the Eastern Caribbean

Mark Moberg

Berghahn Books
NEW YORK • OXFORD

First published in 2008 by

Berghahn Books

www.berghahnbooks.com

©2008, 2011 Mark Moberg
First paperback edition published in 2011

Library of Congress Cataloging-in-Publication Data

Moberg, Mark, 1959–
    Slipping away : banana politics and fair trade in the Eastern Caribbean / Mark
Moberg.
        p. cm. — (Dislocations ; 4)
    Includes bibliographical references and index.
    ISBN 978-1-84545-145-5 (hbk)— ISBN 978-1-84545-197-4 (pbk)
    1. Banana trade—Saint Lucia.   2. Banana growers—Saint Lucia.
3. Globalization—Economic aspects—Saint Lucia.   4. Competition, Unfair.
I. Title.

HD9259.B3S1736 2008
382′.41477209729843—dc22

                                                            2008032704

British Library Cataloguing in Publication Data

A catalogue record for this book is available from the British Library

Printed in the United States on acid-free paper.

ISBN: 978-1-84545-145-5 hardback
ISBN: 978-1-84545-197-4 paperback

For Tawnya

CONTENTS

LIST OF FIGURES

LIST OF TABLES

LIST OF ABBREVIATIONS

ACP	African, Caribbean and Pacific countries
BERU	Banana Emergency Recovery Unit (Government of St. Lucia)
BGA	Banana Growers' Association
BSC	Banana Salvation Committee
COLSIBA	Confederación Latinoamericana de Sindicatos Bananeros
DBCP	1,2-Dibromo-3-chloropropane
EC $	Eastern Caribbean dollar (EC $1.00=US $0.38)
ECU	European Currency Unit
EU	European Union
EUREP GAP	European Retailers' Working Group Good Agricultural Practices
EUROBAN	European Banana Action Network
FLO	Fairtrade Labeling Organizations International
GATT	General Agreement on Tariffs and Trade
HYV	High Yielding Variety
ICCR	Interfaith Center on Corporate Responsibility
ILO	International Labor Organization (of the United Nations)
IMF	International Monetary Fund
IRDC	Inland Reception and Distribution Centre
JBPA	Jamaica Banana Producers' Association
MVDP	Mabouya Valley Development Project
NDM	National Development Movement

NDP	New Democratic Party
NJM	New Jewel Movement
OAS	Organization of American States
ONE	Organization for National Empowerment
PUWS	Percent Units Within Specifications
SLAM	St. Lucia Action Movement
SLBC	St. Lucia Banana Company
SLNFTA	St. Lucia National Fair Trade Association
SLP	St. Lucia Labour Party
SSU	Special Services Unit
STABEX	Système de Stabilisation des Recettes d'Exportation
STEP	Short Term Employment Programme
TQFC	Total Quality Fruit Company
UFCO	United Fruit Company
ULP	United Labour Party
UWP	United Workers' Party
VAT	Value Added Tax
WIBDECO	Windward Islands Banana Development and Exporting Company
WINBAN	Windward Islands Banana Association
WINFA	Windward Islands Farmers' Association
WTO	World Trade Organization

ACKNOWLEDGEMENTS

For several decades now, anthropologists have pronounced the death of the "ethnographic present." This tradition in anthropological writing isolated communities in space and time and excluded from consideration all that was viewed as "non-local" and therefore irrelevant to a hermetically sealed village or tribe. In actuality, the notion that past anthropologists completely neglected forces from outside the community was always something of an exaggeration; even the most doctrinaire British functionalist or American historicist acknowledged, albeit in a cursory way, some aspect of what they identified as "modern change." Conversely, our present concern with power and global structures has not altered the fact that the community remains the basic unit of study for most ethnographers. Their continued focus on local knowledge and practice is, I think, eminently defensible: adopting the community as a vantage point illustrates in a profound and often poignant way the impact of global forces that now penetrate the daily lives of people in even the most remote places.

Yet in setting out on this project, I anticipated something beyond the community study, favoring a multi-sited approach that drew upon the experience and beliefs of culturally and geographically distinct communities and individuals. What lent a measure of coherence to the stories of rural residents in St. Lucia, St. Vincent, and Dominica, political leaders and activists across the region, and supermarket executives and alternative trade proponents in Great Britain was their common involvement in some aspect of the banana commodity chain. Although most of the story is told from the experiences of rural St. Lucians, it is impossible to explain how neoliberal economic policies are experienced in the region solely from their vantage point. At various points along the links that extend from banana producers to the consumers of their products, this approach may sacrifice some depth for an understanding of the whole. Fortunately for those readers who wish to approach this story in greater detail at either end of the commodity chain, there exists both a robust body of earlier ethnographic studies at the village level in the Windward Islands and a voluminous literature on the complicated trade war that has devastated many such villages. Most of this literature is cited throughout the chapters that follow for the insights it provides in the telling of this story.

I learned early on that multi-sited ethnography posed acute logistical problems in gaining entrée to a variety of widely dispersed field sites. Without the generous gifts of patience and knowledge accorded us by individuals at each of these sites, this book would never have materialized. Almost without exception, residents of the Windward Islands were willing to discuss for hours at a time the intricacies of local politics, the economics of banana production, the principles of Fair Trade marketing, and above all, their fears and hopes regarding a trade war that directly affected their well-being yet was completely beyond their control. At the outset, I would like to thank our hosts in each of my field sites for providing comfortable accommodations as well as other assistance and advice. These include Mr. Wellington Daway in Roseau, Dominica, the Daize family in Arnos Vale, St. Vincent, the Lewison family in Kew, Richmond Surrey, Great Britain, and above all Mr. and Mrs. Bruno Hunte and their daughter Keisha in La Clery, St. Lucia. Over successive periods of residence on St. Lucia during a four-year period, the Huntes not only proved to be an inexhaustible source of information about St. Lucian politics and personalities, but became caring friends.

On St. Lucia, this research was facilitated by an institutional affiliation with the Caribbean Agricultural Research and Development Institute (CARDI) in the Mabouya Valley, for which I would like to thank two of CARDI's consecutive team leaders, Lennox Daisley and Ronald Pilgrim. In this course of this research, we recorded 108 extended, semistructured interviews with people in the Windward Islands and United Kingdom. It is impossible to name all of them here, but those whose personal communications were incorporated into the text are listed in the bibliography. They, and dozens of others, gave generously of their time and expertise despite more pressing commitments of work and family. I would like to acknowledge those who provided our initial introduction to the St. Lucian banana industry at the first stages of this project, for they established the foundation on which the subsequent work was built. These include Tony Jn Pierre, Herbert Rosarie, and Nicholas Faisal of the St. Lucia Banana Corporation, Dr. Luvette Thomas-Louisy of WINBAN, and Winston Henry of the island's National Fair Trade Association. On St. Vincent, Sylvester Van Loo of the SVBGA explained the parallel yet distinct organization of that country's banana industry and helped arrange introductions to farmers. Arthur Bobb, Wilberforce Emmanuel, and Hella Lipper of WINFA in Kingstown provided valuable insight into the development of Fair Trade in the Windward Islands. Junior "Spirit" Cottle of the St. Vincent Ministry of Agriculture offered his first-hand experience among those who had forsaken banana production for other, extralegal alternatives. And on Dominica, Errol Emmanuel of the Dominica Banana Corporation invited me along on farm visits that took us to every banana-growing region on the island. I will never forget the spectacular scenery and engaging conversations that we enjoyed on these trips.

Because most of our work took place on St. Lucia and, in particular, in the communities of the Mabouya Valley, we owe a special debt to residents of that island. These include leaders who have made the island's political landscape what it is today, including the late Sir John Compton and Patrick Joseph, both of whom remained as passionately engaged in the fate of the banana industry during their interviews with me as they were in 1993, when they struggled over its future. Since that time, many others have stepped forward to alleviate the distress of those displaced from the industry. For their devotion to this cause and often eloquent assessment of the state of valley communities I extend my deepest respect to Fr. Raymond Laurent, Mecia Boxill, and Deann Geraia of the Catholic Archdiocese of St. Lucia, and Julie Nurse of the Poverty Reduction Fund. In the Mabouya Valley, the farmers and other residents who assisted in this project are far too numerous to mention, but I would like to single out Cornelius Lynch and Fitz Roy and Lucretia Alexander, who provided my initial introductions to many of their neighbors and took me into their homes as a guest and friend.

The 2004 valley survey that comprises much of the analysis in the pages that follow was conducted by a team of dedicated and insightful St. Lucian field research assistants, who translated the survey instrument into Kwéyòl and threw themselves into administering it to 133 farmers between May and August of that year. To Lucien Charles, Tessa Glasgow, and Merlica Charles must go the credit for the survey data presented throughout this book. In the pages that follow, I have employed the actual names of those informants who granted permission for their reproduction in publication; this is the case for all extended interviews listed as "personal communication." For all other informants I have employed pseudonyms, although I have dropped the artifice of pseudonyms for place names, as all would be easily recognizable in any case from newspaper and other accounts of the last two decades.

This research was made possible with the generous support of the College of Arts and Sciences at my home institution, the University of South Alabama, which provided a grant for a pilot study in 2000 and a sabbatical during fall semester, 2002. Field research between 2002 and 2004 was supported with a grant from the National Science Foundation (BCS-0003965). I wish to extend my thanks to the former director of cultural anthropology at NSF, Dr. Stuart Plattner, who supported my application for supplementary funding in 2004 to examine Fair Trade farming in greater depth than had been anticipated when the project began. This manuscript has benefited from the close reading and suggestions from Dr. Doug Midgett, a longstanding mentor and St. Lucia specialist, Dr. Marc Edelman, who reviewed the manuscript for Berghahn Books, and Professors Gus Carbonella, Don Kalb, and Linda Green, Berghahn's editors for its Dislocations series. The enthusiastic support of these readers and editor Dr. Marion Berghahn was a balm of reassurance at a time when I sought a home for the manuscript. The map in this manuscript was skillfully produced by Sarah Mattics of the University of South Alabama, while the figures were prepared by Carol Naquin. However much the research and manuscript benefited from this support and assistance, responsibility for the final product, and the conclusions reached within it, is mine alone.

Throughout the prolonged period of research and reflection that result in a book, authors inevitably experience some unanticipated changes in their own lives. Depending on their personal circumstances, these can either be a disabling distraction or a stimulus to creativity. I am blessed beyond measure to have shared these years with a partner whose intelligence and faith have always spurred me to something greater than what I could accomplish on my own. My wife, Tawnya Sesi Moberg, is an adept ethnographer in her own right and is responsible for much of the initial field research that produced this book. Throughout the process, she has offered unflagging support and critical commentary on the project and the manuscript that resulted. Although she does not share with me all of the conclusions I have reached in this project, there are no pages in which her presence is not felt. It is to her that I dedicate this book.

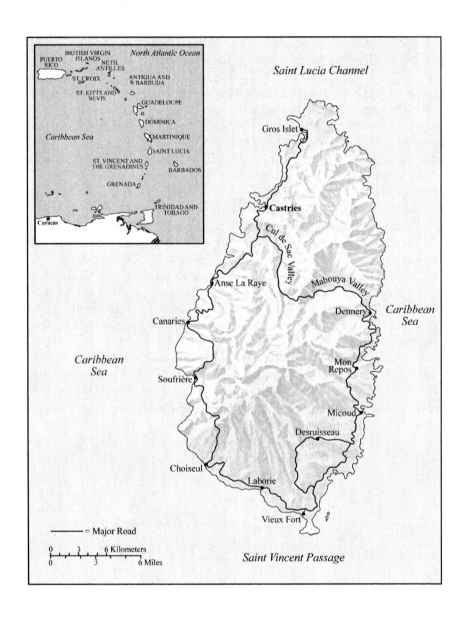

Saint Lucia Channel

North Atlantic Ocean

PUERTO
RICO

BRITISH VIRGIN
ISLANDS

NETH.
ANTILLES

ST. CROIX

ANTIGUA AND
BARBUDA

ST. KITTS AND
NEVIS

GUADELOUPE

DOMINICA

Caribbean Sea

MARTINIQUE

SAINT LUCIA

ST. VINCENT AND
THE GRENADINES

BARBADOS

GRENADA

Caracas

TRINIDAD AND
TOBAGO

Gros Islet

Castries

Cul de Sac Valley

Anse La Raye

Mabouya Valley

Dennery

Caribbean
Sea

Canaries

Caribbean
Sea

Mon
Repos

Soufrière

Micoud

Desruisseau

Choiseul

Laborie

Vieux Fort

Saint Vincent Passage

———— = Major Road

0   3   6 Kilometers

0   3   6 Miles

Chapter One

LINKING THE PERSONAL, THE LOCAL, AND THE GLOBAL

Case studies of individuals reveal suffering, they tell us what happens to one or many people; but to explain suffering, one must embed individual biography in the larger matrix of culture, history, and political economy.

—Paul Farmer, "On Suffering and Structural Violence" (1996)

Dislocations, Societal and First-Hand

My first visit to the Eastern Caribbean island of St. Lucia ended on an unsettling and nearly tragic note. It was the end of May, 2000, and my wife and I were winding up a month of preliminary research on the country's banana industry. On the Windward Islands of St. Lucia, St. Vincent, Dominica, and Grenada, banana production is unique in that it rests almost entirely in the hands of smallholding family farmers. Unlike Central and South America, where bananas are grown on estates often comprising thousands of acres,[1] most Windward Island farmers make a living on plots averaging just a few acres in size. In place of the armies of desperately low-paid and vulnerable immigrant workers employed on Latin American plantations, farmers in the Windwards rely on the labor of family members and a few hired workers, usually their neighbors and friends.

Because of the small scale of their production, relatively high wages paid to their employees, and absence of chemical-intensive methods, Caribbean farmers produce fruit at a unit cost nearly twice that of Chiquita and other Latin American producers. For decades, their survival in a world market dominated by the three major American banana companies had been ensured by a complex system of tariffs, quotas, and licenses that had guaranteed island growers a place in the British market. As a result of a trade war brought by the United States in the World Trade Organization, most of these market preferences were soon to end. Before long, tens of thousands of family farmers would face much more direct competition with Chiquita, Dole, Del Monte, and their vast Latin American holdings. Still to be determined was what form of protection, if any, the WTO would allow in the aftermath of the trade war. We had come to St. Lucia in 2000 to learn how the region's farmers were dealing with that uncertainty and to lay the groundwork for the longer field project that would eventually result in this book.

Given our plans to interview government and industry officials as well as the farmers themselves, we opted to reside in the island's largest town, the capital of Castries, which would afford easy access to both. There we rented the bottom floor of a house in the Biseé neighborhood of town. From our house it was a ten-minute walk to the Gros Islet highway, and then a quick trip via minibus to the banana-growing areas to the south. In these communities, we had encountered farmers who were already traumatized by the changes wrought by the encroaching deregulation of the banana trade, a process begun seven years before with the Single European Market. Many had asked us why a wealthy country like the United States now wanted to strip them of livelihoods that had enabled them to educate their children and to escape the poverty of their grandparents' generation. We could offer little in response to their anguished pleas, other than to tell their story. After four weeks of recording interviews, visiting farms, and combing through government reports and archives, we reviewed our material to ensure that we had enough for a full-fledged research proposal. Two days before our planned departure, we arranged to revisit an industry official to clarify a detail from his earlier interview. Having made an appointment with him that morning, we set off for his office in town.

St. Lucia is a country of breathtaking natural beauty, and for that reason it is justly acclaimed as a tourist destination. Our house was situated toward the top of one of the many hills in town. As we left it that morning, we encountered the now-familiar panorama of sheer verdant slopes to either side of the quiet residential street leading down to the highway and the Caribbean Sea just beyond it. This steep, lengthy walk was one that we had made many times over the previous weeks, but we never tired of the spectacular view it afforded. Those who lived along the street had long been aware of our comings and goings, and many greeted us from their doorways and front yards along the route. In front of us walked a young man who periodically glanced at us over his shoulder. I took no particular notice of him, aware that in Biseé (unlike the tourist areas of the island), white foreigners remained a curiosity for most people.

As we passed an uninhabited area near the highway, the man slowed his pace to come alongside me on the right. I turned, expecting him to speak. Instead, he lunged toward me. He had timed his assault with care, for my escape was blocked by a concrete wall to my left. A machete (known locally as a "cutlass") had suddenly appeared in his upraised right hand. He cocked his arm back and swung it forward, the blade moving swiftly and inexorably toward my upper body. I flinched, fearing a fatal blow, but the blade stopped short just inches from my throat. Meanwhile, with his left hand, he deftly relieved me of my book bag, which I had slung over just one shoulder when I left the house. He was sprinting back up the street before I even realized that my life was no longer in danger.

We never made it to our appointment that morning, being instead diverted to file a police report for the theft of the bag's contents, a few dollars and a camera belonging to my university. I am thankful for my safe emergence from an incident that might have ended very differently, as well as for the fact that nothing like it has recurred over several return visits to the Windwards. On each of our trips to St. Lucia, St. Vincent, and Dominica, we have known steadfast cooperation, patience, and friendship among many banana farmers and others struggling to survive in a changing world economy. Yet I cannot pretend that the incident has not affected me at some deep, lasting level. Years later, I remember the indelible look on the young man's face as his eyes met mine, a puzzling mixture of fear and fury. The memory also involuntarily evokes the same surge of anger I felt in that instant when I thought my life was about to end.

It is perhaps inevitable that victims of crime personalize an event that leaves persisting emotional, if not physical, scars. Yet as anthropologists, the holistic perspective compels us to place any action—whether societal or personal, criminal or charitable, hurtful or loving—within a broader sociocultural context. The robbery that morning was tallied as one of 6,828 "crimes against property" reported to the Royal St. Lucia Police in the year 2000 (St. Lucia 1995–2003). The number of such crimes (mostly theft, burglary, and robbery) had risen on the island nearly 21 percent over the previous five years. In tandem with such offenses, "crimes against the person" (mostly murder, assaults, or threats) had increased nearly 36 percent over the same period, and the incidence of drug-related crimes (possession, cultivation, or trafficking) had exploded by an extraordinary 304 percent. Some crimes on the island achieved international notoriety, as when two emotionally disturbed men attacked worshippers in the Castries Cathedral on New Year's Eve, 2000, bludgeoning an elderly nun to death and using gasoline to set a dozen other people on fire. That story made it to the pages of the *New York Times,* but it was a more prosaic, if no less deadly, crime wave affecting all areas of the country that allowed the island's newspapers to offer up a daily diet of graphic, full-color photos of cutlass and gunshot victims. Meanwhile, St. Lucia's prison population had burgeoned, reportedly doubling between 1990 and 2000 (Francois, personal communication 2004).

Was there a link between the anthropological problem that I had set out to study—the effect of "free trade" policies on Caribbean farming communities—and a surging crime wave that had touched me personally during the course of the study? From the perspective of numerous reports commissioned by the governments of the Windwards and other institutions to prepare for the loss of market preferences, the connection between the two was indisputable. As early as 1997 a survey discerned growing levels of crime, alcohol and drug abuse, domestic violence, and child neglect after the initial effects of market liberalization had forced one quarter of the country's banana farmers from production over the previous four years (Cargill 1998: 14). These trends had especially affected the young, landless men who once made up the rural wage labor force. Lacking ready alternatives to steady work on banana farms, many had drifted to town only to turn to theft and drug sales as a way of life. Perhaps this applied as well to my young assailant. The dislocations from the declining banana industry, the study warned soberly, "threaten to destroy the social fabric of the society" (Cargill 1998: 14). Since then, the hemorrhage of banana farmers has continued. Of more than 9,000 farmers active on St. Lucia in 1992, only 1,400 remained in production eleven years later. Not until the year 2004 did the region's banana production and grower base finally show signs of stabilizing at a level just a fraction of its historic high reached in 1992.

This is an ethnography of a region in transition, one whose story is still being written at the local level throughout the Eastern Caribbean. Because this story originates with the decisions of powerful actors that have restructured the global economy, the experiences of the Windwards could be considered an archetype for communities in much of the "developing world."[2] But although the ideology of free trade predominates worldwide, seldom has it gone unchallenged, nor are its effects everywhere the same, even on adjacent Caribbean islands that have experienced similar macroeconomic processes. Economic restructuring in the Windwards is hardly a novel experience; since the origin of the region's banana industry in the 1950s, it has been felt through a series of ever-greater demands on banana farmers by external agents (see especially Slocum 1996, 2006; Grossman 1998; Moberg 2005). Such demands were first issued by the banana company that purchased their fruit, and they continue to this day with the British supermarkets that remain their sole export outlet. Yet it is the most recent series of mandates, originating with the World Trade Organization, that have called the survival of farming communities themselves into question, for it has dictated an end to the policies that had formerly assured family farmers a small but relatively secure place in the world market.

Globalization and Local Response

The concept of globalization has spread from the scholarly literature into the broader culture to become an almost clichéd description of contemporary social change. These clichés are represented, for example, by anthropology textbook covers that show Amazonian Indians operating laptop computers while dressed in tribal regalia. Such representations aside, if globalization remains an ambiguous concept in many people's minds, it may be because it embraces so many seemingly distinct aspects of daily life. In the Windward Islands, globalization is, like the textbook image, reflected in consumption patterns, behaviors, and a "structure of feeling" that not only lack local precedent, but often sit uneasily beside West Indian cultural patterns based on Afro-Caribbean rural traditions. A generation ago, residents of the Mabouya Valley in St. Lucia relied on kerosene lanterns and candles for lighting, cooked with charcoal in outdoor kitchens, and carried water from wells or a nearby river. A fortunate few owned AM radios, which they tuned to Radio St. Lucia, the country's only broadcast medium at the time. By the time of my research from 2001 to 2004, I was able to arrange interviews with farmers by calling them on their cell phones. Occasionally I arrived at their homes while family members watched BET or Nickelodeon on satellite TV. In the background, North American rap and hip-hop increasingly supplanted the rhythms of calypso, reggae, and zouk that are more rooted in the Caribbean experience.

To some observers, these cultural juxtapositions are striking or even amusing indications that the far-flung corners of the world are becoming more and more alike in aesthetics and consumption patterns under the impact of mass media emanating from the developed nations. At a time when the US and Europe appear to be threatened by terrorism and anti-Western fundamentalism, some North Americans may find solace in the global spread of aesthetics, music, and fashions that originated in the US. Less often considered are the effects of such seductive images and desires in societies where most people lack the means to attain them. In the Windwards, the cell phone has moved from being a status symbol of the very wealthy to a socially necessary marker of modernity for all, much as the color television did in the US forty years ago. On the islands themselves, few seem to question the advisability of very poor people spending US $50 or more per month to maintain such prestigious symbols of modernity.[3] Perhaps this is because, as a St. Lucian teen told me in an accent Americanized for my benefit, "[A]t the end of the day, you're nobody without one." Nor is there any easy way to describe the bewilderment expressed by a devoutly religious banana farmer, who had grown up during the time of kerosene lamps, after he discovered his grandson staying awake late at night to surf internet porn sites. However great the impact of the telecommunications and internet revolutions in the societies that spawned them, it is impossible to overstate the extent to which these technologies create generational and cultural chasms in societies previously governed by entirely different value systems. Indeed, as some have asserted (Barber 1995, Gray 2003), such clashes may *in part* underlie the fundamentalist backlash fueling terrorist acts against Western targets.

Yet this story is less about the cultural dimensions of globalization than its economic and political consequences. In the Windwards, these have been especially destabilizing to cultural traditions built upon farming as a way of life, for in economic terms globalization has threatened the continued survival of that foundation. In one sense, this is a process of great antiquity, for social historians and anthropologists have long documented the ways in which traditional cultural values and social relations were transformed by their incorporation into a unitary world system of production and commerce (Polanyi 1957; Wallerstein 1980; Wolf 1982; Abu-Lughod 1989). This process continues apace in the contemporary world, leading some to question whether globalization is not merely a novel label for the venerable practice of colonial domination (Miyoshi 1993). Yet many scholars insist that there is something quite new about the disorienting pace of contemporary global change, which has resulted in an unprecedented "compression of our spatial and temporal worlds" (Harvey 1989: 240). They describe globalization as a process involving accelerating and unimpeded flows—of investment capital, commodities, and to a much lesser degree, labor—across national borders, to the extent that such borders virtually cease to exist in economic terms (Basch, Schiller, and Szanton-Blanc 1994; Bauman 1998; Greider 1997; French 2000; Brennan 2003). In part, these trends are the outcome of recent technological innovations in transportation and communications. We see this when, for example, American florists import fresh cut flowers from Colombia on 747 cargo planes (Friedemann-Sánchez 2006), US airlines employ reservations agents in the Caribbean to staff their ticketing call centers (Freeman 2000), and broccoli picked in Guatemala is sold in Nashville supermarkets the following afternoon (Fischer and Benson 2006).

While improvements in telecommunications and transportation technology have been necessary for this kind of global integration of production and consumption, they have not been sufficient conditions. In order to implement these changes, it is also necessary to greatly restrict the ability of national governments to regulate investment and trade across their borders. For the economic concomitants of globalization to occur, in other words, governments have to be stripped of most of their *governance* over national economies. This has involved a conscious dismantling of an international consensus dating from the 1944 Bretton Woods (New Hampshire) conference, at which the workings of the postwar economic order were negotiated among representatives of forty-five allied nations. The conference's priorities were guided by the Keynesian doctrines of economic planning then dominant in the United States and Great Britain. In large part so that national governments could achieve their social and political objectives, including the creation of social welfare systems and postwar rebuilding, Bretton Woods established exchange controls that limited the capacity of corporations and individuals to move capital across borders (Helleiner 1994: 164). As the conferees recognized, were corporations and the wealthy able to easily shift their resources from one country to another, governments would be hamstrung in their ability to impose taxation or redistributive policies critical to economic planning.

Following the initial wave of decolonization after World War II, governments in the developing world took advantage of such policies to incubate fledgling national industries or agricultural sectors behind tariff barriers or subsidies. These policies shielded local producers from direct competition with industries and agriculture in the developed countries. The rationale for tariff barriers was phrased in terms of both the economic and political survival of the governments that erected them. Lacking investment capital and technology comparable to that found in the industrialized countries, fledgling industries in the developing world would be destroyed by an unregulated influx of cheaper manufactured or agricultural goods. The goal of "protectionist" policies was to create local industries and agricultural sectors that would generate products for local consumption, reducing the reliance of newly independent countries on expensive imported goods.

Of equal importance to policy makers was the political imperative to shield the rural poor from the onset of competition with industrial agriculture in the developed nations, a process held to fuel landlessness and even insurrection (de Janvry 1981; Ochoa 2000). Trade disputes under this system did occasionally arise between countries, and for that reason Bretton Woods had established the General Agreement on Tariffs and Trade. For five decades GATT provided a framework for regulating international trade among signatory nations by negotiating tariff rates and import duties so that member states retained "reasonable" levels of access to each other's domestic markets.

By the early 1970s, the advent of jet transport and containerized shipping had made it possible for manufacturers to relocate virtually anywhere in the world, greatly reducing the temporal and geographic fixity of production in the then-industrialized countries (Harvey 1989). These developments created a politically powerful constituency, mostly of major corporations in the US and Western Europe, that favored dismantling national exchange controls as a way to expand their investments abroad (Helleiner 1994: 167). These forces secured a critical victory in 1973, when the US government abandoned longstanding fixed exchange rates and allowed its currency to freely "float" against others. Once the world's largest economy had opted out of the Bretton Woods exchange rate system, all other capitalist industrialized nations eventually followed suit.

Yet a significant impediment remained to the unfettered movement of manufacturing and goods across national borders; namely, the reluctance of many national governments in the developing world to lower tariffs and regulations that had protected state-run and -supported industries. Some countries, such as Brazil and Chile during their periods of military dictatorship in the 1970s, courted foreign investors with guarantees of lavish tax concessions, duty-free importation of equipment, and unlimited profit repatriation. But many democratic governments were hesitant to fully open their borders and expose nascent national industries to direct competition with heavily capitalized foreign firms. Their ability to maintain such policies was eroded during the 1980s, which saw an unprecedented debt crisis in much of the developing world.[4] As interest payments ballooned and debt levels became crippling economic burdens, one national government after another turned to the International Monetary Fund for assistance. A multilateral lending agency established at Bretton Woods, initially for the task of postwar rebuilding, the IMF now became a lender of last resort for many indebted countries as they sought to repay private creditors.

As a condition of IMF assistance, national governments are required to conform to Structural Adjustment Programs (SAPs) drafted by IMF staff, in which they virtually turn over all aspects of national economic policy to the IMF. A common condition of structural adjustment is that governments devote as much national income as possible to the repayment of foreign debts. The IMF instructs them to do so by slashing public expenditures, eliminating subsidies for food, medicine, and other assistance to the poor, and removing restrictions on foreign investment—the same policies that could only be imposed previously on local populations by military dictatorships (Rowbotham 1998, Farmer 2003). Structural adjustment further mandates that government-owned national industries and utilities be sold to private investors in order to "free up" revenues for debt repayment, leading to layoffs and reductions in wages among those who retain their jobs, as well as a rising cost of living for consumers of newly-privatized electricity, water and other services.

By the 1990s, the collapse of the Soviet Union and most other centrally planned economies had left standing only one model of economic development worldwide, one that viewed national economic sovereignty as an impediment to the free and unregulated movement of capital and commodities. Embodying the principles of "free trade" and privatization, neoliberalism is now embraced—at least rhetorically—by all of the world's developed countries as an axiom of economic growth. These principles are embodied and enforced by a multilateral agency, the World Trade Organization (WTO), whose binding decisions in trade disputes have replaced the older consensual GATT framework regulating world trade.

Yet if neoliberalism is now nearly everywhere the dominant economic ideology, its effects and implementation are not experienced equally in all places. Among the first anthropologists to situate their ethnographic work in a global context, Sidney Mintz (1977) and June Nash (1981) warned against overly deterministic readings of the world system. What Nash termed the "problem of the passive periphery" in world systems theory, i.e., its tendency to regard conditions in local communities as a reflex of their insertion into the world economy, could apply equally well to globalization perspectives that regard neoliberalism as a monolithic process. With the emergence of neoliberal policies, as Nash (1994) observed, small-scale farmers have often been forced to adapt suddenly to the removal of tariffs and price supports. In some instances, the withdrawal of market protections for small-scale farmers has been mandated by IMF structural adjustment policies. In the Windwards, such measures have been imposed by the WTO at the indirect behest of agribusiness corporations seeking control of markets formerly protected by tariff barriers. Such policies have brought small-scale farmers into price competition with industrial agriculture, which enjoys greater productivity because of its technological intensity as well as "hidden" subsidies, such as agricultural tax credits and price supports in the developed countries. Yet, where states in the developing world have been able to avert WTO trade wars and IMF conditionality, some have been able to retain substantial protections for poor farmers and other rural residents, despite an ostensible commitment to neoliberal ideologies.

More often, though, neoliberal policies have compelled farmers to adapt to the loss of market protections, and their responses to change are situated in local culture and the constraints and opportunities existing in rural communities. Usually unable to compete with much larger corporate farms in deregulated markets, many household-based farmers have indeed withdrawn from commercial farming. A shift toward autarky, or a greater degree of subsistence production and inward self-reliance, may be one response, especially among farmers who are able to retain their land. For others, the effects of globalization have been more disruptive, prompting emigration, seasonal reliance on low wage labor, and in many instances, the production of illicit drugs. Yet in many areas of the world, small-scale farmers are not prepared to surrender their lands and traditional livelihoods, at least not without intense resistance to draconian "free market" measures. It is no coincidence, for example, that the Zapatista rebellion in southern Mexico began on the very day that the North American Free Trade Agreement was to take effect. Zapatista leaders recognized that the dismantling of tariff barriers to cheap imported US maize, one of NAFTA's provisions, would decimate small farmers throughout Mexico (Collier 1994).

As we will see, in that same year of 1993 the Mabouya Valley in St. Lucia also exploded with an unprecedented bout of growers' strikes and rural unrest largely due to falling banana prices after the first wave of deregulation in the European banana market. In recent years, the neoliberal model favored by the United States and the multilateral institutions in which it holds a dominant voice has produced a political backlash throughout the Americas. This has resulted in the election of national governments seeking greater economic sovereignty and the strengthening of a state sector geared toward ensuring social welfare.

Island Politics and an Agency Model of the State

Because this story links the local with the global, and the powerful with the comparatively powerless, we break from the convention of bounded community studies that makes up much of the anthropological tradition. Much of this story will be told from the Mabouya Valley, a region of eastern St. Lucia long considered the island's primary "banana belt." As will be seen, the valley's recent, turbulent history reveals the impact of global forces since the early 1990s as well as determined local responses to them in the realms of both politics and production. This account of events embraces newer anthropological approaches that have supplanted the ethnography of the bounded community. Inspired by Laura Nader's (1974) appeal to "study up," anthropologists today widely recognize the need to situate the communities they study within a broader matrix of institutions and powerful outsiders whose actions affect them. Thus we leave the confines of the valley to examine the contexts in which the decisions and strategies of powerful economic actors are rooted.

Fieldwork for this study involved not only repeated periods of residence on St. Lucia and neighboring islands, but also interviews with UK banana company and supermarket executives involved in the importation and retailing of Windward Islands fruit. In addition, St. Lucia's experience is contrasted with that of St. Vincent, a neighboring banana-producing island where neoliberalism has yielded quite different, if no less dire, consequences for farmers. Finally, particular attention will be devoted to global and local actors, including the US-based Chiquita Corporation, the US government, the WTO, and the companies that trade in Windwards fruit, as well as St. Lucian politicians who hold state power and those who aspire to it. The political aspirations of the latter form a significant unifying theme in this book. As will be seen, office holders and would-be officials have often politically mobilized banana growers desperate for a solution to their economic difficulties. Far too often, their efforts serve to manipulate rural voters into advancing narrow political ambitions rather than addressing farmers' problems. In the wake of such political opportunism, farming communities lie littered with divisive loyalties, distrust, and broken promises, all of which hinder the capacity of the rural poor to recognize their common interests, let alone realize them.

However critically they affect community solidarity and collective action among the poor, the vagaries and maneuvering of island politics are not easily appreciated through prevailing anthropological views of state power. In recent decades, scholars have vigorously debated the nature of the state, especially since the infusion of Marxist and other materialist perspectives into the social sciences during the 1970s and 1980s. These concerns developed in tandem with a rejection of earlier ethnographic descriptions that isolated localities in space and time and neglected the ways in which global forces impinged upon their residents. While a preoccupation with the nature of the state has grown in recent decades, traditional anthropological views on the matter have been conditioned by two longstanding, opposed political theories. Following the seventeenth-century political philosopher Thomas Hobbes and inspired by 1950s Parsonian functionalism, some have argued that states in both the premodern and contemporary worlds are fundamentally managerial institutions, developed to resolve complex economic and political problems arising within large class-stratified societies (Wittfogel 1957; Service 1975; Johnson and Earle 2000). From this "contractual" point of view, states govern more or less equally on behalf of all segments of society, on the basis of an implicit social contract in which their legitimacy derives from the services they provide to the governed. It might be noted that this model corresponds closely to how the leaders and bureaucratic components of the state represent themselves to their citizens; i.e. as rational, impartial "public servants" acting in the interests of society-at-large (Sharma and Gupta 2006: 18). The historical and ethnographic records, of course, reveal that the discourse of state actors, generally crafted to secure their legitimacy, offers a singularly poor guide to their actions. It is the practice of state power, rather than its representation, that concerns us here, for the state most directly enters the lived experience of its citizens through the services (and coercion) that it alternately provides or withholds.

In challenging the contractual view of state-society relations, many anthropologists in recent decades have revised and debated among themselves variants of Marxist political economy. Political economy perspectives ultimately derive from the numerous (and occasionally conflicting) observations made by Marx in the course of his life on the relationship between the exercise of state power and class interests. Within this broader framework, "instrumentalist" theorists regard the state as an entity that rules directly on behalf of elite classes by formulating policies favorable to their economic interests (Fried 1967; Domhoff 1983; Miliband 1983; Foley and Yambert 1989). Hence, state agencies tend to promulgate laws and exercise power on behalf of economic elites and to the detriment of producing classes. Other scholars, in a "structuralist" orientation, concede greater autonomy to the state by viewing it as a means to manage the societal contradictions of capitalism (Poulantzas 1978; Wolf 1982). When developing policies that ameliorate extreme poverty or environmental pollution, for example, state bureaucracies often defy the short-term demands of economic elites, but in the long run their reforms perpetuate prevailing patterns of ownership and economic accumulation. Common to political economy models, whatever their differences, is a view of the state as an ultimately coercive institution that enacts policies furthering the exploitation of producing classes by those who appropriate the products of their labor.

What these older debates have in common is their tendency to ascribe an innate nature to the state, one that is either coercive or integrative, pluralist or class-dominated, contractual or exploitative (Haas 1982; Vincent 1987). Such claims do little to illuminate how those who control the state actually utilize its power, for any state can be shown to be all of these things at different times, exhibiting quite disparate actions toward the populations that reside within its borders. More recent approaches have examined the nexus of state and culture in the ways that state personnel and institutions represent themselves to their citizenry, and the discursive resources deployed by the state to consolidate its power over (and in) society (Sharma and Gupta 2006). Hence, the state's endorsement of an official language for transacting business, or a specific form of literate expression, inherently privileges some of its citizens over others; as will be seen in the St. Lucian case, such practices often lay the foundation for grievances by marginalized groups against those who wield power. This scholarship converges with emerging views that regard modern bureaucracies as social actors in their own right, and their actions and discourse as the primary means by which they enhance their own power relative to their citizenry, either as individuals or members of civil society (Skocpol 1979; Evans, Rueschemeyer, and Skocpol 1985; Foucault 1994; Jessop 1999). Scott (1998) has shown, for example, that strikingly similar "high modernist" initiatives for large-scale social engineering were undertaken by twentieth-century states of starkly distinct ideological orientations. Such efforts were intended largely to deepen citizens' dependence on the state by destroying the bonds of community, kinship, or ethnicity that predated it. This view goes a long way toward transcending earlier, usually teleological arguments over the inherent "nature" of the state. Yet it stops short of answering why states so conspicuously reward some of their citizens over others in terms of resources, policy, or employment. Explicating this issue requires a shift from structure to agency, i.e. a focus not on the nature of state power but on the motives of those who control it.

Regardless of their ideologies, class background, and degree of sincerity or cynicism, those who hold power and those who aspire to it possess a common interest. Once in control of state power, most politicians wish to retain it, and they use the institutions and resources at their command to do so. That power holders seek to perpetuate their positions is obvious to the citizens of most states and central to the assumptions of Enlightenment political theorists such as Machiavelli and Hume (Service 1975: 22). Among the more pointed assertions of this position is the "Iron Law of Oligarchy," developed in 1915 by Robert Michels: "It is extremely probable that a social group which had secured control of the instruments of collective power would do all that was possible to retain that control" (1958: 401). Michels was struck by the paradox that, despite their stated commitment to revolutionary democracy, socialist leaders were as likely to entrench themselves in positions of power as were conservatives. Few anthropologists, with the exceptions of Bailey (1969, 1988) and Boissevain (1974, 1977), have paused to acknowledge this axiom about power holders and consider its implications for the exercise of power.

Adopting Michels, the above-mentioned political anthropologists, and newer variants of state theory as a point of departure, an "agency" model of the state largely regards the policies, actions, and discourse of those who control state institutions as the means by which they perpetuate that control (Moberg 1994). In doing so, power holders entertain policy choices that may reward desired constituents with resources while punishing opponents with options ranging from benign neglect to overt repression. As political economists recognize, politicians require substantial material support to achieve power, and these resources are most commonly provided by economic elites. Yet those who wield the power of the state do so primarily to retain control rather than to consistently reward a single set of class interests. Election (or reelection) to office requires sheer numbers of votes as well as money, and candidates are unlikely to obtain sufficient amounts of both from the same class (Moberg and Sesi Moberg 2005). Politicians, then, engage in never-ending calculations of the political support (both popular and elite) to be gained from their electoral promises and symbolic gestures. A much-cited analysis of US electoral trends (Frank 2004) examines how political strategists seek to maximize voter support by crafting simultaneous appeals to a variety of constituencies, even those whose economic interests conflict, such as lower-income religious conservatives and affluent corporate executives. As shown in the 2004 US elections, such efforts can even secure the election of a president whose taxation and social policies are not only opposed by most Americans, but demonstrably harmful to their well-being.

Because of St. Lucia's small population and its considerable poverty, island political strategies are perhaps more transparent than in the developed North, centering on tangible material promises to specific constituents and communities. Key among these assurances is consideration for government services such as schools, sewer systems, roads, and employment, as well as a punishing denial of such rewards to individuals and communities that fail to back the party that controls the government. With the contraction of government social spending—a common phenomenon in states embracing free market policies and an inevitable consequence of IMF conditionality—the rewards of state largesse persist but have grown scarcer. The effect, ironically, is to heighten competition for those resources that remain. In explaining island politics during 2004, a long-term resident of the Mabouya Valley employed the widely understood metaphor of the "PIP": "[I]f you support the Party in Power, or the PIP as we call it, then you get everything. It's a known fact. And if you do not support the party, you get victimized. I'm not speaking about any one party, but this is how politics work in general here."

Echoing the claims of contractual theory, national governments in St. Lucia as in the rest of the Caribbean publicly assert their intention to govern equally on behalf of all citizens. Behind the scenes, however, a different governing principle prevails, one that Caribbean residents express in the metaphor of the PIP.[5] Retaliation against opposition supporters via the prerogative to provide jobs and services is commonplace after elections throughout the region (see, for example, Ames 1987; Grindle 1977, 1986; Hintzen 1989). Where the membership of political parties mirrors ethnic cleavages, as in Guyana, the direction of state largesse often swings violently in the aftermath of an election, away from those ethnic communities supporting the previous government and toward those supporting the newly elected party. Even where such ethnic divisions are muted or politically irrelevant, as in several of the Windward Islands, post-election victimization is invariably meted out through firings of suspect members of the civil service as well as ritualistic debasement of high profile opponents. Hence, the swearing in of a new government is often followed in short order by humiliating public proceedings known as Commissions of Inquiry that investigate alleged wrongdoing by those who suddenly find themselves out of favor (Midgett 2004). As the following chapters illustrate, the banana industry in St. Lucia has, since its very origin, been inextricably bound with the stratagems of island power holders and those who aspire to power.

In contrast to many scholarly analyses that situate globalization in the workings of institutional structures and anonymous market forces, this book seeks to personify these forces in the motives of powerful, named global and local actors. The decisions and policies that adversely affect Windwards farmers ultimately originate in these actors' desire for control, of either markets or positions of power. Whether the actor in question is the world's largest banana company, the Chiquita Corporation, seeking to acquire the remaining sliver of the European market remaining outside its control, a US president advancing Chiquita's interests at the WTO in exchange for domestic political contributions, or a St. Lucian parliamentarian calculating how to harvest votes from devastated rural communities, few can escape this admittedly harsh assessment.

Notwithstanding the cynicism and self-aggrandizement that propel many of the forces of globalization in the Windwards, and the destructive impact of neoliberal policies on rural communities, this is not a story barren of hope for the future. In recent years, both consumers in the now-developed nations and producers in developing countries have begun to visualize a new global economic order of reciprocity and mutual respect. This is not an order based on the values enshrined at the WTO or, for that matter, the local Wal-Mart. From the free trade perspective that animates such institutions, goods are to be obtained from the cheapest sources available, almost regardless of the social or environmental costs that make such low retail prices possible. In contrast, the growing Fair Trade movement seeks to link consumers and producers in reciprocal relations that benefit both. Here, the exchange between them offers the consumer a good that is produced under socially just and environmentally sustainable conditions, while providing the producer with a price that enables him or her to survive.

Fair Trade is a rapidly emerging phenomenon in the Windward Islands, where thousands of growers now label their fruit as Fair Trade bananas, then use a part of the proceeds from their sales in Britain to develop educational, health care, and social programs of their own design within their communities. Fair Trade is not a panacea for the problems of underdevelopment, and in many respects it falls far short of its promised reciprocity. But in the face of prevailing economic thought, where the "bottom line" is accorded precedence over the well-being and even survival of much of humanity, Fair Trade offers a glimpse of "another, better world," in the words of its advocates (FLO 2004). That world, governed by priorities of social justice and environmental sustainability, has afforded some refuge for Caribbean farmers striving to survive in a rapidly changing global economy. As will be seen in the final chapters of this book, Fair Trade, by providing rural communities with the opportunity and means to plan local development, may also portend a greater degree of autonomy from the machinations of powerful outsiders who attempt to yoke the rural poor to their own personal and political ambitions.

Notes

1. As indicated in Chapter Three, there exists some variability in the size of holdings and ownership structure among banana industries on the mainland of Latin America. In Central America, very large plantations operate either under direct corporate control or under private ownership in contract relationships with US and European exporters. In South America (notably Ecuador and Colombia), smaller farms under private ownership predominate. Yet even Ecuadorian farms—the smallest in mainland Latin America—average about 75 acres (Moberg and Striffler 2003: 19), roughly twenty times the size of the average St. Lucian banana farm.
2. I prefer this usage despite poststructuralist critiques of development discourse (Escobar 1995; for a devastating counterargument see Edelman 1999), and the fact that indices of social welfare in many countries have deteriorated rather than improved in recent decades. Unlike "postcolonial" or "Third World," the term implies participation in an integrated global system, albeit on a basis that is unequal and subordinate.
3. In a similar vein, Sklair poses the "enigma of why poor people, in poor and rich countries, apparently defy economic rationality by purchasing relatively expensive global brands in order to forge some sense of identity with what we can only call, in a rather crude sense, 'symbols of modernity'" (1998: 303).
4. The origins of this crisis, which are beyond the range of this chapter, lie in metropolitan banks' lending policies during the 1970s, designed to generate profits from the dollar-denominated deposits of oil-exporting countries. Concessionary loans offered at low interest rates became crippling debts when a global recession forced interest rates to rise in the 1980s, even as the cost of imported oil continued to increase and demand declined for many of the developing world's traditional exports.
5. At times, particularly when addressing supporters, the façade of equitable governance is publicly abandoned. After St. Lucia's 1974 elections returned the governing United Workers' Party to power, its chairman openly pledged to the party's constituents that "from this time on, the supporters of this government will be taken care of first. Our supporters first, the rest afterwards" (in Wayne 1987: 226). In the weeks and months that followed, there ensued a purge of suspected opposition sympathizers from all levels of public sector employment.

— *Chapter Two* —

AN ISLAND IN HISTORY

The postulation of a world system forces us frequently to lift our eyes
from the particulars of local history, which I would consider salutary.
But equally salutary is the constant revisiting of events "on the ground,"
so that the architecture of the world system can be laid bare.
—Sidney Mintz (1977)

First Encounters: Geography and Culture

Scattered along an arc from Puerto Rico to Venezuela, the Lesser Antilles
appear as specks on a map of the Caribbean Sea and Western Atlantic. The
southernmost chain in the archipelago, the Windward Islands, consists
of volcanic peaks that climb abruptly from the ocean floor to elevations
of more than three thousand feet above sea level. Traces of the seismic
activity that created the islands can be found in the sulphurous vents and
hot springs that rupture the surface on each of the Windwards. On nearly
every island these volcanic sites are known by the place name Soufrière, a
vestige of French colonial exploration throughout the region.

Volcanic activity bestowed on St. Lucia the island's most striking and
widely recognized landmarks. Whether approaching by sea or air, visitors
gain their first glimpse of the island's leeward coast in the Gros and Petit
Pitons, two sheer basalt peaks rising from the Caribbean to an elevation
of more than two thousand feet. Located at 13° 53′N by 60° 68′W, St. Lucia is intermediate in size between the smaller islands of St. Vincent and
Grenada to the south and the larger islands of Martinique and Dominica
at the northern end of the Windwards chain. At its maximum length and
breadth, the island is 27 miles long by 14 miles wide, with a surface area

of about 238 square miles. St. Lucians liken the shape of their island to that of a mango.

Despite its diminutive size (about 3.5 times the area of Washington, D.C.), St. Lucia exhibits marked variability in landform and climate. Northeast trade winds bring moisture-laden air from the Atlantic, resulting in precipitation of up to 250 inches per year at the highest elevations (St. Lucia 2003). In comparison, the island's southern and northern extremities lie miles from any peaks and receive little rainfall outside of the "hurricane season" from June to November. The highest elevations, including the island's highest point at Mt. Gimie (3,218 feet above sea level), consist of multi-storied rainforests rising a hundred feet or more above the forest floor. Here dozens of epiphytic species, mostly orchids and bromeliads, cling to the upper branches of trees. Descending in elevation, both rainfall levels and the density of the forest canopy diminish greatly. Below one thousand feet a lower montane rainforest of smaller trees and broken canopy are associated with dense undergrowth of giant ferns and bamboo. A still lower zone of secondary forest occurs where agriculture or timber-cutting—mostly for charcoal—have altered native plant communities, often resulting in serious erosion on steeper slopes.

Approximately 35 percent of the country's surface area currently remains under forest cover, but this represents a decline of 22.5 percent since 1977 (St. Lucia 2003). Much of this decline resulted from the expansion of commercial banana farming during the 1980s, when farmers extended cultivation into marginal hillside areas poorly suited for agriculture. Belying the lush forest cover at the higher elevations, most of the island's soil is acidic red clay of low fertility and poor drainage (Hunting 1998). Most of the rainfall in highland zones makes it way to the coast in rivers and streams that broaden, fan-like, toward the sea. It is on the river valley floors and adjacent hillsides that freely draining and darker soils of high fertility are found. These are the sites where the most productive farming is practiced.

Traveling across the island brings these variations in climate and landform into sharp relief. Most visitors from outside the region arrive at the Hewanorra International Airport near the southernmost town of Vieux Fort. The south coast is a dry, windswept place of scrub woodland, cactus, and other succulent plants. The trip to Castries, the capital and largest town, takes about ninety minutes on average but varies with the white-knuckled audacity of drivers, who negotiate a twisting two-lane road also traveled by farm equipment and the occasional horse or goat. For the first fifteen miles or so the road clings to the Atlantic (windward) coast, affording a view of fancifully shaped islets, eroded cliffs, and a few hardy if stunted trees that have been sculpted by the constant sharp wind from the east. At regular intervals, the road dips into broad river valleys that empty into the ocean. In the zones of flat, fertile land on either side of the river, a carpet of banana plants extends eastward as far as the eye can see.

At the largest of these valleys, that of the Mabouya River, the road turns inland, running parallel with the river toward its source in the mountains. Farming settlements and a few small grocery and rum shops appear, surrounded by a sea of banana plants extending well up onto the hillsides that frame the Mabouya Valley. A casual observer might infer from the unbroken expanse of green that he or she is in the midst of a massive plantation, but the packing sheds that dot the side of the road indicate farm boundaries at three- to five-acre intervals. What appears to be a single farm, then, is actually a patchwork of hundreds of individually farmed parcels. Closer attention reveals that many of the farms are choked with weeds, their packing sheds fallen into disrepair. This is the first indication of the crisis that has overcome the industry and driven many farmers out of production.

The eight-mile drive from the coastal town of Dennery to the inland settlement of Grande Rivère affords one of the only relatively straight and level stretches along the road from Vieux Fort to Castries. Here drivers often accelerate to breakneck speed to compensate for the slow progress made over the rest of the route. Before long the road ascends into the hills at the head of the valley. The surrounding flora becomes notably more lush and tropical, and the air moist and cool. Soon the last signs of farming are left behind, to be replaced by bird of paradise plants, bamboo, and liana-enshrouded trees that line both sides of the road. Vegetation arches overhead, and for the next several miles the road proceeds under a dense forest canopy. Even the most powerful vehicles struggle with the grade and the abrupt switchbacks that lead over the center of the island, a ridge known as the Barre De L'Isle. From this height, through massive stands of bamboo, one glimpses fleeting panoramas of the western side of the island. Below, as an almost mirror image of the Mabouya Valley, the Cul de Sac region spreads from the highlands down to the leeward shore. The road descends into another sea of green banana leaves interspersed with residences and shops, and the cool, moist air of the mountains gives way to a humid languor unrelieved by the trade winds from the east.

Turning north, the final stretch of road leading to Castries ascends over the Morne Fortune, a crest that stands over 1,100 feet above the town and its harbor. Used as a lookout by both French and British troops in the eighteenth century, the Morne was later claimed by England's colonial officials as a residence offering some respite from the heat and congestion of town. Today it is home to most of the island's economic and political elites. The Morne provides visitors with a spectacular view of the harbor and town, even if their arrival in Castries itself is something of a disappointment in comparison. Having suffered numerous fires in its history, including one that destroyed most of the city in 1948, Castries is now dominated by concrete and glass structures rather than the colorful clapboard construction utilized in most West Indian building. Castries may not physically resemble the towns in the former British West Indies that have retained their colonial architecture, yet of all of St. Lucia's towns, it is the most culturally oriented toward the Anglophone Caribbean. While the division between city and countryside is acute throughout the Caribbean, the distinction between Castries and rural St. Lucia is even more pronounced owing to the differences of culture and language that separate them.

Of the four officially Anglophone Windward Islands (which also include Dominica, St. Vincent, and Grenada), St. Lucia is the most populous, with 166,000 inhabitants, some 62,000 of whom reside in Castries (St. Lucia 2001b). With the exception of Martinique and Guadeloupe, which have the status of French Overseas Departments, the Windward Islands are independent parliamentary democracies associated with the British Commonwealth. Education, government, and most business and local broadcasting are conducted in English, and British standards of parliamentary order and debate animate government proceedings. In recent years, the officially English identity has been overlaid by media influences from the United States, arriving mainly via satellite television.

Yet St. Lucia's official identity masks a complex cultural history rooted in African slavery and torn by colonial rivalries between England and France. Most St. Lucians are fluent in or have at least a working knowledge of English, and English predominates in the city. For most rural residents, however, English remains a foreign tongue second to the language of home, a French-based Creole (known as Kwéyòl or Patwa).[1] Two centuries have passed since France surrendered its claim to St. Lucia, but the island retains an astonishingly powerful tie to the Francophone Caribbean. Both the names of its settlements and surnames of its people are overwhelmingly French. Unlike most former British colonies, the Roman Catholic Church has a longstanding presence on the island and claims the allegiance, however nominal, of most of its residents.[2] Interred in the Castries Cathedral are the French priests who evangelized master and slave alike in the eighteenth century. Jamaican reggae and Trinidadian calypso may predominate on the St. Lucian airwaves, but not far behind are the rhythms of Martinican zouk. Whether in curbside eateries, tourist restaurants, or homes, St. Lucian cuisine draws from both the English- and French-speaking islands. Notwithstanding their membership in the British Commonwealth, then, many St. Lucians look across the water to their neighbors in Martinique, Guadeloupe, and even French Guiana rather than their Commonwealth partners for their overall cultural sensibilities. As will be seen, such ties to the Francophone Caribbean have become increasingly vital to the survival of many rural households no longer able to survive exclusively from own-account agriculture.

Colonial Conflicts and Identities

Surprisingly, given their diminutive scale, the Windward Islands were the object of two centuries of intense rivalry between France and England. Both harbored powerful imperial ambitions that were frustrated by Spain's earlier arrival in the Caribbean. The Greater Antilles of Jamaica, Hispaniola, and Puerto Rico represented the real prize for Spanish colonialism, with their fertile lands and large native populations. In comparison, Spaniards viewed the Windwards as too small and too rugged to warrant permanent settlement, while the fierce reputation of the indigenous Caribs discouraged intensive inland exploration. The few contacts that did occur between Spanish landing parties and Caribs were enough to touch off disease epidemics that decimated native populations throughout the Caribbean.

For both the English and French, St. Lucia's attractiveness resided in its protected deep harbor on the leeward coast at Castries, an ideal site for resupplying ships destined elsewhere. After Britain failed at several attempts to colonize the island, French settlers began to arrive, several hundred by the mid seventeenth century. Both countries agreed at the time that the island should remain a neutral territory, but the presence of these settlers ensured that it would remain a de facto French colony for the next century. British forces seized St. Lucia following the outbreak of war between Britain and France in 1756, but the island was returned to France by treaty seven years later. At that point, more French planters and their African slaves arrived from Martinique to establish cocoa and coffee plantations in the fertile Cul de Sac and Mabouya Valleys.

Over the next fifty years, as Britain and France remained in a more or less permanent state of war, their forces waged repeated battles over the island, causing it to change hands fourteen times. During one period of French control in 1793, newly arrived Republican authorities freed the colony's slaves. A year later, however, British forces invaded and defeated the French garrison. Fearing reenslavement at the hands of the British, former slaves fled to remote areas, where they established heavily fortified Maroon settlements. Assisted by French troops who had avoided capture and inspired by Republican pledges of equal citizenship, the Maroons waged fifteen months of guerrilla attacks on the British garrison, an episode detailed in Breen's (1844) early history as the "Brigands' War." The attacks grew more costly for British forces after the arrival of reinforcements from Republican France. By 1795, guerrilla warfare and disease had driven the depleted British ranks from the island, but they returned *en masse* the following year to reconquer it. In 1797, most of the Maroons surrendered after securing a pledge that they would not be reenslaved. Yet they failed to anticipate that there were other plans for what the English regarded as an insurrectionary population of free blacks. "Glad to get rid of such troublesome 'Citoyens,'" Breen writes (1844: 107), British administrators "formed [the Maroons] into a regiment, which was sent to the coast of Africa." The island was formally ceded to Britain at the end of the Napoleonic Wars in 1814, ending a half century of shifting allegiances.

Having established definitive control over the island, the English sought its thorough cultural and institutional incorporation into the British West Indies. St. Lucia was administered by a governor appointed by the British Colonial Office and was later annexed to the other Windward Islands. In 1842, English was declared the island's official language, and aspects of the legal code were revised along the lines of English common law. British colonialism also reinvigorated, at least temporarily, a plantation system that had been weakened by the earlier abolition of slavery under French authorities.[3] Many French planters who had fled the island during the Republican period returned after 1803 to begin sugar production on estates that had formerly been given over to coffee and cocoa. After the British gained control of St. Lucia in 1814, slavery was reestablished on the island, but given the difficulty of reenslaving an already freed black population, it was limited in practice to slaves imported from elsewhere in the West Indies. By an Act of Parliament, slavery was replaced throughout the British Empire by "apprenticeship" in 1834 and abolished altogether four years later.

Despite British ambitions to remake St. Lucian society, many institutional changes either remained a legalistic veneer over deep-seated French traditions or were eventually reconciled with them. Eager to retain a functioning sugar producing sector and the planters who controlled it, British authorities extended civil rights to St. Lucian Catholics decades before their English counterparts enjoyed similar freedom of conscience (Lowenthal 1972: 29). The imposition of the English language was hampered by the inability or unwillingness of colonial authorities to establish schools in rural areas, and by the fact that formal education, where it existed, remained in the hands of French-speaking priests. Hence, while British authorities often lamented that court proceedings, government business, and interactions between administrators and populace usually required Kwéyòl translators, they did little to foster the learning of English in rural areas until the mid twentieth century. English-speaking Afro-Caribbean and East Indian laborers were imported throughout the nineteenth century both to ameliorate shortages of plantation wage labor and to facilitate the spread of English (Richardson 1997: 41). As a mechanism of cultural change such efforts failed conspicuously, for the children of immigrants usually grew up speaking Kwéyòl and were absorbed into the broader St. Lucian population. Finally, while St. Lucian laws were revised, they retained aspects of the Napoleonic Code that differed in crucial ways from English common law. If St. Lucia remains distinct from the rest of the former British West Indies by its culture and heritage, provisions in its legal code have resulted in a pattern of land tenure and livelihood also contrasting sharply with other Commonwealth Caribbean nations.

Even more than other West Indian societies, St. Lucia is a place of cultural hybridity. Little outward evidence remains to distinguish the once ethnically and geographically distinct populations that, willingly or not, have arrived on the island's shores since prehistory. Unlike neighboring St. Vincent and Dominica, St. Lucia no longer has an identifiable Amerindian minority, as its few surviving Caribs had intermarried with free blacks by the late eighteenth century. There are just a handful of the commercially prominent Chinese, Portuguese, and East Indians found in much of the Anglophone Caribbean. Syrians and other Arabs own many of the shops in Castries but often decline to identify with St. Lucia at all, many of them returning to the Middle East after retiring from the retail trade. Although many St. Lucians bear the surnames of the island's past plantation elite, the white members of these families are long gone, most having returned to metropolitan countries. As a result, the island is home to one of the most thoroughly creolized societies in the Anglophone Caribbean. Approximately 98 percent of the population is identified as having African ancestry (St. Lucia 2001b).

The absence of ethnic distinctions in the population does not, however, imply that St. Lucia is free of discrimination and the color prejudice that feeds it. With few exceptions, the island's urban political and economic elite tend to be lighter-skinned than the general population. They are also more oriented toward Great Britain and the United States in their language, behavior, and consumption patterns than they are to practices in the rural areas of their own country. Until recent decades, island elites deigned to speak Kwéyòl only poorly or not at all, reinforcing a patronizing view that it was appropriate only for colorful proverbs and communicating with the uneducated in rural areas. A local journalist summarized such attitudes as they existed in the late 1960s among Castries residents, although vestiges of these views are readily apparent today among many city dwellers:

The poor, barefoot, uneducated, unsophisticated, shy people in the out-districts ... looked up with awe and fawning respect to the well-dressed, well-spoken and better read city folk – the people who could boast of electricity, who met and hobnobbed with people from abroad, who went or probably might have gone to college ... The out-districts were a Never-Never land where people walked silently and uncomplainingly in misery and neglect, where people waited hand and foot on leadership and direction, and the occasional word of wisdom from the city folk of Castries. (Quoted in Lewis 1968: 150–151)

If a gradual shift is underway in the urban elite's view of rural traditions, so that a cabinet minister now delivers a campaign speech peppered with Kwéyòl expressions rather than one entirely in standard English, it may reflect more of a change in strategic thinking than an actual appreciation for village culture. Regardless of their low standing in the eyes of middle- and upper-class Castries residents, rural residents have avidly exercised their vote since receiving the electoral franchise in the waning years of colonialism and thus wield a considerable degree of control over the avenues of power. As will be seen, the recent political history of St. Lucia, and its banana industry in particular, cannot be understood apart from the efforts of aspiring office holders to acquire power by mobilizing the grievances, and thereby the votes, of rural residents. In the process, urbane Castries politicians have learned that if they openly disparage the language, identity and sensibilities of rural constituents they do so at their own grave risk.

Sharecropping and Family Land

It is an adage both in the social sciences and conventional wisdom that when the rich and poor come into conflict the latter usually come up short. The history of export agriculture in much of the world amply illustrates this point. Throughout much of Latin America, wherever small-scale farmers compete with plantations to sell their crops, their lands are often absorbed over time into larger commercial farms. Thus stripped of their landholdings, many former peasant proprietors become rural wage laborers rather than farmers, while those even less fortunate must make do with the uncertain returns of artisanal production, urban or transnational migration, drug trafficking, or a host of other precarious survival strategies.[4] These trends relate both to the vagaries of the markets in which export producers participate, and to farmers' disparate access to political power. Export prices of crops such as coffee, cocoa, bananas, sugar, and citrus are notoriously unstable: while consumption levels and fashions in the developed countries fluctuate widely, supplies of such crops usually outstrip long-term demand, in large part because of the absence of effective supply management among numerous producers in geographically dispersed areas. Further, the long-term prices for the inputs required of export production—fertilizer, herbicides, pesticides, and machinery and equipment—tend over time to increase relative to crop prices (De Janvry 1981). Lacking the cash reserves and access to credit enjoyed by large commercial estates, small-scale farmers are less able to survive periods of low prices and, unable to pay their bills, may find their land seized by creditors. Once alienated from the peasantry, these lands invariably end up in the hands of more economically robust large farms. More blatantly, however, agricultural elites may simply confiscate peasant lands for their own use, secure in the knowledge that government authorities will uphold their actions as legitimate or at least not worth a legal challenge.

This model of rural socioeconomic change formally originated in the work of the Russian Bolshevik leader and political theorist V.I. Lenin (1964), but it has become known in the literature of economic anthropology and political economy as social differentiation theory (Roseberry 1985; De Janvry and Vandeman 1987; Cancian 1992; Cook 2004). According to this perspective, household-based cultivators tend over time to diverge into two separate social classes: a tiny group of successful commercial farmers who expand their landholdings and scale of production, and a much larger mass of former peasants, now landless and reduced to providing the wage labor on commercial farms. The model describes how, in layperson's parlance, "the rich get richer and the poor get poorer" (Smith 1984). In the 1920s, a group of Russian agricultural economists led by A.V. Chayanov (1966) challenged this view of the inevitable disappearance of the peasantry, asserting that household agriculture could hold its own in competition with larger farms. For one, they argued, household units of production enjoy lower overhead costs as they rely on unpaid family labor rather than wage workers. Secondly, unlike commercial entities that require a given level of profit to remain in business, peasants have an intense, almost mystical attachment to the land and will work unimaginably long hours to satisfy their needs. Finally, Chayanov observed how peasant communities often engage in institutional and ceremonial practices that periodically redistribute wealth among their members, thereby providing something of a safety net for their poorest residents. For challenging what had become economic orthodoxy in Stalin's Soviet Union and the ensuing policy of forced collectivization, Chayanov was accused of counterrevolutionary conspiracy in 1930 and shot nine years later. Rediscovered after decades in obscurity,[5] his work has inspired scholars to investigate why peasants seem to stubbornly persist in the midst of commercial agriculture (see Shanin 1972, 1986; Sahlins 1972; Durrenberger 1984; Kerblay 1987; Bernstein and Byres 2001).

The predictions of social differentiation theory, readily borne out through much of Latin America (De Janvry 1981; Deere and De Janvry 1981), do indeed fall short of the Eastern Caribbean reality. On St. Lucia, a system of land tenure based on plantation production in the early nineteenth century has steadily given way to small-scale independent peasant production. The last vestiges of the plantation system were swept away by state-sponsored land distributions during the 1970s, although the system as a whole had been moribund for at least a century. Moreover, in contrast to Latin America, where landholdings have usually become more inequitable with the expansion of commercial export agriculture, that expansion has not led to the consolidation of land in fewer and fewer hands on St. Lucia. To an extent, Chayanov helps us to understand why social differentiation has not occurred in the manner predicted by political economists. The innate qualities and trajectories of the peasant household, including its famously intense "attachment to land," account in part for this tendency. More importantly, the peculiar institutional, cultural, and political context in which St. Lucian farmers have worked since the time of slavery has led to the emergence of an unusually resilient, if distinctive, pattern of land tenure on the island.

The experience of slavery in the West Indies fueled contradictory attitudes toward agriculture, many of which are still evident today. In the years immediately after abolition in 1838, during which sugar plantations operated with wage labor, planters lamented their difficulty in recruiting workers. Ex-slaves evidenced little desire to continue working for their former owners to produce a crop that had become synonymous with servitude. Most freedmen sought to distance themselves as much as possible from plantation slavery by seeking wage work or a trade in town, and some viewed farming as a distinctly less desirable livelihood because of its past connotations. Yet for most former slaves, gaining some personal control over land acquired an urgency that could never be fully appreciated by those who had not been enslaved (Marshall 1993: 100). Occupying, or preferably owning, a parcel of land to support oneself was equated with an irrevocable status of freedom. The outcome of the ex-slaves' passionate reaction against the plantation system and its connotations of servitude was that a West Indian peasantry was "reconstituted" from African origins and New World innovations (Mintz 1974: 132).

After 1838, West Indian planters were critically weakened in an economic and political sense, and for sheer survival were forced to reconcile themselves to the freedman's desire for independence. The decision of the British Parliament to abolish slavery was an early indication of their eroded political standing at home. The savvier, more politically connected merchant class in Britain increasingly viewed the West Indian plantation system and the tariffs that protected it as an archaic hindrance to the importation of cheaper commodities from outside the British Empire. If the abolition of slavery was the first battle in the war between colonial protectionism and free trade, the British merchants won decisively again with the Sugar Equalization Act in 1846. The act eliminated tariffs that sustained the price of West Indian sugar and allowed for the free introduction of much cheaper cane sugar produced in Cuba and the Dominican Republic, as well as beet sugar from the European continent. Earnings on West Indian plantations collapsed as a result and planters found it increasingly difficult to pay wages that would retain a free work force. Throughout much of the region, planter-dominated legislative councils, which were intended to fill an advisory role vis-à-vis colonial governors, attempted to retain laborers by restricting access to alternatives, either by refusing to initiate surveys of otherwise salable Crown land or by imposing heavy taxes on smallholders (Bolland 1981; Marshall 1985). In the Windwards, however, where rough, remote terrain provided opportunities for ex-slaves to occupy land as squatters while evading legal authorities, planters were forced to accept alternatives to wage labor in order to remain in production at all.

Soon after abolition on St. Lucia, the plantations' inability to attract wage laborers had led to the widespread adoption of *metayage,* a system of sharecropping with roots in medieval France. Under this arrangement, planters divided their estates among tenant farmers (*metayers*), who at the end of each year delivered cane from their individual parcels to the estate mill for processing. The terms of *metayage* were governed by a contract negotiated between the estate owner and individual sharecropper. Usually *metayers* preferred oral contracts because they were reluctant to affix their mark to any document, fearing that it might revoke their freedom. One written 1848 contract survives, however, and specifies that the estate owner was to provide the *metayer* with three acres of land on which to grow sugar for six years, in exchange for a share of one-half of the total production (Adrien 1996). In addition, the *metayer* was provided with land on the periphery of the plantation to grow staple crops ("provisions") and erect a house. The *metayer* was also given an advance, to be deducted from his gross production at harvest time before shares were determined. Finally, after the estate manufactured sugar from the *metayer*'s cane, he was given the value of his share of production in cash consistent with the current market price.

The *metayage* system was adopted on a few estates elsewhere in the West Indies, but only in St. Lucia did it become the primary basis of export agriculture after slavery. Adrien (1996) speculates that it was embraced by much of the rural population because it corresponded with traditional patterns of landholding and reciprocity distinctive to the island. On St. Lucia, land was commonly shared among kin in a system of land tenure known as family land (in Kwéyòl, *ti familie*). Under these arrangements, when a proprietor died intestate (i.e., without a valid will), all heirs inherited an equal share of the holding. The land would ordinarily not be subdivided, but every heir would theoretically retain rights of access to the parcel. Indeed, no portion of it could be sold to a new owner without the stated agreement of all co-owners, a daunting requirement when dozens of individuals may claim rights over a single parcel after the passage of several generations (Bruce 1983; Cole 1994). Frequently, some heirs would temporarily relinquish their rights of cultivation to others in exchange for a negotiated share of the produce grown on the land. Here the resemblance to formal sharecropping becomes apparent (Barrow 1992).

On St. Lucia, access rights to family land and labor alike were widely shared among rural residents. In a practice known as *coup de main* (in Kwéyòl, *koudeman*), farmers entered into informal agreements to provide voluntary reciprocal labor on each other's parcels on alternate days. Because it was most widely practiced among kin, *koudeman* often joined together cultivators on family land parcels, resulting in complex patterns of sharing in both labor and produce. Similar patterns of labor exchange (known also as *koudeman* on Dominica and as "swap labor" on St. Vincent) are practiced elsewhere in the Caribbean, and some have attributed them to antecedent African practices (Barrow 1992). Although family land tenure is found—at a much lower incidence—elsewhere in the Anglophone Caribbean, only on St. Lucia was it institutionalized in inheritance law, which specifies that all children inherit property equally unless a will indicates otherwise (Bruce 1983). This requirement is derived from the Napoleonic Code and differs from other West Indian inheritance laws, which usually specify the eldest legitimate son as the sole legal heir. The Napoleonic provision persisted in the St. Lucia Civil Code of 1897, despite the earlier British revision of St. Lucia's laws, and undoubtedly accounts for the much higher prevalence of family land on the island (Bruce 1983: 17).

Given the requirement that all heirs agree upon its sale, family land is rarely if ever sold. Hence, a key mechanism of social differentiation—the transfer of land from peasant to plantation via sale—becomes blocked by legal preconditions. Family land tenure has long been disparaged by agricultural experts who view it as a disincentive to investment and development (see Crichlow 1994: 24), but from the viewpoint of the rural poor it forms, in Lewis's memorable phrase, a bulwark "without which [they] would be naked against the blasts of life" (1968: 153). Even where land is individually owned so that family tenure creates no impediment to sale, the intense attachment to land as a symbol of independence persists in the form of extraordinarily high land prices throughout peasant areas of the Caribbean. Many small proprietors, even when faced with the prospect of being unable to survive in farming, remain loath to sell their land at any price.

Similarly, over time *metayage* strengthened peasant farmers relative to the estates that purchased their crops. The alternative to *metayage* was squatting on Crown lands in remote areas, a practice that authorities could do little to prevent.[6] Estate managers recognized that squatting deprived them of both labor and production, so they were rarely able to negotiate with *metayers* from a position of strength. In addition to the income derived from their share of production, *metayers* could hire themselves out at slack times and sell crops from their provision grounds. Adrien (1996: 31) mentions the case of a *metayer* who earned £60 in 1845 from his provision grounds alone, not including his share from land under *metayage*. This occurred at a time when the average agricultural worker earned slightly over £10 annually in full-time wage labor.

Earnings of this magnitude permitted many *metayers* to accumulate wealth and purchase land, which sold at between £2 and £20 per acre on the island in the 1840s. According to the 1897 West India Royal Commission that investigated land tenure in the British Caribbean, over the previous half century the number of peasant landowners on St. Lucia had increased by 4,655 individuals, or 346 percent. The commissioners concluded that the large majority of these landowners "were formerly labourers on sugar estates who, under the metayer system, purchased plots of land with their proceeds of their share of sugar" (in Adrien 1996: 37). Over time, the number of *metayers* declined relative to the number of independent peasant landholders, not all of whom produced cane for sale to factories. This afforded the remaining *metayers* still greater bargaining power in negotiating contracts with landowners. The equal shares arrangements of the nineteenth century gave way to contracts in which *metayers* retained two-thirds of production by the early twentieth century, and eventually four-fifths by the final years of the arrangement in the 1950s (Adrien 1996: 37).

Creating a Peasantry

Notwithstanding the direct occupation of much of the colony's land by *metayers* and peasant landholders, all of St. Lucia's sugar refining remained in the hands of estate owners. In addition, the estates retained the richest bottomlands in the Mabouya, Cul de Sac, and Roseau Valleys under plantation production. In the course of the nineteenth century, nearly all of the original French planter families confronted bankruptcy and sold their lands to British merchants in town (Romalis 1975). Management of the estates rested in the hands of appointed overseers who negotiated contracts with *metayers* and supervised wage laborers on plantation lands. *Metayers* gained some degree of autonomy because of their control of provision grounds, but wage laborers were in a decidedly disadvantaged position. Whether from tacit agreements among the managers of St. Lucia's three large estates to suppress wages, or from the continuing malaise that affected sugar prices well into the twentieth century, agricultural wages on the island remained stagnant for generations (Lewis 1968: 148). Convened to investigate labor relations in the wake of region-wide strikes during the 1930s, the Moyne Commission concluded that on "the smaller and poorer islands, rates for agricultural labour have advanced little beyond the shilling-a-day introduced after emancipation" (in Acosta and Casimir 1985: 45). The commission pointed out that farm wages on St. Lucia and St. Vincent were the lowest in the region.

Like the rest of the West Indies, St. Lucia was periodically wracked by rural labor unrest from Emancipation through most of twentieth century. Worker discontent centered on agricultural wages that not only failed to satisfy the basic needs of their families, but fell steadily behind the rising cost of living, which was closely tied to imported commodities. After 1884, when cheap European beet sugar flooded the English market, sugar prices in the Windwards plunged into a deep depression that persisted for decades. Charged with investigating the impact of these trends on the islands' economies, members of the 1897 West India Royal Commission were shocked by the levels of infant mortality and even starvation prevailing among farm worker families (Richardson 1997: 25). At least as troubling to the commissioners was the bitter resentment that the islands' wage-earning populations expressed toward the remaining white elites, with an attendant fear that their deepening misery would trigger a social explosion that threatened British political control altogether.[7] Yet such desperation was much less evident among the smallholding segments of the islands' populations, many of whom had retreated from sugar production in favor of subsistence crops and produce that could be sold on town markets. The commissioners concluded with a recommendation designed to bolster political stability as much as the welfare of the working population; that is, the settlement of plantation workers "on small plots of land as peasant proprietors" (in Richardson 1997: 212).

The recommendations of the West India Royal Commission were received coolly by planter-dominated colonial governments in much of the region, and where the plantation sector remained relatively viable, as in Barbados, they encountered prolonged planter intransigence (Lewis 1968: 89). In the Windwards, though, where planters were comparatively weakened in both an economic and political sense, some of the recommendations made their way eventually into policy (Acosta and Casimir 1985). On St. Vincent, for example, an ambitious settlement program was embarked upon, while on St. Lucia the commission report signaled a more laissez-faire attitude toward those who squatted on government land. Throughout the Windward Islands, plantation production retreated to the estate lands immediately surrounding sugar mills, and smallholdings increased dramatically in numbers during the early twentieth century. The region continued to experience occasional labor conflict, notably during another period of prolonged depression in the sugar industry during the 1930s (Bolland 1995). Following its investigation of labor relations in the region, the 1937 Moyne Commission recommended that West Indian workers be granted the right to collectively bargain through trade unions. Although the 1897 and 1937 commissions were intended to strengthen colonialism through reform, they established the preconditions that eventually led to the dismantling of British rule in the Caribbean. The West India Commission recognized that extending land to the landless conferred some political legitimacy, a view shared by the St. Lucian leaders who wrested power from Britain decades later. These men had risen to prominence in the trade union movement encouraged by the Moyne Commission, and they consolidated their political support by challenging the remnants of the plantation system.

Much as it lent an imperative to creating a politically stable peasantry, the prolonged depression in the sugar market had reconciled colonial governments to the urgent need for agricultural diversification. At the invitation of St. Lucia's colonial administration, the Swift Banana Company, a United Fruit subsidiary, purchased land in 1925 to produce bananas for the US market. The government encouraged smallholders to produce bananas for sale to Swift, even offering instruction to farmers on how to cultivate the crop. By 1927, however, Panama Disease (*Fusarium oxysporum cubense*, a highly contagious soil-borne fungus) had decimated many of St. Lucia's banana-producing lands, causing the company to abandon the island. In 1933, the island's banana trade was revived with the arrival of the Canadian Banana Company, another United Fruit subsidiary. That company's offer to purchase all fruit in good condition for immediate payment sparked a dramatic increase in banana plantings. Because the banana cultivar most widely grown on the island remained the disease-prone Gros Michel, however, Panama Disease again broke out and infected many farms. By 1941, disease and a shortage of shipping due to World War II conspired to once again wipe out banana production for export (Romalis 1975: 230).

Despite these inauspicious beginnings, banana production resumed in 1948 when Antilles Products Ltd, an independent Irish company, negotiated a contract with the St. Lucian government to purchase one million stems of bananas over fifteen years. This time the company insisted upon plant varieties that were resistant to Panama Disease (initially Lacatan, and later the Giant Cavendish that is the basis of the banana trade today). A team of agricultural experts from Britain visited in 1951 to recommend the creation of a Banana Growers' Association (BGA) as an entity that would represent the interests of growers and provide services such as credit, inputs, pest control, and insurance. Yet Antilles Products received only tepid support from island governments in its bid to develop an export industry, reflecting administrators' fears that another collapse might occur after a few years of expansion (Romalis 1975: 231). Unlike previous attempts to export bananas, Antilles Products was oriented to the European (Irish and Belgian) markets, later securing agreements to export fruit to Britain. In 1954, Antilles Products was acquired by John van Geest, a Dutch investor who had developed a lucrative fruit and vegetable business in England.

Partly because of his greater stature in the English market and greater success in organizing shipping between the Windwards and Britain, Geest received a measure of enthusiastic UK government support that had been withheld from earlier initiatives to export bananas. For the British government in the waning years of colonialism, the promotion of Windwards banana production satisfied a number of critical political and economic objectives. Foremost among these was the continuing preoccupation with political "stability" rooted in island livelihoods based on smallholding farming, a legacy from the 1897 West India Commission recommendations. Yet the creation of a Caribbean banana industry also satisfied political and economic objectives closer to home. By the 1950s, the Windwards had become chronically and deeply dependent on grant-in-aid assistance from Britain, so the infusion of export earnings from banana sales was thought to offset some of the economic burden that the islands created for the central treasury. Moreover, most other bananas in the UK market were imported by Fyffes Ltd., then a wholly-owned subsidiary of the United Fruit Company. Geest's British-based importing operations were thus seen by the government as a significant counterweight to the American banana multinational that had sought—often by ruthless measures—to establish monopoly control of both the supply and retail markets in which it operated.

The Emergence of Party Politics

The [Crown Colony] system was a perfect instrument for the degradation of political life, for it gave the illusion of power without the reality of responsibility, and turned decent men into rancorous citizens.
—Gordon K. Lewis (1968)

In advocating the recognition of trade unions, the 1937 Moyne Commission laid the groundwork for the first mass political movements on St. Lucia and the native-born politicians who were to lead them. The rise of trade unionism also coincided with universal adult suffrage, which was introduced to the colony under Britain's Labour government in 1951. Previously, St. Lucians who wished to vote for the members of town boards and the legislative council were required to demonstrate functional literacy in English as well as minimum property and income requirements. Under Crown Colony provisions in effect since 1936, the island's chief governing body was its legislative council, composed of five elected "unofficial" members who served beside the "official" majority of eight members appointed by the governor of the Windward Islands (Wayne 2002: iii). Under such circumstances, as Lewis noted in his scathing critique of Crown Colony governance, "the popularly elected element was unavoidably cast into the role of an opposition whose fractious behavior would never be quelled by the requirement, and the opportunity, to take responsibility itself" (1968: 101).

Fewer than 25 percent of all St. Lucians were eligible to vote for unofficial members under the literacy requirement, a direct result of the lack of schools in rural areas of the island where most of the population lived (Da Breo 1981). It is no coincidence, then, that St. Lucians who held office or aspired to it were urban, educated, and largely of middle-class origin. With the introduction of universal adult suffrage during the 1950s, the rural Kwéyòl-speaking majority was now incorporated into the political process in a way that middle-class English-speaking politicians could no longer afford to ignore. Regardless of the motives that drew them into the labor movement, aspiring political leaders found that mobilizing rural voters was inextricable from engaging in trade union activity targeted at a newly enfranchised rural majority.

The St. Lucia Cooperative Workers Union was initially organized in Castries, but during the 1950s it enjoyed its greatest success in recruiting members and organizing strikes among workers on the remaining sugar estates. The union was led by George F. L. Charles and John Compton, two elected members of the legislative council who also spearheaded the development of the St. Lucia Labour Party (SLP). Charles and Compton assumed leadership of the 1957 strike against the Dennery Factory estate of Denis Barnard in the eastern Mabouya Valley and the Cul de Sac and Roseau estates of Harold Devaux. One of the few remaining members of St. Lucia's white plantocracy, Barnard was notorious for the harsh, humiliating treatment of workers on his farm, including, according to strikers, his sexual exploitation of workers' wives and daughters patterned after the medieval prerogative of *droit du seigneur* (CO 1031/2809b). The highest-ranking British official in residence, Administrator J. K. R. Thorp, officially opposed the strike and deplored the involvement of legislative council members in it. In private, however, he complained in a dispatch to the Windward Islands governor that the planter's retrograde attitudes served only to aggravate anti-colonial sentiments on the island. Barnard, he wrote, "still lives in a world which vanished many years ago, and he retains an outlook and behaves in a manner which is feudal in the extreme, and which cannot possibly continue to exist in the West Indies as they are today without causing disaster" (CO 1031/2809b). Such attitudes, he argued, played directly into the political strategies of Charles and Compton, who, not coincidentally, represented the very Cul de Sac and Dennery constituencies in which striking workers resided.

In this light, it is worth quoting Thorp's communication at length, for it illustrates how politicians responded to universal adult suffrage by drawing upon social injustice and racism as major electoral campaign strategies. Indeed, with some modification the passage could well stand for the subsequent history of St. Lucian electoral politics:

> Politics in St. Lucia are conducted on an entirely amoral basis, and it can be said with but small exaggeration that few of our present leading Labour politicians would consider for a moment that ... the general welfare of the population should take precedence over their own urgent need for votes ... [T]he evolution of the sugar industry has resulted in a situation whereby the normal clash between workers and employers has become enmeshed in political intrigue and personal animosities ... [B]oth Mr. Harold Devaux and Mr. Denis Barnard are not only employers, as such, but for long past have been the object of continuous and bitter vote-catching attacks as being the arch-prototypes of the old style ruling class, with which in the minds of the masses Government is still identified. The Labour politicians do all they can to encourage this outlook which suits their purposes. For both Mr. Charles and Mr. John Compton a major upset in the sugar industry can be shown to imply a final struggle by the masses to overthrow the power of the 'white man' (a term which in St. Lucia includes coloured property owners). This was a heaven-sent political opportunity, which from their point of view could not be missed. (CO 1031/2809b)

Yet if colonial officials feared that intransigent planters strengthened the hands of ambitious politicians, they seemed oblivious to how their own actions also inflamed anti-colonial sentiments. Finding their demands for higher wages ignored by the estates and dismissed as "impractical" by Thorp, Charles and Compton organized picket lines and roadblocks to prevent the introduction of strikebreakers willing to harvest cane and bananas. Colonial officials reacted to these "disturbances" in exactly the same fashion as their nineteenth-century predecessors: by importing more than one hundred heavily armed police from Barbados and Grenada to threaten and arrest strikers. This strategy consciously drew upon the deep-seated sense of cultural superiority that Anglophone West Indians evidenced toward their Kwéyòl-speaking counterparts. Officials also requested the dispatch of a naval destroyer, the HMS *Bigbury Bay*, for further intimidating effect. By the late 1950s English officials were outwardly reconciled to local self-government, but their private communications reveal the same racist arguments that had long justified the denial of self-rule to the West Indies. Commenting on the impending arrival of the destroyer, a functionary in the Colonial Office wrote that "a warship ... has, quite apart from the access of armed strength it provides, an immediate calming effect in the kind of sudden violence which can arise among the volatile inhabitants of these islands, and its mere presence restores morale and helps to prevent isolated incidents from developing into more serious class or colour strife" (CO 1031/2808).

Compton and Charles's decision to extend the strike to workers who loaded banana stems onto freighters forced a reluctant government to mediate the conflict. Whereas sugar had become but a marginal part of the island economy by the late 1950s and was soon to disappear altogether, a strike in the banana industry threatened the colony's largest source of export earnings. After six weeks of negotiation a new wage contract was signed that covered both estate workers and banana carriers. The dispute catapulted Compton and Charles to national political attention as the saviors of the rural working class, the barefoot, largely illiterate Kwéyòl-speaking farmers and wage laborers often derided by Castries residents as "country bookies" (equivalent to "rubes").

Compton's image had been especially burnished from a confrontation in which he and Barnard had drawn guns on each other, and from his subsequent arrest and conviction for threatening the estate owner. He had become, according to Charles, "a symbol" to the nation, and hundreds converged on his trial in Dennery out of solidarity (1994: 55). Thus it proved galling to the urbane, London-educated Compton that the more provincial Charles, a former timekeeper and clerk, was selected as the island's first chief minister when Britain granted internal self-rule in 1961. Compton had briefly quit the SLP during an earlier leadership dispute, but this time, rather than serve in a government that he did not head, he left the SLP and never returned. For the remainder of his political career, he and Charles, as well as Charles's successors in the SLP, were to vie bitterly for the nation's leadership. Compton was to emerge more often as the victor in such struggles, thanks to his recognition of the critical role that rural residents and the banana industry could play in his political ambitions.

"A Quiet Revolution"

After John Compton and several allies in what was deemed the "intellectual wing" of the SLP government left the party in 1961, he expanded his constituency by establishing an opposition party, the National Labour Movement, and acquiring a position on the executive board of the five thousand member–strong Banana Growers' Association. For eighteen months Compton served both in the legislative council and as the BGA's director, a position offering an unrivaled platform for his political ambitions. Compton rallied support among wage laborers and farmers by inveighing against the SLP's "betrayal" of the working class for its association with the remaining sugar estate owners. For such claims, Compton was often denounced as a "communist" by the island's business-dominated press, despite the fact that he assiduously cultivated middle-class allies from Castries in his bid for power (Da Breo 1981: 58).

When the government introduced legislation prohibiting political party leaders and members of Parliament from holding executive positions in the BGA, small-scale growers accurately perceived the proposed law as an attack on their ostensible champion within the organization. Ironically, the bill also proposed to expand the representation of small-scale farmers on the executive board, but this point was lost among the many who believed it to be exclusively targeted at Compton. Although the SLP won a short-term battle against Compton in the BGA by forcing him off the board, it proved to be a Pyrrhic victory. Gauging the deep unpopularity of the measure with rural voters, two SLP cabinet members who had earlier voted for it now resigned from the government and joined with Compton. Charles was forced to call elections, which John Compton's newly organized United Workers Party (UWP) won handily with extensive support in rural areas (Da Breo 1981: 60).

With the exception of a three-year period in the early 1980s, Compton was to hold office as chief minister, premier, and finally prime minister from 1964 until 1996.[8] Having risen to power in part by challenging government interference in the BGA, he did not, as many supporters expected, seek to repeal the legislation prohibiting officeholders from also holding executive positions in the association. Mindful that such a position had proven critical to his own political ascent, he was determined to deny similar opportunities to potential opponents within the BGA (Da Breo 1981: 60). Yet the mobilization of small-scale growers that led to the election of the UWP government also created a newfound sense of small-grower empowerment within the BGA. Mounting debts due to the construction of a lavish new BGA headquarters and defaults on loan payments heightened divisions between small growers and the middle-class professionals who dominated the executive, as each blamed the other for the BGA's financial straits (Romalis 1975: 236). When Premier Compton approached the Canadian government for financial aid to offset BGA debts and the effects of declining world banana prices, Canadian assistance came on condition of an industry-wide efficiency study designed to reduce costs and improve profitability.

Completed in 1967, the consultant's report recommended severe reductions in the number of fruit buying centers, BGA staff, and delegates representing district branches. Most of these changes would negatively affect small growers both economically and in their representation within the organization. The report also recommended converting the BGA into a statutory organization, with the government holding seats on the board of directors and claiming the right to dissolve the board at its discretion. Although the so-called "professional" members of the BGA (mainly large-scale and absentee farmers) largely supported these measures, they were overwhelmingly opposed by the vast majority of the membership, which consisted of small growers. Aware of the political consequences of direct interference in the BGA's business, Compton appeared to remain aloof from the association's internal divisions, but he had privately agreed to the Canadian consultants' terms as a condition of assistance. The membership voted to replace the entire board of directors, but in the end the BGA was left with little alternative but to accept the proposed changes. In what appeared to be a move coordinated with the release of the report, the local branches of all three metropolitan banks in the colony (two of them based in Canada) suddenly cut off credit to the BGA to force acquiescence to its terms (Da Breo 1981).

Under the terms of the BGA's reorganization in 1968, a nine-member board of directors was established. Voting for board members had earlier occurred on an at-large basis, culminating in a sweep of all the seats by small-scale farmers in 1967. Following the BGA's reorganization, seats were apportioned according to the members' scale of production, with all farmers classified by acreage as small-, medium-, or large-scale producers. Two seats on the board were allotted to farmers representing each category, while the government appointed the remaining three board members. Small farmers, defined as those holding ten acres or less, comprised over 85 percent of all growers but were now represented by just two of the nine positions on the executive. The BGA's reorganization had strengthened the government's control and lessened small-grower participation, but it was not entirely "the final defeat of mass small grower democratic action," as an earlier observer predicted (Romalis 1975: 237). Rather, having found their voices silenced within the BGA, small growers in later years turned to new leaders who challenged the association from the outside to express their grievances. By the 1990s, this strategy had brought many small growers into open conflict with Compton's government and the BGA that it controlled.

Recognizing the key role that farmers played in his electoral successes, during most of his term in office Compton retained for himself the portfolio of minister of agriculture and publicly flaunted his own identity as a banana farmer. During his tenure, Compton engineered the dismantling of the remaining agricultural estates in the Mabouya, Roseau, and Cul-de-Sac Valleys. By 1961, the Devaux family had sold the latter two estates to Geest Ltd., which converted them from sugar to banana plantations operated with wage labor (Compton, pers. comm. 2004). Similarly, the Dennery lands had been converted to bananas by the early 1960s. By the end of the decade, the estate had passed to one of Barnard's sons, who evidenced little interest in the farm and offered to sell it to the government. Compton seized the opportunity to convert the valley estates to small farms, recognizing the potential to solidify his constituency through land grants and cheap credit. Such allocations would permit former wage laborers to become independent farmers in a flourishing banana industry. To accomplish this transformation he utilized the Sugar Price Stabilisation Fund that had been provided to the colony by the British government on the recommendation of the Moyne Commission (Compton 2003: 10). The fund had remained unused, as the price of St. Lucian sugar had never fallen below world market levels. With the demise of the sugar industry, Compton argued that the remaining revenues should provide seed money to create thriving small-scale banana farms out of the moribund estate system.

Using such funds, and with the help of the Commonwealth Development Corporation, Compton's government purchased the Geest holdings and Dennery estate and subdivided them into five- and ten-acre parcels. These lands were made available to squatters and wage laborers on the basis of long-term credit, with payments deducted automatically from the recipient's banana sales. The most ambitious of these efforts, known as the St. Lucia Model Farms Project, took place during the 1970s in the Roseau Valley, which was occupied almost entirely by wage laborers lacking experience as own-account farmers (St. Lucia 1987). The Model Farms initiative entailed a land distribution and extension program that developed five-acre farms from a former Geest estate and then transferred them to program recipients, who were literally taught by extension agents to become banana farmers. In the Cul-de-Sac Valley, lands were transferred to individuals who had greater farming experience and therefore required less in the way of preparation. The Mabouya Valley Development Project

(MVDP) of the 1980s and 1990s fell somewhere between these poles in terms of the provision of services. A major goal of the MVDP, which remained unfulfilled despite substantial national and international financial support for the effort, was an effort to "regularize" land tenure by replacing family land with individual titles (OAS 1991). Much as the multiple and conflicting demands to parcels precluded market sale, they also hindered bureaucratic efforts to individualize land tenure.

Years later, Compton noted that the land settlement projects were not universally welcomed and had led to a break with his former allies in the labor movement. "Roseau was always a difficult area," he recalled.

> It was an area where there was always some kind of struggle. Any politician who wanted to run for election, they would get a public address system and go down to Roseau and whip them up … Because the trade unions did not have a lot of power, so they wanted this pool of restless laborers who they could exploit at election time. Now if these people converted from being laborers into farmers, they had a stake in the system. You can't call a strike … [W]hen we were using the funds [for land settlement], this unholy alliance of the former estate owners and the unions, they came together, they wanted to share the money. To hand out the money to the laborers so you can have a great party on Saturday night. So I said, no, let me … use it as seed money for the Quiet Revolution. (Compton, pers. comm. 2004)

Viewed in light of the agency model mentioned earlier, Compton's recollections reveal the transformation of his political strategies as he moved from labor militant to head of government. Having risen to power through the same tactics that he later deplored in others, he consolidated his position by establishing an economically stable and politically quiescent rural voter base. His strategy of transforming a restive anti-colonialist working class into a stable political clientele was nothing less than the delayed fulfillment of the 1897 West Indian Commission's proposals. In the process of extending land to the landless, he remade himself from a "communist" labor agitator into "Daddy Compton," a benevolent father figure who claimed personal credit for the prosperity enjoyed by rural communities during the heyday of the banana industry. Compton's "Quiet Revolution" was to be measured not by the socialist and anti-colonial rhetoric of his years in the labor movement, but by the substantial dwellings, private vehicles, and well-nourished children abounding in banana-producing communities. Such scenes of economic tranquility were calculated to return his United Workers Party to power in election after election. What he failed to calculate was that the same strategies that fueled his rise to power could be used against him when the fortunes of the banana industry began to decline decades later.

Notes

1. In addition to standard English and Kwéyòl, a West Indian English–based Creole is also spoken on St. Lucia, more commonly in town than in rural settings. A teacher who worked as a census enumerator in the rural Mabouya Valley in 2001 stated that about 60 percent of the valley's adult residents are fluent in English (Mathurin, pers. comm. 2004). For residents between the ages of twelve and forty, almost all of whom have had some formal schooling, that figure exceeds 90 percent, but it drops off sharply for older residents.

2. Past colonial rivalries are also expressed in forms of cultural expression distinctive to St. Lucia. During the early nineteenth century, many rural communities witnessed the rise of La Rose and La Marguerite societies, sodalities within local Catholic parishes that represented the warring colonial powers. Both societies had elected positions of royalty, and in their heyday their members met weekly to play music, sing, and dance. The celebrations of the groups differed stylistically, and in annual pre-Lenten competitions, La Rose, representing the "English" faction and La Marguerite, representing the "French," vied for community recognition. According to older residents, these traditions had died out in the Mabouya Valley by the 1970s.

3. Independently, Napoleon had reestablished slavery throughout France's remaining Caribbean colonies in 1802, and it was to persist until 1848 (Dubois 2004).

4. Exceptions to these trends are numerous (see Kay 1974), but most arise as a result of political intervention designed to ameliorate the loss of peasant lands. Hence, various forms of peasant struggle and ensuing redistributive policies by reformist states have resulted in more equitable land distribution, at least for a period of time, in places such as Mexico, Costa Rica, and Ecuador. These trends are also confounded by the fact that smaller, more capitalized farms are usually more profitable on a per-acre basis than much larger farms operated along the lines of traditional haciendas, which employed archaic technology and were geared mostly for local markets.

5. Chayanov's work had disappeared from Soviet libraries by the time of his imprisonment, but before then had been translated into Japanese. It was almost entirely unknown in the English-speaking world until its translation from Japanese into English in 1966.

6. Squatting in remote areas is widespread to this day, and is believed to account for most of the island's marijuana production.

7. Commissioners' fears of an impending uprising were probably not exaggerated. In the 1865 Morant Bay rebellion in Jamaica, dozens had been killed during an armed insurrection arising in part from resentment over rents and low wages in the island's sugar-growing areas as well as continued white legal and political privilege (Heuman 1994: 44–46).

8. Many island political observers were astonished in December 2006, when the 81-year old Compton once again led his party to power in general elections, decisively defeating the incumbent SLP led by the much younger Kenny Anthony (see Chapter Six).

— Chapter Three —

BANANANOMICS
Work and Identity among Island Growers

Don't cas your eye nor turn your nose,
Don't judge a man by his patchy clothes,
I'm a strong man, a proud man, an I'm free,
Free as dese mountains, free as dis sea,
I know myself, an I know my ways,
An will sing wid pride to de end o my days
Praise God an m'big right han
I will live an die a banana man.
—Evan Jones, The Song of the Banana Man (in Young 1993)

The Importance of Independence

Asked what they like about growing bananas for a living, St. Lucian farmers almost invariably speak of the independence it offers them. The ability to earn a livelihood without being subject to the arbitrary demands of others is a widely held value in Caribbean society. In this respect, many of the observations that Browne (2005) makes of the importance of personal autonomy in Martinican Creole culture apply equally well to St. Lucia and the other Windward Islands. A desire for independence is as deeply rooted in West Indians' historical experience as is their famously intense attachment to land. Stripped of their identity and personhood during centuries of slavery, Afro-Caribbean people have struggled ever since emancipation to reassert their humanity. The painstaking attention that islanders accord their appearance in public may be seen as one such assertion, a symbolic inversion of the time that their forebears were dressed in rags and denied any form of personal adornment. Such attitudes have persisted as well among West Indians who have left the islands for other places. St. Lucians who long ago settled in London, Toronto, or New York are reluctant to part with the fragment of land "back home" that once signaled personal independence and a bulwark against plantation servitude.

When speaking of their livelihoods, St. Lucian banana farmers also offer up a litany of complaints. Their earnings are too little for the amount of work they perform, inputs are costly and scarce, the specifications for fruit handling and packaging are excessive and arbitrary, and the industry's leaders are corrupt and overly political. Yet when compared with other livelihoods available on the island, banana farming trumps every alternative because of the independence it affords. Rural St. Lucians speak of being able to determine their own hours of work, to come and go on the farm as they please, and to retain for themselves all of the monetary benefits of their labor. In contrast, when farmers mention those who work in factories, businesses, or tourism, their comments and tone of voice evoke pity for the dependent condition of wage earners. "When you work for wages, you are only working to make money for somebody else," Lucretia Alexander, a Mabouya Valley resident, volunteers. "They want you as a slave, to do their bidding alone. Why should you work for them any harder than you have to? But when you work for yourself, you keep the profit in your own pocket." Interestingly, farmers such as Alexander often compare employers to slaveholders, even when, like her, they themselves employ wage workers on their farms.

Often the ideal of personal independence conflicts with the conventions of sharing that inform how family farms and, more generally, household economies operate elsewhere. The ideal of the "family labor farm," in which most productive labor is performed by household members on a non-wage basis, constituted Chayanov's model of the peasant household and remains the basis of the US Department of Agriculture's definition of the family farm (Barlett 1987). Yet this ideal is rarely encountered on St. Lucia or elsewhere in the Windwards. Among the 133 Mabouya Valley banana farmers surveyed during fieldwork in 2004 (Table 3.1), ninety-four (71 percent) utilize no unpaid family labor, other than their spouses.[1] Occasionally, older farmers will subdivide a portion of their farm among their adult children so that each can derive some personal income from an individual plot. If they work on their parents' plot, adult sons and daughters who reside at home are usually paid at the same rate as workers having no relationship to the owners (customarily EC $40 [US $15] per four- to six-hour day, or the equivalent of US $20 on harvest days, when the working day extends to eight hours or more). Among common-law and married couples, farms are generally run jointly, but in some instances a farmer will pay wages to his or her spouse for the work they perform. This is

Table 3.1 | Characteristics of Banana Farmers (n = 133):
The Mabouya Valley, 2004

	Min.	*Max.*	*Mean*
Age of farmer	23	83	44.9
Household size	1	11	5.1
Years of school	0	20	7.5
Years farming here	1	65	20.8
Number of parcels farmed	1	4	1.2
Acreage in bananas	0.5	10	4.3
Avg. monthly income from other crops	0	$5,000	$361
Boxes shipped in previous fortnight	5	503	75.6
Gross sales in previous fortnight	$105	$6,858	$1,183
Wages paid in previous fortnight	0	$1,500	$340
Net earnings in previous fortnight	0	$2,606	$643
Percent of assets from banana sales	10	100	62.2

Source: Author's survey data
All figures in Eastern Caribbean dollars (EC $1.00 = US $0.38)

especially true where the registered banana grower and farm operator is a woman whose husband works beside her on the farm rather than in an off-farm job. Although family members are usually paid for their labor, not a few growers prefer to hire nonrelatives rather than kin, who they believe will expect favored treatment.

The cash basis of most farm labor, including that of household members, is offset to some extent by persisting patterns of nonmonetary labor sharing and family land tenure. Despite past concerted efforts by the St. Lucian government to formalize individual land tenure, family land continues as the basis of many rural households' livelihoods. The Mabouya Valley was the site of an ambitious but ultimately unsuccessful Organization of American States (OAS)–funded program for individual land titling during the 1980s.[2] As of 2004, thirty-eight out of the 133 surveyed banana farmers (28.5 percent) in the valley continue to retain some access to family land, almost always in addition to other parcels that they own or rent individually. Although based in principle on sharing among kin, family land often engenders conflict when there are different understandings among family members about access rights to land and crops. Theoretically, whoever plants and tends a crop on family land has the exclusive right to harvest it, but occasionally kinsmen help themselves to each others' produce without securing permission.

More commonly, conflicts arise over rights of access to coconuts, bread-fruit (*Artocarpus altilis*), citrus, and other tree crops that were planted years ago by now-deceased family members. Ostensibly, rights to tree crops are inherited equally, like family land itself. They may be harvested by all beneficiaries of a particular parcel, but opinions as to what constitutes a fair division of the harvest usually differ among heirs. Allegations of prae-dial larceny, or crop theft, are widespread in the Mabouya Valley, where it was reported by 65 percent (86 out of 133) of surveyed banana grow-ers. Many farmers assert that praedial larceny has increased in tandem with local economic difficulties in recent years, but other accounts sug-gest that the practice has always been widespread. Forty years ago, Lewis identified crop theft as one of the major hurdles facing small farmers in the Windwards, even asserting that "stealing produce from vegetable and fruit plots is less a habit than an ingrained way of life for the West Indian rural proletariats" (1968: 149).

Farmers report that by far the greatest amount of theft occurs among subsistence crops on family land parcels. Bananas are occasionally stolen, although most likely for home consumption rather than sale because of the costs involved in boxes and packaging, as well as the elaborate han-dling required for exported bananas. Rumors and suspicions abound about alleged perpetrators of crop theft, but farmers can rarely prove their suspicions as thefts invariably occur under cover of darkness or when the farm is otherwise unoccupied. Naturally, suspicion often turns first to those who are most familiar with the layout of a particular parcel, the crops grown on it, and the victim's work habits; that is, the fellow heirs with whom a farmer cultivates a family land parcel. Valerie Hyacinth, a Grand Ravine farmer who shares a parcel with two other family mem-bers, strongly suspects that the coconuts from the trees that she planted are secretly harvested by her sister, Victoria, on Saturdays when Valerie attends all-day services at the Adventist church. "Now I ask you," Valerie gestured angrily as she pointed out her recently harvested trees, "who else know where I am going to be each and every Saturday? Who else got an excuse to be on the farm? And it only on Saturdays that she thief the coconut them." The accusation, which Victoria denies, has led the sisters to stop speaking to each other, an uncomfortable situation when they find themselves at work together on the farm.

Despite some farmers' claims that reciprocal labor, or *koudeman*, has nearly died out, twenty-nine out of 133 farmers (21.8 percent) indicate that they currently share unpaid labor with friends or family in other house-holds. Although individual *koudeman* arrangements vary, it usually takes the form of an informal agreement among two farmers to swap a day of labor per week on one another's farms. Some farmers even bring with

Figure 3.1 | Women such as Mrs. Andrews (left) comprise more than 30 percent of all St. Lucian banana growers. She is visited here by extension agents from the Ministry of Agriculture.

them the workers they regularly employ on their own farms, with the understanding that the favor will be reciprocated the following week. Such arrangements last as long as both farmers believe them to be beneficial, and they are equally likely to be established with friends or relatives. One farmer reports that he has swapped labor with his *compère* (his son's godfather) every week since the son's baptism twenty-four years earlier. Most of those who engage in the practice cite a reduction of their wage expenses as its major advantage.

Many indicate that local involvement in *koudeman* has increased since the mid 1990s in tandem with increases in the costs of production. "Back in the time of Green Gold, that thing [*koudeman*] had almost disappeared. There was a lot of workers then and there was never any trouble paying them," one farmer in his sixties observed. "But now, we're rediscovering some of the things our parents and grandparents did when there wasn't so much money to go around." When asked why they don't practice labor sharing, farmers who refrain from *koudeman* say they are reluctant to take time away from their own farms every week to contribute work on another person's farm. Several also express a belief that would-be *koudeman* partners might take advantage of them by returning less work than they receive from the arrangement. Some point to longstanding friend-ships that have ruptured over such accusations. Still others state a desire to avoid any obligation that limits their independence. In the words of one farmer, "I wouldn't work for another man for a salary. Why should I work for him for free? Doesn't that sound like slavery to you?"

As a widely held cultural value, the desire for independence is equally strong among farmers and their employees alike. This preference for self-employment also contributes to labor scarcity and numerous complaints among farmers about the work ethic of their employees. Farmers often speak in derisive tones of the alleged disinclination for hard labor among their workers, often mimicking—however unconsciously—the complaints recorded among white planters following Emancipation. As one grower said in exasperation, "It's not enough that we have to pay them $40 per day, but we have to provide them with their lunch, too. And if the lunch I cook is not sufficiently scrumptious, they complain for the rest of the day and might not come back the next morning!" Unmentioned in such complaints, of course, is the viewpoint of the workers themselves, most of whom have also been harmed by the declining earnings from banana farming. The daily farm wage of EC $40–50 has not increased in more than a decade, farm owners now experience much more difficulty meeting their payrolls than in the past, and workers cannot always count on being paid on time, or even at all. Having no land or capital commitments to ba-nana farming, many experienced banana workers have left the valley alto-gether in recent years to pursue other livelihoods. As will be seen, among these alternatives are drug-related activities permitting both a high degree of personal independence and earnings undreamed of by farm workers, albeit at the risk of arrest and violence. Nonetheless, the few "success stories" that circulate of men who became suddenly and unimaginably wealthy as a result of taking a few risks undoubtedly reduce the allure of farm work for some of the young men who remain in the valley.

Ironies of the Production Process

Windwards farmers may describe themselves as free agents in compari-son to wage workers, but ironically they are far from independent in de-termining how to grow bananas. The actual ways in which they use their land, labor, and other productive resources are heavily constrained by the expectations of the Windward Islands Banana Development and Export-ing Company (WIBDECO),[3] Geest's successor and the company to which they have sold their bananas since 1994. For those growers who have be-come certified Fair Trade producers in recent years, WIBDECO's demands have been augmented by an additional set of even more stringent expectations in the realm of production (see Chapter Ten).

As is true for nominally independent farmers worldwide, Windwards banana growers participate in a globalized market controlled by corporations seeking ever greater standardization within each of their product categories (Watts 1990; Grossman 1998). Agribusiness corporations, including the three largest US-based banana companies, increasingly seek such homogenization through means other than direct control of production. Because the actual growing of fruit entails the riskiest and least profitable components of the commodity chain, the companies now prefer in many areas to consign production to nominally independent farmers. Product standardization in turn is gained through direct or indirect control over the contract farmers who produce commodities for them (Little 1994). Such controls are typically exercised at the point at which agricultural commodities are transferred from the grower to the corporate buyer, where rigorous inspection standards penalize growers who deviate from company expectations. Some observers claim that contract farmers in the current world economy are exposed to such relentless standardization and routinization of their activity that they are little more than "disguised proletarians" (Clapp 1994). Among Windwards growers, this characterization greatly understates the variability of banana producing strategies, growers' discretionary use of their time and land, and the degree to which farmers openly resist or subtly ignore the demands made upon them by extension agents. Because all these actions arise from the relative independence that farmers zealously seek to protect, they are correspondingly less available to wage workers.

For reasons discussed in the next chapter, the standards to which Windward Island farmers must conform in order to sell their fruit are increasingly determined by large Latin American plantations, which now produce 75 percent of all bananas exported worldwide. Simply put, because Windwards fruit competes with Latin American bananas for a share of the British retail market, island growers who fail to produce fruit of comparable quality will find themselves shut out of the export market and thereby excluded from commercial banana farming altogether. The independence that farmers celebrate in their livelihood is a cherished ideal, but it is also one that has eroded considerably in recent decades as the demands for quality and standardization have increased. In order to attain these standards, farmers must employ far more technology, labor, and inputs to grow marketable bananas than they did even a few years ago.

A useful illustration of the steadily increasing demands made upon farmers is the official Grower's Manual produced by the island Banana Growers' Associations (BGAs) and WINBAN, the Windward Islands Banana Association,[4] the former chief field experiment and extension agency for the industry. In 1966, a manual produced by the St. Vincent BGA contained 19 pages of instructions covering all aspects of production and harvesting. A WINBAN manual of 1981 designed for all of the region's growers was slightly longer, at 21 pages. The WINBAN manual of 1986 increased to 43 pages, and the one currently used by farmers, issued in 1993, involves 107 pages of instructions covering production, harvest, and post-harvest procedures (Grossman 1998: 126). For St. Lucian farmers in particular, about 35 percent of whom lack functional literacy in English, interpreting the Grower's Manual is a daunting task. Accordingly, the text of each step in the manual is written at about the third-grade level and accompanied by ample illustrations.

Although bananas grow luxuriantly throughout the tropics, the plant must be cajoled to yield the perfectly shaped, blemish-free fruit that consumers in North America and Europe take for granted. Not a few farmers describe growing bananas as comparable to "taking care of babies," in that both require painstaking attention if they are to yield good results as they grow up. Usually, St. Lucian farmers replant bananas after their third year of bearing fruit, by which time the plant's yield has declined. Replanting is typically done over a section of a farm whose plants were all established in the same year, but an alternative is "restocking," in which individual plants are replaced as their yields decline. The Grower's Manual recommends that plants be placed eight feet apart to ensure that leaves from one plant do not brush up against, and therefore bruise, the fruit growing on another. If the manual's recommendations are followed, an average acre on a farm will contain about seven hundred banana plants.

The Grower's Manual was extensively revised and lengthened during the 1980s, when most banana producers were becoming reliant on a number of powerful chemical agents to control pests and secondary growth. Many of these chemicals were first introduced by a UK-funded initiative, the Banana Development Program, that sought to "technologically modernize" small-scale farming in the Windwards. In its earliest stages, a banana plant is susceptible to infestations by nematodes, a variety of microscopic worms that feed upon the plant's roots, eventually killing it. From the time of planting and every four months onward, powerful nematicides are injected into the soil around the base of the plant to control such pests.[5] Other pests, such as the banana borer, a black weevil that consumes the plant's roots and corm, are controlled with a variety of insecticides sprayed directly onto the plant. From the time that a new field is planted until a dense canopy of banana leaves is established, farms are also highly vulnerable to weeds that can choke off new growth. Most farmers control weeds using herbicidal sprays, with Gramoxone (paraquat) and Round-

Up (glyphosate) being currently the most popular. Fungal infestations that threaten bananas, particularly yellow leafspot, are controlled through aerial spraying paid for by charges levied against all banana growers. Although extension agents have routinely recommended the use of these and other chemicals on farms, their actual usage varies considerably from farmer to farmer, with the exception of aerial spraying, over which the farmer has no control.

Many of the chemicals that extension agents routinely recommended for use on banana farms during the 1970s and 1980s, including the nematicide Nemagon (also known by its active ingredient DBCP, or dibromochloropropane) and insecticides aldrin, heptachlor, and DDT, have long been known to pose significant threats to human and animal life.[6] The governments of the Windward Islands now prohibit their importation, although there has been no official acknowledgement of the risks of using them, nor any attempt to calculate the toll that such chemicals may have taken on farmers who handled them or on the downstream communities whose sources of drinking water were contaminated. During the 1980s, farmers went through a quick succession of four chemicals used to control nematodes, each abandoned by extension agents when evidence emerged that it posed unacceptable health risks. Farmers say that they were rarely informed of the reasons that one chemical ceased to be available and another was offered in its place. Almost all continued to use the banned varieties of chemical as long as their own stocks remained. More than a decade passed between the promotion of chemical-intensive methods by regional governments and extension agents and their first efforts during the 1990s to inform farmers and community members about the hazards of farm chemicals when handled improperly. Edme Celestine, an elderly farmer residing in Dennery, described how he and other farmers noticed tingling sensations, insomnia, and uncontrollable nervous tics after using Nemagon, one of the most highly toxic and widely used nematicides during the 1970s and early 1980s. His wife described how village children, until recent decades, played in the clouds of chemicals deposited by crop dusting aircraft. "We were not really informed of how dangerous these chemicals were," Mr. Celestine recalled.

> And the level of chemicals that was being put into the soil … we were not told how much to use. Now where you should have put something like 10cc, instead you put 20 or 30 because you want production. And you were told, well, this is for production, so you think the more you put the more production you'll have. And after a while you find that our water source was not even fit to drink because of the level of nematicides that go into the soil and run into the river and so on. By then all the fish and crayfish were gone from the river. (Celestine, pers. comm. 2004).

Today, farmers are required to record and publicly display on a placard the quantities and types of chemicals used on their farm, in part because of the rampant overuse of farm chemicals in the past. Yet many farmers acknowledge that their present use of chemicals, often far *below* currently recommended levels, has declined not because of greater industry regulation, but because low fruit prices have made it impossible for them to afford the chemicals they once were able to buy. An extension agent for the St. Lucia Banana Corporation (SLBC), the island's largest fruit buyer, stated that fewer than 15 percent of conventional valley farmers apply herbicides and nematicides at recommended rates.[7]

Similarly, farmers' use of land often varies dramatically from the official industry recommendations. Approximately 32 percent (42 out of 133) of the surveyed St. Lucian banana growers practice polyculture to some extent; that is, cultivating at least some food crops within their banana farms. In this respect, farmers' planting practices continue to defy the recommendations of extension agents and government officials, who have insisted since the very origins of the industry in the 1950s that Windward growers plant "pure stands" of bananas to maximize productivity per unit of land and input application. Their arguments often fall on deaf ears among rural residents who recognize the environmental and cost advantages of intercropped fields. Planting low-growing crops among banana stems can partially diminish secondary growth, thereby reducing the need for weeding. On hillside farms, intercropping also helps to control soil erosion. A wide variety of food crops are grown locally, either within banana farms or separately. By far the most popular of local food crops are generically identified as "ground food." These are starchy tubers such as yams, sweet potatoes, tannia (*Xanthosoma sp.*), and dasheen (*Colocasia esculenta*). Vegetables known generically as "greens," including cabbages, tomatoes, cucumber, carrots, and peppers, are also occasionally interplanted with bananas. Finally, many farmers maintain some tree crops in their banana fields, including mangos, citrus, breadfruit, and coconuts.

To the further chagrin of extension agents, farmers who engage in polyculture are now usually reluctant to apply chemicals in levels approaching their recommendations (or even at all) in proximity to their food crops. Many, for example, will wait until they have harvested their food crops before using nematicides and herbicides, and in the meantime will weed by hand using a cutlass. Similarly, because a dense canopy of banana leaves inhibits the growth of low-growing food crops, some farmers maintain a distance greater than eight feet between banana plants to allow more light to reach their other crops. But whether or not food crops are interspersed with bananas, all farmers recognize the importance of regular fertilizing. Fruit borne by unfertilized plants is underweight and badly shaped, and

Figure 3.2 | Food crops (cabbage) interplanted with bananas on a St. Lucian farm, against the advice of industry officials.

is almost always rejected for sale. While not a complicated procedure, fertilizing at recommended levels is exhausting work that requires hauling 100-pound bags of fertilizer onto farms twice a year. The average farm in the Mabouya Valley comprises 4.3 acres in bananas, which, at recommended levels, would require more than six thousand pounds of fertilizer annually. Despite their recognition of the importance of fertilizer, not a single farmer in the sample of 133 applies fertilizer at these levels.

As banana plants grow, their roots send up a succession of suckers that are smaller versions of the main stem. About five months after planting, farmers begin "desuckering" their farms, trimming off all but one of the suckers from each plant. The one that remains, known as a "follower," will produce the second crop of bananas. Follower selection is critical to continuously high production on banana farms, but it is not intuitively obvious. Tempting as it might be to eliminate all but the largest follower, many farmers have found instead that selecting one that faces east, thus receiving more sunlight, often yields greater bunch sizes. Usually the first crop is borne after nine months of growth, after which the main stem is cut down to be succeeded by the follower. Each follower attains a greater height than its predecessor, so that by the third crop, farmers usually have to use ladders to perform much of the work related to the developing bunch. Similarly, because the increasing height of plants and the weight of their fruit bunches (60 pounds or more) make them vulnerable to toppling during high winds, farmers prop up taller plants with twine and stakes. On the island's many hillside farms, using a ladder to tend banana plants is a precarious and even dangerous procedure in which the farmer often has to wrap one leg around the plant's stem to keep from falling.

Bananas develop from a cluster of blooms emerging from the large bud, or "navel," that appears on a stem seven to eight months after planting. About thirteen weeks elapse between the appearance of fruit on a banana plant and its readiness for harvest. When the bud appears, farmers tie a colored plastic ribbon to the emerging stem. The color for a particular week is established in advance by WIBDECO and is consistent for all farms on the island. As the flowers shrivel, a banana develops at the base of each bloom. To enhance the appearance of the fruit for sale, farmers remove the dry, blackened petals from the developing fruit. Soon after this stage, known as "deflowering," they slip a blue-tinted diothene (polyethylene) bag over each bunch. The diothene sleeve reduces insect damage and speeds up maturation time, while the tint alters the wavelength of sunlight to help produce an evenly colored bunch.

Each week, St. Lucia is visited by a freighter that docks in the southern port of Vieux Fort to pick up the island's bananas. It stays in port for two days (typically Tuesdays and Wednesdays), during which farmers all over the island select and harvest their fruit. Introduced in 1996, the ribbon system of fruit identification was designed to standardize fruit quality by making fruit selection easier and ensuring that all of the island's harvestable fruit is shipped at an optimal time. Like all other aspects of certification once described as voluntary, the ribbon system is now followed by virtually all growers. Each week, WIBDECO and the island's fruit companies announce via radio, television, and newspapers the color of that week's harvest, as well as the color to be used for all emergent fruit.[8] Theoretically, farmers need only to identify harvestable stems of fruit by the color of the ribbon that is attached to them. The timing of harvests is critical, for fruit that is ready to be shipped one week is likely to be "over grade" and unsaleable the following week.

In comparison to the relatively leisurely five to six hours daily that most growers work on their farms between harvests, the two weekly harvest days are full of frenetic activity. Harvesting ("selecting") the fruit itself is entrusted to the most experienced and skilled field worker on the farm, for the slightest misstep can lead to fruit being rejected for sale. Fruit "selectors," as well as those who carry the fruit to the packing shed, are invariably male. Women, on the other hand, predominate in the post-harvest operations within the shed itself, although some men may also work beside them. After a selector has identified a harvestable stem by its specific ribbon, he lifts the blue diothene bag and exposes the fruit for cutting. He uses a curved grading knife to cut off lowest "hand" of the stem. This is then cut into several clusters, each consisting of four to seven "fingers," or individual bananas joined to a "crown." Considerable care is required to make smooth cuts in the crown (to enhance its visual appearance and reduce the possibility of fungal infection) and to prevent the stem's sticky latex secretions from blemishing the fruit peels. The clusters are inverted and placed on a clean banana leaf that has been positioned beforehand on the ground at the base of the plant to catch the latex oozing out of the cut crown. After they drain for about ten minutes, another worker places the clusters in a tray lined with diothene bags and banana leaves to cushion the fruit on its way out of the field. The trays, which can hold up to fifty pounds of cut fruit, are carried on the head, the worker usually needing assistance to raise it into carrying position.

Since 1993, all fruit exported from the Windwards has been handled and packaged using a procedure known as the "cluster" or "mini-wet" pack. Since its adoption, every Windwards farmer has been required to construct an open-sided shed where the harvested bananas are packed. Women perform most of the washing and packing, to highly exacting specifications. Prior to harvest, farmers procure the number of pre-printed cartons that they consider sufficient for that week's yield. Until the end of the 1990s, all cartons were printed with the logo of the UK banana importer Geest, but most are now labeled for the specific British supermarkets in which the fruit is to be retailed. While one worker assembles and stacks the cartons in a corner of the shed, another soaks clusters of bananas in a tub containing water and Imazalil, a water-soluble fungicidal powder. The solution is intended to prevent crown rot, a fungus that attacks the stem joining individual bananas in a cluster. Washing also removes any insects, spiders, or small lizards that happen to hide among the bananas. While the treated fruit drains, a packer places a brown paper liner into a box, followed by a clear polyethylene bag to cushion the bananas and maintain some internal moisture. From the array of fruit on her sorting table, the packer carefully selects clusters of the size and shape appropriate to the particular pack type on which she is working. After completing a row of clusters, she folds the paper and polyethylene liner over it and begins assembling another row. When the box is filled to capacity, she ties the plastic liner closed, puts the cover on the box, and attaches a sticker with the farm's registration number. Although packing appears straightforward enough, it is a procedure requiring the utmost care to ensure the placement is neither too roomy nor too snug. Packing that allows excessive movement of fruit during shipment will result in bruising, as will boxes in which fruit is crowded too tightly. Finally, after a box is filled it must be weighed exactly to specifications. The Geest boxes in which bananas were traditionally shipped each weighed 42 pounds gross. Off-weight boxes are reopened and clusters added, subtracted, or rearranged until the box reaches the specified weight. On an average-sized (4.3 acre) farm, any given week's harvest and packing will require between six and ten hours, depending upon the amount of labor available to the farmer.

Since 2000, there has been a pronounced shift in sales from the wholesale to the supermarket trade and accompanying creation of store-branded niche markets. Accordingly, packaging has become even more complex. Five major supermarket chains in the UK now stock store-branded bananas from the Windwards, as does a major supermarket in Switzerland (which sources its bananas mostly from Dominica). Since the supermarket trade now requires specific branding of fruit, each chain insists on the use of its own boxes of varying weights. In addition to boxes of differing dimensions and design, each store also has its own product specifications, including the additional step of packaging individual clusters of fruit in cellophane bags targeted at distinct market segments. Hence, in any given shipment a farmer may package loose clusters, as described above, in 42-pound Geest boxes, children's ("fun-size") bananas in cello bags for Sainsbury's in that chain's 28-pound boxes, and Fair Trade bananas (also in distinctively marked cello bags) for Waitrose in that chain's 32-pound boxes. Not only are farmers responsible for mastering the store-specific requirements of each pack type, but they must pay for all related packaging, from the boxes down to the supermarket cello bags and the oval store-brand stickers they attach to each cluster of bananas.

The final step in the sale of bananas involves the transportation of fruit to a buying depot, where it is either purchased or rejected by WIBDECO for export. In the Mabouya Valley, about 40 percent of all farmers own pickup trucks, most of which were financed through a low-interest government loan program during the 1980s. Few of these original trucks, it seems, have been replaced with newer models, and many farmers have become quite resourceful at extending the useful life of their now vintage, if often decrepit, vehicles. Most farmers attribute their inability to procure new transportation to both the declining earnings of the banana industry since the 1990s and their current difficulties obtaining loans for farm-related purchases. Prior to delivery, farmers and their workers carry their packed banana boxes to the nearest road (astute farmers construct their packing sheds as close as possible to roadside). The majority of farmers lacking vehicles of their own arrange for their friends and neighbors to transport their fruit for sale, at a going rate of one EC dollar (US $0.38) per box.

The boxes are strapped down in the truck bed and delivered to the nearest of two Inland Reception and Distribution Centers (IRDCs). The IRDC at La Caye, near the mouth of the Mabouya River, accepts deliveries from farmers on the eastern half of the island. The other, at Osdan in the Cul de Sac Valley, accepts deliveries from the western half. At each, about a dozen fruit "buyers" (inspectors employed by WIBDECO) evaluate samples of fruit from every farm. Fruit that is accepted for sale is loaded onto semi-tractor trailers and trucked to the port at Vieux Fort for shipment to Southampton, England. Farmers receive an itemized receipt indicating the numbers and types of boxes accepted for sale minus the costs of packing materials and any inputs and credit obtained from the banana company. Their receipts can be redeemed for cash at the headquarters of the banana company, although direct deposit of net earnings is an increasingly common choice among growers. Boxes of fruit that are rejected by WIBDECO, invariably over the vehement objections of growers, are occasionally purchased by local buyers (sometimes disparaged in Kwéyòl as *kòbo*, or "vultures") who wait in trucks outside the gates of the IRDCs. Such fruit, considered unsatisfactory for the European market, finds its way to supermarkets in Castries or occasionally is sold at a steep markup at stores in Barbados or Antigua. Farmers sell fruit at a loss to local buyers, who pay about EC $6.00 (about US $2.25) per box, less than half the price of the lowest-priced fruit destined for the UK wholesale market. If the cost of labor is factored in with packaging materials and inputs, this price is about 60 percent below the farmers' costs of production. Not uncommonly, and especially when the grower attempts to deliver fruit on the second shipping day of the week, the limited demand in local and regional markets is already sated, the "vultures" have flown from the scene, and the farmer is left with no alternative but to dump his or her rejected fruit at a total loss.

The Erosion of Personal Control

Technically speaking, many of the instructions contained in the Grower's Manual carry the force of law. In 1986, the government of St. Lucia passed the Banana Protection and Quality Control Act (simply known as the Banana Act), which attempted to legally regulate the conditions under which bananas are grown on the island. In effect, the act codified as law most of the recommendations contained in the then-current Grower's Manual, even declaring failure to follow the prescribed methods a punishable offense.

Although the Banana Act angered farmers by its presumed interference with their production decisions, it might be seen more accurately, following Scott (1998), as a case of a state overreaching its authority. Neither the government nor the island's Banana Growers' Association possessed a number of extension and enforcement agents sufficient to inspect the more than ten thousand farms then operating on the island. By the time of her study of St. Lucian banana farmers, Slocum (1996) noted that there had been no known cases of government authorities using the act to direct farmers' production decisions through the threat of prosecution. Significantly, during the widespread farmer unrest in 1993, when falling prices led to a growers' strike and angry protests against the BGA and government, the act was never invoked despite the fact that it could easily have been used to punish protest leaders.

Finally, while the act persists even today in the St. Lucian legal code, its specifications have been rendered as obsolete as the 1980s Grower's Manual on which it was based, for the procedures it mandates have been entirely superseded by a new system of post-harvest handling. Rather than actually setting out to control banana farmers' production decisions, it is more likely that the St. Lucian government's motive in passing this unenforceable legislation was to persuade the British government, Geest, and WINBAN that it took their oft-stated concerns about fruit quality seriously. In the end, this symbolic gesture may have had little effect on growers except to further antagonize and predispose them for the mass protests that convulsed the island in 1993.

Notwithstanding the lack of actual legal enforcement over farmers' decision making and the variability that farmers exhibit in production decisions, throughout the Eastern Caribbean growers have had no choice but to adopt a succession of innovations introduced to the industry by WINBAN from the 1960s through 1990s. Most of WINBAN's research during this time focused on post-harvest handling of bananas, as this was considered to be the most critical component in fruit quality. As each innovation in handling was introduced, it was accompanied by changes in the way that fruit was purchased from farmers, leaving them with no alternative but to observe the new practices. Further, each change has progressively shifted responsibility for fruit selection, handling, and packaging from external agents (importers and the Banana Growers' Association) to the farmers themselves. Accordingly, the innovations have steadily increased the demands on farmers' labor and required them to purchase new, costly inputs and supplies.

Older farmers speak of the banana industry between the 1960s and 1980s as a time of "Green Gold," when production entailed relatively few costs and little wage labor. In those days even poorly managed farms could turn a profit, and many town residents with full-time employment but little farming experience adopted banana production on the side as a secure second income. Most of the post-harvest handling of fruit at the time was conducted by workers employed by the BGA, who were paid from a "cess" (dues) levied on farmers from each box of bananas they sold. Growers cut whole stems of fruit and transported them to literally dozens of boxing stations scattered throughout banana-producing areas of the island. At each station, BGA workers cut ("dehanded") the fruit from the stems, washed the hands, and boxed them for export.

Believing that the transportation of fruit to boxing stations was contributing to quality problems, in 1980 WINBAN began to close the stations and transfer responsibility for post-harvest handling to growers. The post-harvest innovation introduced at that point was the Crown Pad pack, in which growers dehanded fruit, attached a latex pad containing fungicide to each crown, and then packed the fruit on their own farms in cardboard boxes. The introduction of the Crown Pad system increased production costs for growers, all of whom saw their returns reduced by the cost of boxes, pads, and additional labor for packing.[9] The requirement that each farm have a packing shed was not yet in force, but in practice farmers had to provide some minimal shelter on their farms for workers engaged in packing, which necessitated additional labor and expense in construction. Although the Crown Pad proved effective in controlling crown rot, it proved unsightly to English consumers, many of whom preferred Latin American bananas treated with fungicides and lacking the pads. In response to consumer preferences, Geest called on WINBAN to develop an alternative method of fungus control for Eastern Caribbean bananas.

WINBAN's solution was the "mini-wet pack" introduced throughout the Windwards in 1993, which replicated on a farm-by-farm basis procedures already in place on Latin American plantations. The "mini-wet pack" resulted in a dramatic increase in labor and input costs for farmers. In 2000, supermarket-branding and cello-packing were introduced, requiring that clusters be packaged in cellophane bags and boxes bearing the logos of the particular UK supermarkets in which they are sold. These innovations further added to the complexity and cost of production. Whereas all bananas packaged until then had been placed in identical 42-pound Geest boxes, each of the five supermarkets that now handle St. Lucian fruit has a distinctive "pack type," i.e., specific requirements in terms of packaging and box weight. With the exception of some farms contracted specifically as sources by a single supermarket, most growers now must sort and package their fruit according to the requirements of two or even three simultaneous "pack types" for a given harvest.

All of these changes in post-harvest handling have been imposed without recourse for banana growers. Other costly innovations in production have been introduced on an ostensibly voluntary basis, although in practice farmers wishing to survive in the export market have had little alternative to accepting them. Until the early 1990s growers were paid an identical price for all fruit that met Geest's standards of acceptability, with the best bananas receiving the same price as minimally acceptable fruit. But in 1991, a new three-tiered pricing system was introduced that tied quality scores to fruit prices, with the aim of providing an incentive for growers to improve their quality beyond minimally acceptable levels. The three price categories were replaced in 1996 by a farm certification program introduced by WIBDECO (which had taken over WINBAN's extension functions). Under this initiative, "certified" growers were granted preferential rights to sell supermarket-branded fruit, which commands a much higher price than loose clusters. Growers hoping to enjoy the benefits of certification were required by WIBDECO to construct a packing shed with a cement floor, partially enclosed walls, and solid roof; to regulate and record their chemical usage on a chart posted on the shed wall; and to meet an array of standards with regard to farm maintenance and cleanliness. Compliance with these requirements was gauged through an onsite inspection by a WIBDECO certification officer and through the growers' attainment of consistently high quality scores upon sale.

Uncertified fruit is sold on wholesale markets, where it fetches a price well below most farmers' costs of production, while only bananas from certified farms are designated as "premium" fruit that is packaged by super-

Figure 3.3 | St. Lucian Fair Trade farmer packing specialty bananas for the Sainsbury's chain in Great Britain.

market brand. If the fruit from a certified farm receives poor quality scores upon inspection, the farmer may receive a visit from the WIBDECO certification officer as well as a warning notice. If he or she receives three consecutive low scores, the farm will be decertified and its fruit consigned to the wholesale market. Given present costs of production, it is doubtful that there remain any farmers today able to survive exclusively from sales on the wholesale market. Innovations such as the certification program that were introduced as "voluntary" have thereby eventually become requisite for all farmers who wish to remain in the export market. For example, most of the original components of certification, including the construction of a substantial packing shed with a cement floor and the recording of chemical usage, are now mandated under EUREP-GAP requirements, which all farmers had to adopt in order to export fruit to the European Union after 2004.[10] Meanwhile, with all of the island's remaining farms effectively meeting certification criteria, the primary incentive offered by certification—the exclusive right to ship supermarket-branded fruit—is no longer guaranteed to all farmers who have made these changes.

It is in the sale of fruit to WIBDECO's buyers, rather than a formally legislated process such as the 1986 Banana Act, that control is most effectively asserted over growers. At a minimum, 20 percent of most growers' shipments will be inspected upon arrival at the IRDC. A buyer will inspect all of the clusters in the first ten boxes of a hundred-box shipment by removing each cluster from its box and examining it closely for defects. Inspectors evaluate fruit with respect to some twenty dimensions of size, shape, color, scarring, and other measures of quality, few of which are apparent to the untrained eye. Buyers will accept for purchase boxes of fruit that score at least 85 PUWS ("Percent Units within Specification"), meaning that 85 percent of all the clusters in a box exhibit no defects with regard to visual characteristics or dimensions. It takes about four minutes to inspect each box in its entirety. If the first ten boxes are satisfactory, the next ten boxes may merely be opened but not unpacked. Should this secondary inspection reveal no problems, the entire shipment is accepted. In practice, it is rare for an inspection not to result in some rejected boxes. At the buyer's discretion, inspection is carried out for as many cartons as necessary, and in some instances, if the quality of the first ten boxes is poor, the buyer will opt for a 100 percent inspection.

In recent years, St. Lucia's banana industry has been plagued by several plant diseases that lead to rejected fruit, the spread of which are often attributed to the indirect effects of the industry's privatization in 1997. Among these are the Yellow Sigatoka (leafspot) fungus, which causes premature ripening of fruit. Leafspot can be identified from fruit whose peel has already begun turning yellow after harvest. All such fruit is rejected, as it will be a total loss by the time it arrives in the UK some two weeks after harvest. Another, even more costly disease, known as Green Ripe, leads to a rejection of the entire consignment because its presence can only be confirmed when fruit is cut open. As one buyer stated, "[Y]ou could have 200 boxes, and we'll give all of it back to you, because we don't know where is the rest of the fruit. The fruit came from a stem, but we don't know where the other fruit from the same stem might be in your shipment." A few St. Lucian farms were quarantined by WIBDECO after an outbreak of Green Ripe in 2002: a ban was placed on sales by the farms until they were entirely replanted, effectively forcing their owners out of business.

Buyers are employed by WIBDECO and work just two days per week, although their shifts may run twelve hours or more. Their earnings, at a minimum of US $190 per fortnight, compare very favorably on an hourly basis to the wage paid for most work on the island. Yet banana buying is difficult work, not only because of the extensive training and patience required to evaluate export-grade fruit, but because it is accompanied, more often than not, by contentious and stressful exchanges with farmers. Growers stand directly across the table from the buyers who inspect their fruit. Most buyers come from banana-growing families in the Mabouya and Roseau Valleys and are personally acquainted with the farmers whose fruit they grade (though IDRC management does not permit them to buy fruit from immediate family members). Farmers whose fruit has been rejected will occasionally appeal the buyer's assessments with the IRDC foreman, but he almost invariably backs up the buyer's decisions. On occasion, buyers report being verbally or even physically threatened by angry farmers. To discourage such threats and occasionally remove belligerent growers, a detachment of police is posted near each IRDC on shipment days.

Farmers and buyers are inevitably at cross-purposes because of the handsome bonuses that WIBDECO pays to buyers for the quality of the fruit they purchase on behalf of the company. The fruit that is inspected and purchased in St. Lucia is inspected again upon arrival in Southampton. The unique buyer's code and farm registration number on each box allow WIBDECO's UK-based inspectors to trace every box of fruit back to a particular farmer, and also allows them to determine whether the St. Lucian buyer was doing his or her job thoroughly. Fruit quality inevitably deteriorates as freighters proceed from St. Lucia to procure more fruit from Dominica, where holds are opened and shipments exposed to the elements. Since the company anticipates some degree of further deterioration during the ensuing two-week voyage to England, the minimally acceptable grade for a box arriving in Southampton is 75 PUWS. Island buyers who attain that average score among all of the fruit they purchase will receive an annual bonus amounting to about US $350. Hence, buyers have an overriding incentive to "grade hard"; that is, to reject all possibly questionable fruit before it leaves St. Lucia, to ensure that they qualify for a grading bonus. Similarly, should fruit that was accepted in the Windwards be rejected when it arrives in Britain, the farmer that produced it will be targeted for a 100 percent inspection the next time he or she delivers fruit for sale.

However much they resent aspects of the inspection process and what they often view as arbitrary harshness by buyers, many farmers speak with pride of attaining consistently high-quality fruit. Inspection is a highly public event, with other farmers present to witness the buyer-grower interaction and final evaluation. Farmers not infrequently comment (unfavorably) on the abilities or aptitude of other growers whose fruit has been downgraded or rejected. Referring to a neighbor who had preceded him at sale and suffered the rejection of fifteen boxes out of his shipment of sixty, one Riche Fond grower commented, "I would be ashamed to deliver fruit in that condition. He argue at first, but in the end he [was] just so humiliated that he take his slip and drive straight away. Never say a word and never look nobody in the eye."

In addition to being a source of satisfaction, high quality scores offer the added benefit of expediting the sale and inspection process once a grower's favorable reputation among buyers is established. Indeed, a handful of growers who have maintained consistently high scores are allowed to deliver their fruit with little or no inspection. The vast, less fortunate majority are without much recourse when their fruit is rejected for sale, but many attempt to subtly influence the process before it begins. Lucien Charles, a La Caye buyer in her early twenties, noted the considerable lengths to which some farmers go to get their fruit through inspection. One of the first women to be trained as a buyer, Charles recalled that many male farmers deliberately chose her inspection line when she began work. "They never seen a woman buyer before, and they thought I would be easy," she laughed.

> First they try to charm me. When that didn't work, they try to intimidate. Man, I tell you, some of those guys learn pretty quick that day! Some of them, though, they're so smart. You know, you cannot check all the boxes because if you check each one you would never finish your work. The farmers know this, so some of them they arrange their boxes so the first ones off the truck are the best quality. They hoping that I won't look further. Well, you might get away with that once or twice, but sooner or later we find out when the shipment reach England. Then we write 'T' on that farmer's card. That's 'T' for target; that means we give him 100 percent [inspection]. St. Lucia, you know, is a small island, and you can't fool people forever. (Charles, pers. comm. 2004)

Thus, in the work of fruit buyers such as Lucien Charles, Windwards growers find both their autonomy and earnings increasingly disciplined by the relentless pursuit of aesthetic perfection and other measures of "fruit quality." Such constraints, as noted above, are imposed indirectly by the Latin American banana sectors and US corporations that dominate the global market for the fruit. Despite the globalization of these aesthetic criteria, participants in the Latin American and Caribbean banana industries operate in very distinct worlds. It is to that contrast and the history behind it that we turn next.

Notes

1. See Chapter Ten for discussion of survey and sample.
2. Advocates of agricultural modernization in the St. Lucian government, WIBDECO (the Windward Islands Banana Development and Exporting Company), and external development institutions believe that the practice of administering land jointly among heirs creates disincentives for the full utilization of agro-chemicals and other "farm improvements." This assumption derives from the neoclassical economic assertion that farmers will not willingly invest in new techniques if the benefits will also accrue to non-investing "free riders." Unable to secure the agreement of all co-heirs to transfer title to a single owner, past initiatives such as the Mabouya Valley Development Project have all failed to significantly reduce the prevalence of family land on the island.
3. Since 1994, when it bought out Geest Industries, WIBDECO has overseen the distribution and marketing of bananas from the Windward Islands. WIBDECO is owned by the producers' groups of each of the four Windward Islands and the governments of the islands. WIBDECO also entered into a joint partnership with the UK-based Fyffes banana company to buy out Geest's wholesaling business in England. This venture, known formally as WIBDECO UK, is referred to as Geest in the islands because that label continues to be used to retail most Windward bananas.
4. WINBAN was established in 1958 as a regional organization acting as liaison between Windward Islands farmers and the British market. Its role was to negotiate contracts with Geest, administer aid programs and insurance, and conduct research aimed at improving yields and quality. WINBAN was replaced in 1994 by WIBDECO, which, as noted above, assumed much more involvement in the actual shipping and importation of bananas.
5. These recommendations do not apply to Fair Trade farmers, who are prevented by the rules of Fair Trade certification from applying nematicides (as well as most herbicides) because of their environmental effects.
6. DBCP was banned in the United States in 1979 but continued to be used by US banana companies in Central America as late as 1993 (AP 2007). According to St. Lucian farmers, Nemagon was withdrawn from local use in 1983. Between 2001 and 2004, several dozen lawsuits were filed on behalf of thousands of disabled Central American farm workers and their families against the US banana multinationals and chemical manufacturers, for DBCP-related illness and fatalities. The plaintiffs contend that the com-

panies routinely exposed them to heavy doses of the chemical up to thirty years after DBCP's health effects (including cancer, sterility, paralysis, severe birth defects, and kidney failure) had been scientifically established (Bérubé and Aquin 2005). In 2003, Nicaraguan courts awarded 500 plaintiffs US $489 million in damages against Dole, but the company refused to pay and countersued the banana workers for fraud (Leahy 2006). Three years later, after a federal judge in Galveston, Texas, agreed to hear twenty-five such cases, Dole settled most of the lawsuits for an undisclosed amount before going to trial (Dole 2006). Windwards farmers are included among plaintiffs in several civil suits against Dow Chemical, manufacturer of DBCP, pending in Los Angeles federal court. In the first of these, a jury awarded $2.5 million in damages to five Nicaraguan banana workers poisoned by the chemical.

7. As will be seen, Fair Trade farmers are prohibited by certification from using such chemicals at all.

8. While the majority of broadcast television and radio programs in St. Lucia take place in English, Kwéyòl dominates in all programming related to the banana industry.

9. Although the BGA suspended the packing of bananas at boxing stations and reduced its workforce to some extent, many of the former BGA fruit packers were incorporated into the association's bureaucracy in other capacities. Despite its lower operating costs after the closure of the stations, the BGA did not lower its cess levels on farmers.

10. The European Retailers Working Group, known as EUREP, represents the main supermarkets to which Windwards farmers export their bananas and other produce. They have developed common standards and procedures for Good Agricultural Practices, or GAP. Ostensibly developed to ensure food safety, EUREP-GAP entails nearly forty pages of phyto-sanitary and worker-related criteria with which Windwards farmers were expected to comply by the end of 2004. See discussion in Chapter Six.

— Chapter Four —

ST. LUCIA IN
THE GLOBAL BANANA TRADE

The opening up of new markets, foreign or domestic ... incessantly revolutionizes the economic structure *from within,* incessantly destroying the old one, incessantly creating a new one. This process of Creative Destruction is the essential fact about capitalism. It is what capitalism consists in and what every capitalist concern has got to live in.
—Joseph A. Schumpeter (1942)

Two Industries, Two Lives

Imagine for a moment that you are Calixte Jn Baptiste, a 59-year-old resident of Derniere Riviere, a settlement of about three hundred people in the Mabouya Valley.[1] Your farm occupies three acres of land on the steep slopes that rise from the northern end of the valley floor. It is not, even by island standards, an optimal place to grow bananas. You are reminded of that fact every two weeks when you, your adult sons, and two hired workers harvest fruit for sale. Even under the best of circumstances it is difficult to climb and descend farm trails on a twenty-degree gradient. Not infrequently you and your workers do so while carrying trays laden with fruit. When afternoon downpours turn the trails into slick rivulets, the occasional slip and fall is much more than a painful and embarrassing hazard of hillside farming, for every such misstep causes the loss of an entire carton or more of fruit. Bananas that have been dropped will betray telltale bruises within a few hours, rendering them completely worthless by the time they reach the buying depot. With the passage of years, your agility and strength have ebbed somewhat, so that more and more of the harvesting labor has to be turned over to younger men who work for wages.

You look with some envy on your neighbors who cultivate farms on the relatively flat bottomlands, for they enjoy higher yields, fewer losses, and lower wage expenses. You consider yourself fortunate when an acre of your farm produces eight tons of fruit in a year; the bottomland average of eleven tons seems frustratingly just out of reach.

On non-harvest days, farm work proceeds at a steady but relaxed pace and is usually finished by mid afternoon. During the two harvest days every fortnight, however, you and your crew work long hours to cut, wash, grade, and package all fruit that is ready for sale. After the last stems are harvested and boxed, the bed of your pickup truck groans under the weight of some fifty cartons. They rise to a height of nearly eight feet and are secured by a tarp lashed to the vehicle with bungee cords. The distance from your farm to the IRDC at La Caye is ordinarily a short trip of eight miles, but on harvest days you drive in slow motion, arduously navigating the valley's rutted feeder roads to avoid any further bruising to your fruit. Once there, your truck joins a queue of dozens of other farmers, each anxiously waiting to deliver their fruit to the buyers, who grade a sample of their produce. The inspections always reveal some boxes containing sub-grade fruit, the entire contents of which are rejected for export. Farmers whose fruit has been turned down in large quantities argue, beg, and imprecate against the buyers, who stand impassively behind their verdicts. After witnessing many such scenes, it is your turn to approach the buyer's inspection station, where you receive the signal to unload your cargo. The buyer rejects only two cartons from the sample of fifteen that he opens. You are thankful this percentage is low enough to rule out an inspection of the entire harvest.

By the time you arrive home after midnight, you have been at work for sixteen hours. After inspection you were provided with a receipt indicating the net value of all of your cartons accepted for sale. After paying your workers, your earnings allow you to clear your family's expenses until the next harvest and to set some money aside for your granddaughter Teresa's First Communion. Around you stand the symbols of what most islanders would consider a comfortable middle-class livelihood. You grew up in the Mabouya Valley, but Derniere Riviere today is nothing like the place of your birth. Long ago the village of thatched roofs, candlelight and lanterns, well water, and pit toilets was replaced by a community of substantial cement and masonry houses, electricity, and running water. In school you never went beyond Standard Two (the equivalent of fourth grade in the US), and to this day you remain less comfortable speaking in English than in the Kwèyól of the countryside. In contrast, one of your daughters has finished her nursing degree at the island's community college, and your sons are well on their way to completing secondary school; all

Figure 4.1 | Transporting bananas from field to packing shed, Mabouya Valley.

navigate the English-speaking culture of Castries and beyond with greater ease than most residents of the village they left behind. Thanks to the local health clinic and water treatment plant, the intestinal contagions and other infections that swept away so many children when you were young are almost unknown to your granddaughter's generation. Entering your house in the early hours, you see the carefully arrayed satin dress, white leather shoes, gloves, and veil that your wife has purchased for Teresa in Castries. Except for the wealthiest people, celebrations of First Communion were far more modest in the village of your youth.

Now imagine that you are Calixte Jn Baptiste's counterpart in the Republic of Honduras, 52-year-old Justo Martínez. Unlike Jn Baptiste, you are not a farm proprietor in your own right but a laborer on the Boca del Tigre estate of 2,000 acres in the lowlands near the Caribbean coast. The plantation you work on is one of many carved from the jungle in the coastal department of Atlántida. Whether viewed from the ground or air, the adjacent plantations merge into a monotonous swath of banana cultivation occupying nearly 100 square miles of flat, fertile land. The average farm in the department exceeds 700 acres in area. Many are now owned by wealthy private investors rather than the US-based banana corporations that previously controlled almost all production. Boca del Tigre, once directly owned and managed by Dole Foods, was sold in 1995 to a private grower who continues to market his fruit through that company. While the farm's products bear the same label as before, conditions on the farm itself have changed dramatically since the transfer of ownership. Immediately after the sale, the new owner nullified the farm's contract with the banana workers' union, one that had been in force since a nationwide general strike in 1954.

On the two harvest days per week, the farm rings with the hollow, metallic sound of the cableways moving thousands of banana stems through the fields. Nearly all Honduran farms are crisscrossed with steel cables suspended by braces at a height of about seven feet. Boca del Tigre alone has several miles of cableway, all converging on a central packing shed. On harvest days the farm employs more than five hundred workers, each assigned a specialized niche in an industrial-scale division of labor. Selectors identify fruit for harvest, cutters separate the sixty- to eighty-pound stems from banana plants, and haulers (*junteros*) carry the stems to the cableway. Once each stem is hung on a hook suspended from rollers, other workers carefully remove the blue diothene bags in which the fruit has been maturing while on the plant. When a "train" of thirty or more stems has been assembled, a *cablero* ("cableman") attaches a line from the train to a leather harness around his waist and begins to slowly pull the train to the shed. Each train may have a ton or more of bananas suspended from it and is towed as far as half a mile to its destination. A single *cablero* may make this trip twenty-five times or more in a thirteen-hour shift. It is debilitating work but also the most highly paid production labor on the plantation, and farms never lack young men hoping to accumulate some quick money as *cableros* before their mid twenties, when their backs give out. When the fruit trains arrive at the shed, the stems are transferred to a predominately female work force whose job it is to separate individual hands, grade, wash, and pack the fruit in cartons for export.

Not including supervisory personnel, there are nine categories of production work on the farm, each paid at a distinct piece rate. As a general farm laborer, you bring home earnings of about 80 Lempiras (about US $4.00) per day, a wage that has declined by a third since the union was broken. After deductions are made for your purchases at the farm commissary, you are frequently left owing money to your employer at the end of each week. The prospect of sending children to school, much less owning a home, is simply out of the question, given your modest earnings.

Scanty wages are not the only consequence of the farm's change in ownership. At no point have conditions on Central American banana farms been safe for workers, most of whom are routinely exposed to pesticides with poorly documented health effects. Like thousands of other banana workers in Honduras, you have been left sterile from years of exposure to Nemagon, and you have seen many of the children born in the vicinity of the farm endure the paralysis, contorted limbs, and other horrifying stigmata of DBCP-related birth defects. Their plight, together with the prevalence of untreated malaria, dysentery, and HIV, compounds the general atmosphere of misery prevailing on the farm. Geographically isolated, lacking diversions other than binge drinking and brothels, and crosscut by ethnic and national antagonisms carefully nurtured by management, the farm workforce is prone to explosive outbreaks of seemingly random violence.[2]

Since the outbreak of Black Sigatoka leaf fungus in Honduras in 1993, Boca del Tigre has been sprayed from the air with the cancer-causing fungicide Chlorotlalonil on a weekly basis. Union agreements had once ensured that crop-dusting aircraft operated only when workers were absent from the fields, and that management provided protective clothing and masks for those who handled and applied farm chemicals. Under the new management, agreements and national laws designed to regulate chemical exposure are now openly flouted, and you are expected to continue at your tasks even as crop dusters deposit their noxious chemical trails around you. Not a few of your fellow workers have sickened from chemical exposure and been forced to quit, but the abrogation of union contracts and closure of nearby smaller farms has left a pool of desperate unemployed workers ready to take their place. The intensive chemical use on Boca del Tigre may take a heavy toll on its workers, their families, and the environment, but it has boosted farm productivity dramatically. The estate on which you work regularly attains annual production levels of twenty-five or more tons per acre, three times that of a St. Lucian hillside farm. Yet it is doubtful that Calixte Jn Baptiste or any other St. Lucian banana farmer would willingly trade his place with yours.

Origins of the Dollar Area and ACP Trading Blocs

Despite their common involvement in banana production for the world market, Calixte Jn Baptiste and Justo Martínez appear to inhabit different worlds. Almost all banana production on St. Lucia and the other Windward Islands takes place under the conditions experienced by Jn Baptiste. Farms are independent, family-run operations that employ household members and at most a few wage laborers. The average size of a banana farm in the Mabouya Valley is slightly over four acres, and 75 percent of the island's farms consist of less than ten acres of land (OAS 1995; St. Lucia 2002). Levels of mechanization and input use on such operations are very low by global standards, and farms instead rely heavily on labor-intensive methods, raising the costs of production per box to between two and three times that of Ecuador, the world's largest producer (Paggi and Spreen 2003: 14). This is above all the case for the many farms that cling to the steep slopes of the islands' mountainous landscapes. On St. Lucia, 43 percent of all banana farms are located on slopes of twenty degrees or more (Kairi Consultants 1993). The cableways and elaborate division of labor that make Central and South American farms resemble "banana factories" are nowhere to be found in the Caribbean.

Throughout Latin America, banana plantations occupy hundreds to thousands of acres of flat, fertile terrain. At the upper end of this scale are the Central American farms remaining under the direct control of the three large US-based banana corporations. Increasingly, corporate ownership and management has been supplanted by contract farming, as the US banana companies abandon the riskiest segments of the commodity chain (production) for the most profitable (marketing). In Ecuador, where slightly smaller private farms predominate, the buyer's role is played by Grupo Noboa, a consortium that makes up the world's fourth largest banana exporter. Yet any commercial banana farm in Central or South America dwarfs its counterpart in the Windwards. A single farm owned by Chiquita (formerly United Fruit) along the Costa Rica–Panama border comprises as much land as the entire acreage under bananas among all

11,000 St. Lucian farmers in 1992, the industry's peak year of production (see Bourgois 1989: 4). At the root of the high productivity of Latin American farms are notoriously exploitative and dangerous working conditions, as reflected in the experience of Justo Martínez. In addition to the human health problems caused by chemical contamination, the environmental costs associated with banana farming in Central America include deforestation, topsoil erosion, contamination of aquifers, and extinction of untold species of native plants and animals. Central American farms ooze with the detritus of industrial agriculture: pesticide runoff destroys aquatic life, and millions of chemically-laden blue diothene bags litter the landscape or are incinerated in black, oily clouds of smoke.[3]

How can the same export crop yield misery and environmental destruction in one region and a reasonably comfortable standard of living in another? The difference is attributable to the distinct ways in which Caribbean and Latin American bananas are exchanged on the world market, which has long been structured in two separate trading blocs affect their participants in starkly disparate ways. The Dollar Area (Latin American) and ACP (African, Caribbean, and Pacific) banana blocs were formalized in the late 1940s, but they hark back to the very beginnings of the export banana industry in Central America during the nineteenth century.

From its origins in the 1870s until the eve of the twentieth century, the US-bound banana trade was highly decentralized. Fruit was grown on privately owned banana farms of widely varying sizes scattered along the humid Caribbean lowlands from Costa Rica to British Honduras (now Belize). Control of the trade resided in the hands of schooner and steamboat captains who procured the fruit directly from farmers and shipped it to New Orleans, Mobile, and other ports on the Gulf of Mexico (Soluri 2005: 28). Centralization of the trade began with the incorporation of the United Fruit Company (UFCO) in 1899 from the merger of three steamboat lines linking Central America to the US market. The company's founder, Minor Keith, had already accumulated large landholdings in Costa Rica, Honduras, and Guatemala as government concessions in exchange for the construction of railroads.[4] With its incorporation, United Fruit became a vertically integrated company controlling all phases of production, rail and ship transport, and wholesaling of bananas. From its inception the firm was known for its relentless pursuit of monopolies, particularly with regard to the purchase and shipping of fruit. A favored strategy was to buy the produce of independent growers in competitive markets at higher prices than the company's rivals offered, thereby garnering most of their output. Short-term losses from such price hikes were offset by profits generated in markets where the company had already secured a monopoly. Once United Fruit's rivals had withdrawn from the market, the company was free to dictate often ruinous prices and marketing conditions to private growers. By 1905, most of the remaining independent banana growers in Central America were already tied to exclusive contracts with United Fruit after rival shipping companies had either been acquired by United Fruit or driven to bankruptcy through predatory pricing (Moberg 2003: 146). The company's stranglehold over marketing earned it the epithet of *el pulpo* (the octopus) throughout Central America, while its ability to dominate the region's governments and flout their national sovereignty lent them the dismissive label of "banana republics."[5]

United Fruit's marketing monopolies placed independent producers at a disadvantage, but in the end it was disease that sealed the fate of the region's small-scale banana farms. In the years after 1910, producers of the Gros Michel variety—at that time, virtually the only variety grown for export—were increasingly afflicted by a mysterious disease that caused leaves and stems to yellow and die. Farmers who replaced diseased plants with healthy suckers found that the replacements soon withered away as well. Taking its name from the locale in which it was first described, Panama Disease was traced to a soil-borne fungus (*Fusarium oxysporum f. cubense*) that quickly spread to previously healthy farms via seasonal floods, human contact, transplanted suckers, and even the use of tools from infected farms. Following the conversion of diverse tropical forest ecosystems into Gros Michel monocultures, the disease spread like wildfire across Central America.

As established plantations died away, United Fruit was forced to relocate its sites of production to new, uninfected regions, a practice that Soluri (2005: 70) likens to "shifting plantation agriculture." With each such relocation, the company dismantled rail lines and other infrastructure to deny their use to competitors, few of whom, in any case, possessed the capital and landholdings required to establish new farms every five to fifteen years (Bourgois 1989: 16). Small-scale producers—even those whose farms remained unscathed by the disease—found themselves forced out of production as United Fruit suspended rail service to affected regions or even uprooted tracks for use elsewhere. By the 1940s, small- and medium-scale production for export (i.e., farms of less than 100 acres) had virtually ceased to exist in Central America, in large part because of the enormous cost of controlling *Fusarium* and a more recently introduced disease, Yellow Sigatoka (Soluri 2005: 116). Although some efforts were made to introduce disease-resistant varieties, former company plant scientists claimed that United Fruit "dragged its feet" in developing alternatives to the Gros Michel, mainly because each time the company relocated its operations, it enhanced its monopoly over marketing and production (Bourgois 1989: 16). It was not until the 1950s that the Giant Cavendish, a variety that was

Fusarium-resistant but required far more delicate handling because of its thin peel, replaced the Gros Michel on United Fruit plantations. The Giant Cavendish remains virtually the only variety of exported bananas today, prompting renewed concerns about the lack of genetic diversity in one of the world's most important commercial and subsistence crops.

United Fruit's monopolistic practices engendered intense opposition among labor activists and nationalist politicians in Central America, to which the company responded with bribery, coercion, and assassination (see Bourgois 2003). Repeatedly the company sought to defeat strikes by importing English-speaking black workers from the West Indies to undermine labor solidarity among Spanish-speaking mestizos. The legacy of this strategy persists in the strained and occasionally explosive ethnic relations between the two groups along the Caribbean coast of Central America today (Bourgois 1989; Purcell 1993; Moberg 1997).

The company's growing monopoly over the US banana market had not escaped notice in Washington, D.C., either. In 1909, United Fruit was partially broken up under US anti-trust laws, resulting in the creation of Standard Fruit (later acquired by Castle and Cooke, and now known as Dole Food Corporation). A 1972 anti-trust suit also forced the company to sell some of its lands to the Del Monte Corporation (McCann 1976: 42). During the 1970s, United Fruit merged with another food conglomerate and was reorganized as United Brands, eventually changing its name to Chiquita. In an effort to rehabilitate its image and avert both the tumultuous labor relations on its plantations and the risks of production, Chiquita has since sold off some of its Central American holdings and emphasized its shipping and wholesaling activities. Meanwhile, independent producers and exporters in Ecuador and Colombia have also slightly eroded the control of US-based banana companies over Latin American production. Yet if the current actual landholdings of the three major US banana companies are but a small remnant of the millions of acres they controlled at their peak in the 1930s, the companies remain powerful economic and political players on the world market. As will be seen, in the mid 1990s the company's political influence at the highest levels of the US government was undiminished from forty years earlier, when it had persuaded the US to engineer a coup d'état against the democratically elected government of Guatemala.

Providing all of the bananas sold on the US market, the Dollar Area bloc trades exclusively in Latin American fruit, most of which is handled by the three large US-based banana multinationals. Although the US remains the single largest banana market in the world (it consumes 31 percent of the world's exported bananas), the Dollar bloc extends into Asian and European markets as well (Raynolds 2003: 29). While the ACP bloc has historically centered on the European market, even here Dollar Area producers dominate, providing about 64 percent of the bananas consumed in Europe (Raynolds 2003: 30). Chiquita, Dole, and Del Monte among themselves control 67 percent of the world trade in bananas, and when the smaller Ecuadorian and Colombian exporters are added to the equation, the Dollar bloc in its entirety constitutes more than 75 percent of all world trade in bananas (Raynolds 2003: 30). Clearly, by virtue of its scale of production, the Dollar Area bloc is able to set the price at which bananas are bought and sold worldwide.

Whereas the Dollar Area is the creation of the US-based banana companies, the ACP bloc emerged from European imperial politics and trade practices intended in part to curtail the influence of the US companies in European markets. The introduction of onboard refrigeration on transatlantic steamers at the end of the nineteenth century opened the European market to banana producers in the Americas. Colonial administrators seized upon growing British demand for bananas to resolve some of the longstanding social and economic problems experienced by Britain's West Indian colonies. Among these were the lack of economic alternatives to a sugar industry that had declined since the abolition of slavery, and island populations that were growing politically restive because of deteriorating economic conditions. Yet a major obstacle stood in the way of an economically viable smallholder-based banana industry under British direction: by the beginning of the twentieth century North American firms already controlled most of the transatlantic shipping of bananas and were extending control over the UK market as well, to the exclusion of British importers.

To counter United Fruit's rapidly growing dominance over the transatlantic trade, in 1901 the British government set aside 75 percent of the domestic market for an English firm, Elders and Fyffes Ltd., predecessor of today's Fyffes PLC (Thomson 1987: 80). Because Fyffes was a shipping firm and operated no farms of its own, Great Britain promoted smallholder production in Jamaica and provided subsidies to the company to supply the English market via its refrigerated ships. Yet what was intended to secure, in mercantilist fashion, both a colonial source of bananas for the domestic market and control of that market by British interests soon fell prey to United Fruit's ambitions. The US company amassed shares of Fyffes even as British government officials guaranteed much of the domestic market to what they believed to be an English company. By 1910 UFCO had emerged as a majority owner of Fyffes, and within two more years had acquired the remaining shares as well (Davies 1990: 82). British authorities were alarmed by the fact that UFCO now controlled, either directly or through its subsidiary, virtually the entire domestic banana market.

To thwart UFCO's ambitions, the Imperial Economic Committee recommended in 1926 that Britain turn to the Windward Islands as a source of fruit, advocating an industry of small- and medium-scale producers joined in growers' organizations under government auspices (Grossman 1998: 36). The committee viewed banana production in the hands of smallholders as a way to economically and politically stabilize the deeply impoverished Windwards while supplying the needs of a growing British market; indeed, the project meshed nicely with the 1897 Royal Commission's recommendations favoring smallholder agriculture as the basis of island economies. As noted in Chapter Two, however, these early efforts in the Windwards proved short-lived due to repeated infestations of Panama Disease and then a lack of shipping during World War II.

In Jamaica, the colonial government countered UFCO's ensuing control over the island's banana exports by organizing banana growers into a cooperative, the Jamaican Banana Producers Association (Holt 1992: 351), or JBPA. Securing government-guaranteed loans during the 1920s, the JBPA operated a modest fleet of ships between Jamaica and nearby US ports. Forced to compete with the association for the island's fruit and facing a small but growing threat from the Jamaican producers over some retail markets in the US, United Fruit was determined to crush the JBPA with the same tactics it had already perfected in its conquest of Central America. Its profits secured in other markets, the company enticed Jamaican growers with prices far exceeding those of the cooperative. For some time the JBPA maintained the loyalties of its members, but in 1934 a hurricane vastly reduced yields on most of the island's farms (Holt 1992: 353). Despite appeals by the co-op's management to resist the company's overtures, many farmers affected by the storm succumbed to UFCO's higher prices.

Having lost a significant share of its suppliers, the co-op was soon facing bankruptcy. By 1935, it was forced to submit to UFCO's terms in the price war. These included the co-op's withdrawal from all US markets, its conversion from a cooperative to a shareholding firm, and an agreement to not exceed the prices paid by United Fruit for Jamaican bananas (Sealy and Hart 1984: 77). Soon after the former co-op had surrendered to the company's demands, UFCO slashed its prices for Jamaican fruit to levels comparable to those paid in Central America. Through its Fyffes subsidiary (which exported Jamaican fruit to the UK), United Fruit retained de facto control of the British banana market both in terms of sourcing and importation until 1940, when banana imports ceased because shipping had been diverted to the war effort.

As domestic demand for bananas soared after five years of wartime deprivations, the British government once again promoted banana production in the Caribbean and elsewhere.[6] Government support for the Windward Islands industry was at first ambivalent, reflecting continued shipping problems and a fear that previous failures would repeat themselves. But as both production and official support had grown by the early 1950s, the British government was careful to award the concession for Windward banana exports to a firm that remained outside of UFCO's sphere of influence. As seen earlier, that company was Antilles Products, later to become Geest Industries. Geest's entry into the banana trade dramatically reduced United Fruit's dominance of the British market, and Jamaica's share of British banana sales fell by nearly half between 1938 and 1959 (Clegg 2002: 82).

Because production in the Windwards is spread over thousands of farms, the industry has always lacked the advantages of the vertical integration found in Central America. When a single company controls all aspects of production and transportation, the technical requirements of export production (for example, the use of inputs, aerial spraying, construction of roads, and implementation of pest control measures) can be easily and uniformly coordinated over a large region. Since the time of Panama Disease, the monocultures associated with banana production have remained prone to a host of plant diseases and pest infestations requiring concerted and coordinated responses. Similarly, the shift to the Giant Cavendish variety required a revolution in the handling of fruit, which was now shipped in boxes rather than on whole stems. Such changes could be imposed by fiat on corporate-run farms.

Lacking the vertical integration of Dollar area producers, banana farmers in the Windwards turned to a statutory organization, each island's Banana Growers' Association, to help them satisfy new technical demands. Because each farmer is an independent producer, the BGAs lack the direct control over the production process that United Fruit's management is able to impose over its plantations. To implement the technical requirements demanded by export markets, the island BGAs attempt to mimic the banana companies' vertical integration. They do so by using their control over credit, extension, and marketing to cajole and occasionally coerce farmers into adopting innovations, even when the need for such changes originates in export markets and is poorly understood at the local level. The result has often been confrontation between producers and their ostensible representatives in the BGA, rather than seamless and effective integration. Yet such confrontations, reflected in tumultuous leadership elections and contentious BGA membership meetings, are also testaments to the greater degree of democratic decision making enjoyed by Windwards farmers, compared to those who work on corporate-controlled farms in Central America.

Externalities or "Protectionism"?

Born of a political and economic imperative to stabilize colonial societies, the Caribbean banana industry was never regarded as one that could compete openly with Dollar Area bananas. Rather, Caribbean farmers have always owed their survival to their insulation from direct price competition with the likes of Chiquita. The Windward Islands enjoy none of the natural or economic endowments from which Chiquita has benefited. Thousands of farms dispersed over a rugged terrain permit no economies of scale and few of the capital improvements, such as irrigation, cableways, or mechanization, that have enhanced plantation yields in Central America. Yields are further suppressed by low levels of capital investment on the part of farmers, the most notable consequence of which is an inability or reluctance to use chemical inputs at the levels common to Central American farms. Indeed, as the fortunes of the Windwards banana industry have waned since the early 1990s, many farmers have cut back on their herbicide and pesticide use to save money, resulting, if unintentionally, in near-organic conditions on many farms.

From their abundance of land, cheap labor and inputs, the Dollar Area banana sectors exported in excess of 10.2 million tons of fruit in 2004, dwarfing the 110,000 tons exported from the Windward Islands in that year (FAO 2005). With per acre yields averaging about a third of those attained in Honduras or Costa Rica, Windward Island farms experience production costs between US $400 and $700 per ton, compared to $150–200 per ton in Central America (Raynolds 2003: 37). Yet such elementary accounting overlooks the total costs of production with regard to social and environmental sustainability. The devastating environmental, public health, and social consequences of Central America's monoculture plantation production are largely absent from the Windwards. Until recently, farmers and their wage workers earned a livelihood that permitted them what is locally regarded as a middle-class standard of living.

Economists define the environmental and social costs of production that are not reflected in the market price of a product as an "externality," an expense that is not recorded in cost-accounting but is instead borne by the public at large or by future generations (Acheson 1989: 354). For example, when someone purchases a cheap personal computer, the price he or she pays does not reflect the damage done by the many pounds of heavy metals released into the environment when it is manufactured or discarded in a landfill.[7] Similarly, consumers in developed countries benefit from the low prices of Dollar Area bananas, which fail to reflect the costs of their production with respect to human rights, human health, and the environment. Because the prices at which bananas trade on the market ignore such externalities, ACP fruit is always at a disadvantage compared to bananas grown in Latin America. Some attempts have been made in recent years to educate retailers and consumers about the externalities involved when they purchase cheap Dollar bananas rather than the fruit grown on Windwards farms. Shipped in boxes printed prominently with the phrase "Ethically Grown Bananas," the less than 2 percent of the world's exported fruit originating in the Windward Islands (Paggi and Spreen 2003: 10) is a disquieting reminder that the vast majority of the world's bananas are grown under highly unethical, though profitable, conditions.

To rephrase the above, the costs of environmental and community sustainability are "internalized" by island growers; that is, the cost of protecting the environment and human rights is reflected in the higher cost of their fruit. Such fruit can only be sold in markets where the purchase price of bananas similarly internalizes all the costs of their production. Historically, this has been achieved through a complex system of tariffs, quotas, and licenses intended to raise the European retail price of Dollar Area bananas to levels comparable to the production costs of ACP fruit. To advocates of free trade—the doctrine that commodities should be exchanged across national borders without regard to the conditions under which they are produced—such markets are considered "protectionist." Under the neoliberal doctrines that now dominate global trade policy, protectionism is considered a flawed strategy that perpetuates inefficiency in production and prevents consumers from realizing the benefits of goods that can be produced more cheaply elsewhere. Unacknowledged in such claims is that "efficiency" and low production costs for most globally traded commodities are usually achieved through high external costs, such as conditions that abuse human rights and the environment where those commodities are produced. That a corporation can manufacture goods more cheaply with child or prison labor in China than by unionized workers in the United States must not, under neoliberal doctrines, limit the right of that company to freely move its products across national borders. Moreover, such doctrines are no longer mere opinions held by academic economists but now carry the weight of enforceable law in international trade. For many low-skilled industries, one effect of such policies has been a "race to the bottom" as manufacturers seek to source their products from places offering the lowest wages and least restrictive environmental policies, leading necessarily to a reduction in workers' earnings and environmental quality worldwide.

Until 2000, the marketing of bananas in the European Union (EU) was governed by a succession of treaties first negotiated in Togo, West Africa, in 1975 and known as the Lomé Convention. Lomé was intended to provide

Figure 4.2 | Boxes of Windward Island bananas are marked "ethically grown" to distinguish them within the supermarket setting.

preferential access to the European market for forty-six (later expanded to seventy) developing countries that were formerly colonies of Europe. Among its many provisions, the convention stipulated that all bananas from ACP countries could be imported into the EU free of duty, while a 20 percent ad valorum tariff would be levied on imports of Dollar Area fruit (Tangermann 2003: 26). Yet what purported to enact common priorities for trade masked quite divergent interests among European states. Countries such as the UK, France, Spain, and Italy, all of which maintained strong historical ties to banana producers in former colonies or overseas departments, sought preferences over and above Lomé in the form of market quotas that restricted the importation of low-cost Dollar Area fruit. On the British market, these measures were manipulated to maintain prices that covered the production costs of growers in the Windwards and Jamaica. Countries lacking former colonies, such as Germany, Austria and Sweden, lobbied for and obtained an exemption from the common tariff and refused to impose quotas of any kind. Thus these countries allowed for completely unimpeded access by Dollar Area importers, which provided virtually all of the fruit on their respective markets. In between the extremes of the UK and Germany were countries such as Denmark, Ireland, Belgium, and the Netherlands, which imposed no quotas restricting Dollar Area fruit but maintained the common 20 percent tariff (Tangermann 2003: 28). Although all European countries subscribed to Lomé's tariff exemption for ACP fruit, in practice Dollar Area bananas dominated European markets everywhere except in those countries, such as the UK, that imposed additional import quotas.

The creation of the Single European Market in 1993—itself a significant neoliberal policy objective—was intended to remove virtually all barriers to trade between EU member states. In line with this aim, the substantial national differences in banana trade policy were to be negotiated out of existence in favor of a continent-wide import regime. During highly contested negotiations, Germany and other nations that relied heavily on Dollar bananas demanded modifications favoring Latin American suppliers in order to retain low prices on their domestic markets. The resulting New Banana Regime (Regulation 404, adopted in July 1993) represented a complex compromise between countries that sought continued Dollar Area imports and those wanting to protect traditional ACP suppliers.

Under the new provisions, Dollar Area and ACP countries were awarded import quotas to Europe based upon their "historic" export levels. Within its quota of 858,000 tons, all ACP fruit was imported duty-free, as was all fruit imported from overseas departments of European states, such as Martinique and Guadeloupe. Dollar Area producers were collectively granted a two million–ton quota (later increased to 2.2 million tons), on which a 75 ECU (European Currency Unit)[8] per ton tariff was imposed. Dollar Area imports above those levels were subject to steeply higher tariffs of 680 ECUs per ton (Raynolds 2003: 40), a level that in effect constituted an import cap as it rendered all such fruit prohibitively priced on European markets. Importers were granted transferable licenses for duty-free ACP and Dollar Area fruit within the 75 ECU tariff. Because of effective restrictions on Dollar Area imports, the latter license categories were potentially valuable to importers and reportedly changed hands at between US $4 and $7 per box of fruit in the first year after the new regime was instituted (Tangermann 2003: 39). The licenses were predominately awarded to "traditional" importers, a distribution that favored EU-based firms such as Fyffes and WIBDECO. However, the provision also benefited US companies, such as Dole, that purchased fruit from both Dollar Area and ACP sources and had import operations of their own or established partnerships with European importers. As the parent company of Fyffes, Chiquita had long retained substantial access to the European market because of Fyffes's sources of supply in the ACP countries. Having sold off its Fyffes subsidiary in 1986, however, Chiquita later found itself disadvantaged in terms of ACP access under the Single Market provisions.[9]

The negotiation of a common banana trade policy took place against the background of an expanding European retail market. Dollar Area producers long ago saturated the US and Canadian markets, but to accommodate the growing worldwide demand for bananas they have dramatically expanded their production to take advantage of newly opened markets. Among these have been Japan, the former USSR, and the Middle East, but the fastest-growing market since the 1980s has been Europe, which now consumes 33 percent of all bananas produced for export (Paggi and Spreen 2003: 11). Upon introduction of the transferable license provision, large quantities of Dollar Area fruit were for the first time allowed onto the European market without corresponding increases in ACP imports. Increased production on Latin American plantations fueled a global oversupply of fruit, much of which made its way onto European markets. Between 1989 and 1992, the volume of Dollar Area bananas entering Europe increased from 1.71 million to 2.34 million tons (Clegg 2002: 128). The result was a downward spiral of retail prices in Europe, with a corresponding decline paid to producers in the Dollar Area and ACP regions alike.

On balance, the changes under the Single European Market have occurred at the expense of Caribbean producers, even if traditional ACP importers have benefited from the licensing provisions (Anderson, Taylor, and Josling 2003: 141). Prior to the unified import regime of 1993, the Windward Islands produced 65 percent of the bananas consumed in the UK (Nurse and Sandiford 1995). By striking down the earlier country-specific restrictions in the UK and other EU member states, the new provisions under the Single European Market drastically reduced that amount: by 2002, just 17 percent of the British retail market was comprised of Windward Island fruit (Jean 2004: 24). In the early 1990s, as the outlines of the New Banana Regime were being negotiated, the Dollar Area companies consciously sought to inflate their later import quotas, which have a changing year-by-year reference point, by flooding the European market. This strategy drove down the retail price of bananas throughout Europe and was a significant factor in forcing Windward Island producers out of business after 1992. Finally, by expanding their sources among ACP producers in Africa, two of the three US banana companies have been able to make corresponding increases in duty-free Dollar Area imports. US companies now import nearly 33 percent of the ACP fruit entering Europe.

With these practices, Dole increased its market share in the EU from 12 to 18 percent during the 1990s and Del Monte increased its share from 7 to 10 percent (Taylor 2003: 85). The strategies of Dole and Del Monte also assured that the ACP retained a steady share of the European market (fluctuating between 34 and 37 percent in the mid 1990s) (Raynolds 2003: 41). In effect, this was achieved by a transfer of ACP quotas from the Windward Islands to Africa, from which the US companies sourced an increasing amount of exported fruit. Having sold its Fyffes subsidiary and failing to obtain new ACP suppliers, only Chiquita lost out under the trading regime, seeing its share of the growing European market decline from 30 to 15 percent (Raynolds 2003: 41). Such trends were unprecedented and unacceptable for a company founded on the pursuit of an ever-greater market share. Chiquita's response to its declining position in the European market was to mount a full-fledged assault on the EU trading system, and with it the livelihoods of Windward Island banana farmers. If Chiquita were to have its way, Calixte Jn Baptiste would find himself competing directly to sell his bananas on the world market with the employer of Justo Martínez.

How to Get Your Case to the World Trade Organization

Despite the fact that two of the three US banana companies had successfully navigated the New Banana Regime to expand their share of the European market, Chiquita vociferously argued that EU trade policy discriminated against US corporations doing business in Europe. The company claimed that EU provisions had cost it US $400 million in lost revenue.[10]

Until the mid 1990s international trade disputes of this sort had been directed to the General Agreement on Tariffs and Trade (GATT), a forum that permitted trading partners to air grievances and negotiate mutually acceptable solutions. Established in 1948, GATT endorsed the principle of free trade between nations but required that trade issues be resolved by consensus, including consent by all the parties to a dispute. When GATT representatives created the World Trade Organization (WTO) in 1995, the doctrine of free trade acquired a tough enforcement mechanism through its dispute settlement process. Technically, any government that felt that its manufacturers' exports were discriminated against by a trading partner could file a suit with the WTO alleging unfair barriers to free trade. When the WTO trade panel finds on behalf of the plaintiff, it directs the defendant country to remove or modify the offending policies. If that country refuses, the government that brought the suit is permitted to impose tariffs or restrictions in reprisal until the original policy is changed. It is through the WTO that free trade doctrines acquire the force of international law. Because its decisions can override national statutes regulating the flow of goods across borders, the WTO has effectively transferred control over trade from sovereign nations to an unelected body of policy makers. The WTO's critics point out that this body supersedes the ability of citizens to restrict, through their elected governments, the importation of goods manufactured under conditions that they deem to be socially or environmentally harmful.

Since the WTO's formation, the body has been heavily involved in trade disputes between the United States and Europe, most of which have been initiated by US corporations challenging EU trade restrictions. In 1989, the European Union imposed a ban on the importation of beef injected with recombinant bovine growth hormones (rBGH). The hormones, which are manufactured by the Monsanto Corporation in the United States, are used to increase milk yields in dairy cows. Although the hormones were eventually approved by the US Food and Drug Administration, their use remains controversial from the perspective of many scientists and public interest groups in both the US and Europe. They have been linked to increased antibiotic levels in milk (the hormones increase udder infections, which are treated with antibiotics), an early onset of menarche in girls who consume the milk, and even to the development of cancer among those who consume hormone-treated milk and meat (BGH Bulletin 2000). Monsanto approached the US trade representative, a presidential appointee who investigates trade complaints on behalf of US businesses, to challenge the EU's ban on hormone-injected beef. The US government subsequently filed suit with the WTO arguing that the ban was an unfair barrier to US beef exports. The WTO rejected EU concerns about the health effects of rBGH, ruled in favor of the United States, and authorized US $116.8 million in punitive tariffs on European agricultural goods entering the US (French 2000). The trade dispute between Europe and the US over rBGH illustrates how any country or trading bloc whose environmental or public health policies violate the doctrine of free trade must either rescind those policies or face severe consequences for their own export industries.[11] In the case of bovine growth hormone, the EU has repeatedly opted to uphold its ban, despite the heavy costs incurred by its own agricultural sectors for doing so.

Since 1974, Section 301 of the US Trade Act has empowered the US trade representative to investigate allegations of unfair trade practices and to pursue action against foreign governments whose policies "burden or restrict U.S. commerce" (Grier 2005). The underlying assumption is that restrictions on US exports potentially hurt all US residents by impairing businesses' ability to operate at full employment. Given that only a handful of US citizens are employed in the production of bananas (mainly as managers on Latin American plantations) and that Chiquita's exports to the EU are not of US origin, it may seem that Chiquita occupied tenuous grounds at best to invoke Trade Law 301. That was also the initial opinion of Mickey Kantor, President Clinton's trade representative, when Chiquita first requested an investigation into EU banana trading policy. Indeed, upon taking office in 1993, the Clinton administration had reassured Caribbean nations that it supported the existing EU regime, probably recognizing that a failed Caribbean banana industry might increase drug trafficking and illegal immigration into the US.

Chiquita was not easily discouraged by Kantor's lukewarm reception to its case, and historical precedent was clearly on the company's side in its ability to bend government policy to its wishes. Four decades earlier, Chiquita's predecessor, United Fruit, had single handedly persuaded the Eisenhower administration to order the CIA to overthrow Guatemalan President Jacobo Arbenz after he had redistributed some of the company's lands to peasants. That the company was able to use the CIA on its behalf stemmed from the fact that two of its largest stockholders held key foreign policy positions in the Eisenhower administration.[12] Similarly, Chiquita's CEO in the 1990s, Carl H. Lindner, was a man of exceptional wealth (his net worth then was estimated at 800 million dollars) and political clout, and he did not shrink from deploying both to obtain a favorable hearing on behalf of his company (Barlett and Steele 2000). Throughout 1994, Mickey Kantor was visited by a succession of congressional leaders, all of whom relayed their urgent concerns about European banana trade policy. They included Senators Trent Lott (R-MS), John Glenn (D-OH), Robert Dole (R-KS), Mitch McConnell (R-KY), Mike DeWine (R-OH), and Richard Lugar (R-IN), all among the most powerful US senators of the 1990s. What they had in common, other than the fact that no bananas are grown in their home states, was that they were also recipients of lavish campaign contributions from Lindner or companies controlled by him (Barlett and Steele 2000). Lindner and his interests donated almost one million dollars to congressional candidates during 1993 and 1994, making him one of the largest contributors during that election cycle (Stovall and Hathaway 2003: 153). The Chiquita CEO was so grateful for Senator Dole's efforts on his company's behalf that he lent him his private jet while Dole campaigned for president.

But it was not until Lindner, a lifelong contributor to Republican Party causes, became more bipartisan in his spending habits that he clinched Mickey Kantor's support. Between 1994 and 1996, Lindner and his various companies contributed nearly half a million dollars to the Democratic National Committee and several state Democratic Parties (Rosegrant 1999: 10). President Clinton so appreciated these contributions that he extended to Lindner an invitation to dine at the White House and sleep over in the Lincoln bedroom (Myers 2004: 82). Unstated, of course, is what other gestures of appreciation were exchanged for the contributions. It is safe to say that regardless of who won the 1996 presidential election, Chiquita's interests were sure to be upheld by the White House and its appointed trade representative. In this respect, political contributions made for distinctly bipartisan bedfellows.

Following months of pressure from members of Congress who were recipients of Lindner's contributions as well as several meetings with the CEO himself, Kantor reversed his earlier skepticism about Chiquita's case. In October 1994 he authorized the Trade Law 301 investigation that Chiquita had requested (Stovall and Hathaway 2003: 153). After arranging another $100,000 contribution to the DNC several weeks later, Lindner sent a warm letter of appreciation to the trade representative, addressed therein as "Dear Mickey" (Barlett and Steele 2000). In 1996, Kantor initiated a formal complaint before the WTO that the European Union's banana trade policy discriminated against US corporations.

To allay criticism that the complaint was filed narrowly on behalf of a company that employed few US nationals and produced no exports from the United States, additional parties to the suit were recruited by the Clinton administration. These included the Hawaii Banana Industry Association (a miniscule entity representing a total of 1,400 acres of banana farms that have never exported bananas to Europe), as well as the governments of Ecuador, Honduras, Guatemala, and Mexico. These governments were aggrieved because none had been given EU import quotas under a 1995 revision of the New Banana Regime. Two countries that had consented to the new framework, Costa Rica and Colombia, were now pressured by punitive legislation authored by Senator Dole to withdraw from the regime and join the US-led complaint to the WTO (Clegg 2002: 150). Both Dole and Del Monte (now Chilean-owned, but based in Florida) refused to join the suit, raising doubts about its charge that the EU discriminated against US corporations. Yet in September 1997, the WTO Dispute Settlement Body issued a ruling that EU banana regulations violated free trade principles by allocating preferential licenses to the traditional ACP importers Fyffes and Geest (WIBDECO UK).

The next several years saw the EU fighting, and losing, a succession of rearguard actions to preserve remaining protections for ACP fruit against the concerted stance of the United States and its partners in the complaint. The EU revised its banana policies in 1999 in an attempt to reach compliance with the WTO ruling. The new proposal maintained existing tariffs and quotas for ACP and Dollar Area fruit, but allocated new country quotas and reallocated import licenses. This was an attempt to both satisfy Ecuador's claims that it had been discriminated against earlier in the allocation of quotas and enable Chiquita to act directly as a fruit importer in the manner of Fyffes, Geest, Dole, and Del Monte. Chiquita rejected these revisions, and Charlene Barshefsky, Kantor's successor as US trade representative, returned the case to the WTO, which upheld the US objections. This time, the WTO authorized the US to impose US $191 million in trade sanctions against the EU and granted Ecuador the right to impose $202 million in sanctions (Josling 2003: 188).[13] The EU again modified its re-gime in 2000, eliminating country quotas altogether and allocating import licenses on a first-come, first-served basis. After consulting directly with Chiquita, Barshefsky again rejected the EU proposal.

In 2001, Chiquita and the US government finally agreed to an EU pro-posal that, after a transitional tariff quota arrangement, moved to a tariff-only system to be fully introduced at the beginning of 2006. Under these arrangements all country quotas were eliminated, and the only remaining protection for ACP fruit was an exemption of the first 750,000 tons from tariffs applied to all other banana imports (Tangermann 2003: 61). With this "tariff only" agreement, Chiquita had achieved its objective of remov-ing any limitation on the amount of Dollar Area fruit that it could import into Europe. The agreement signaled a formal end to the "banana wars," as the trade dispute had become known on both sides of the Atlantic. Al-though the US and Ecuador suspended their trade sanctions against the EU, issues that vitally affected Windward Islands growers remained un-resolved even as the tariff-only system was introduced. Most significant of these was the size of the tariff to be applied on Dollar Area imports as of January 1, 2006. Up to that date, the first 2.7 million tons of Dollar Area fruit was subject to a tariff of €75 (US $90), rising to €680 for each ton imported above that level. In August 2005, the EU announced that under the new system, all but the first 750,000 tons of ACP fruit would be subject to a tariff of €230 (then about $280) per ton. After an appeal by the United States, the WTO ruled the revised tariff to be illegal, leading the EU to revise it downward to €187 ($226) per ton. This, too, was rejected two months later by the WTO. With just a month remaining until the tar-iff-only system was to begin, the EU announced a tariff of €176 ($206) per ton. This tariff went into effect on all Dollar Area banana imports at the beginning of 2006.

The decision of Honduras and Panama to mount a formal challenge to the new tariff, together with the Bush administration trade representa-tive's statement that he was "very disappointed" at the size of the tariff, portends further conflict (US 2005). With several Latin American countries insisting upon a tariff no greater than $75 per ton, the EU and the Dollar Area producers remain far apart. Profound uncertainties about the future of the market persist among the remaining growers on the Windward Is-lands, where many feel that their fate is being decided by powerful forces and agents entirely outside of their control. In 2000, several months before the US presidential election and a year before the end of the banana wars, a few growers even expressed hope during my conversations with them that US voters might elect a president who would look more favorably on the Caribbean. I declined to tell them that Chiquita had safeguarded its interests in the previous election by contributing to both candidates and was likely to do so again.

Ironies of Dependent Development

Coming soon after the Single European Market forced banana prices in the Windwards below production costs for the first time in history, the added injury of the US suit before the WTO prompted disbelief and outrage across the Caribbean. Using one of the Bush administration's own rhetorical tools against it, St. Lucian Prime Minister Dr. Kenny Anthony denounced the US government in 2003 as "economic terrorists" (*The Voice* 2003c: 4) and went on to label the WTO ruling "a capitulation ... to sheer greed" (Anderson, Taylor, and Josling 2003: 147). Many Caribbean leaders argued that the social problems resulting from the banana industry's demise would be so catastrophic as to lead the US to regret its actions. Predictions of widespread unemployment, out migration, drug trafficking, and political violence were widely voiced both in the Caribbean and among the EU's defenders of trade preferences. The words of Edison James, then Dominica's prime minister, are representative in this regard: "[C]lichés like 'desperate times call for desperate measures' and 'a hungry man is an angry man' may sound banal, but they cannot be ignored. Peace in our region and peace in the world depend on the humanitarian dispensation of justice, and the action which has been taken against us in the WTO is not justice" (Anderson, Taylor, and Josling 2003: 147).

Even regional leaders with no direct stake in the banana industry, such as Guyana's President Dr. Cheddi Jagan, reacted angrily to the WTO case. In what seemed like a scarcely veiled threat to a visiting US trade delegation, Jagan warned that "[i]f bananas disappear, our people will have no choice but to produce marijuana and ship it north ... and not only marijuana; we'll be sending refugees" (*The Voice* 1996: 5). The intensity of such rhetoric was more than matched by the region's farmers themselves. As one angry St. Lucian grower put it while poking his finger at my chest, "If you corner even a peaceful animal and threaten it, it will have to bite to protect itself." Elected governments, opposition parties, farmers' organizations, and news media throughout the Caribbean exhibited a rare degree of unanimity in decrying the verdict, and all called upon the EU to find some way to preserve the protected status it had historically granted the region's banana exports.

As Midgett (2003) points out, there is some irony in the vehement response of Caribbean nationalists to the impending removal of a protected market for the region's bananas. Just a decade earlier, most commentary and analyses about the Windward Island banana industry had regarded it as a neocolonial arrangement that stifled independent development for the region's agricultural producers. Trouillot, for example, viewed the independence and material well-being of Dominica's banana growers as illusory. Instead, he characterized growers as disguised wage workers producing surplus value that was extracted by Geest, in turn impoverishing rural communities of the island and suppressing food production (1988: 181ff.). Similarly, Slocum (1996) viewed the St. Lucian state and BGA largely as extensions of Geest, conspiring on its behalf to force rural residents to produce bananas for the world market.

In these analyses, whatever economic development occurred in banana-producing communities was entirely dependent on the structured subordination of the Windwards in the world economy. The implication of such views was that the banana industry left the Windwards worse off than they otherwise would have been, as the protected market had prevented the islands from becoming agriculturally self-sufficient. To an extent, these arguments are empirically and logically defensible, even if they do not reflect the views of banana growers themselves. Production for export undoubtedly has occurred at the expense of local food production: as Grossman (1998) demonstrated for St. Vincent, in choosing to allocate their land and labor between an easily glutted domestic market and a seemingly endless market for bananas, farmers inevitably picked the latter. Such academic analyses notwithstanding, the angry response of island governments and news media to the WTO ruling, as well as the deep pessimism that descended on banana-growing communities in its aftermath, suggests that islanders find the impending changes to be anything but liberating.

A further irony in the region's response to the WTO ruling was its incredulity, considering that the fragile basis of the islands' banana industry and its dependence on a protected market had been widely recognized almost from its inception. As early as 1963, bananas accounted for 80 percent of St. Lucia's export earnings, a doubling of the industry's economic contributions in just seven years. Addressing the annual meeting of the island's BGA in that year, the government's minister for trade and industry described the banana sector's phenomenal recent growth as a "mixed blessing." He warned the island's growers that "there is much doubt as to the long term economic potential of the industry on the grounds that the present price levels in the United Kingdom are much higher than world prices and might be substantially reduced if dollar quotas were liberalized or if there were tariff reductions" (BGA 1963: 19–20). Similarly, a representative of Geest told the group that "there is no guarantee that dollar fruit will always be limited by the existing quotas," and that the island's growers should concentrate on producing quality fruit that would "make the industry viable in the most competitive market" (BGA 1963: 24). A confidential memo circulated within the British government in 1963 actually agreed with the later US position in the trade war, anticipating that the US government was likely to "urge the removal of specific restrictions on the Dollar [Area] trade, arguing rightly that they are discriminatory" (DO 200/19a).

Over the next forty years there were to be numerous government-funded studies on the economic status of the industry, the workings of the BGA, and the livelihoods of island farmers (e.g., St. Lucia 1973, 1980, 1990; ULG 1975; Kairi 1993; Cargill 1995, 1998). With few exceptions the resulting consultants' reports mentioned the precarious nature of Dollar Area quotas in Europe, predicted that they would eventually come to an end because of US pressure and European consumers' desire for cheaper bananas, and stressed the need for the industry to either diversify or enhance its competiveness. Yet no substantial commitment of government or EU resources to prepare for that time was made until after the Single European Market had already eliminated many of the market preferences for Caribbean bananas. Indeed, island governments undertook little concerted action to salvage their banana industries until the WTO had already issued its ruling. For the island of Grenada, which has ceased exporting bananas altogether since 2004, such measures were too little and came too late.

After 1993, as the industry saw its traditional market preferences stripped away, there was general agreement within government and among industry leaders (that is, representatives of the banana companies and WIBDECO) that the banana industry could survive only by increasing its yields and quality. There was, in other words, an understanding that farmers had to conform to the expectations of the world market by changing the ways in which they grew and packaged bananas. This would require the introduction of new technologies, methods, and inputs, many of which, it was anticipated, farmers would reject out of hand. That farmers resist attempts to improve fruit quality and yields is a long-running theme in official discourses of the banana industry in St. Lucia and the other Windwards. This argument is articulated most often by educated, English-speaking residents of Castries who are employed in the industry in some managerial or bureaucratic capacity. It invariably draws upon the substantial cultural and linguistic gulf separating administrators from the Kwéyòl-speaking and often unschooled rural residents who make up the bulk of the farming population. The most charitable variant of this discourse traces the industry's woes to high rates of illiteracy and lack of English proficiency among farmers, factors that are believed to hinder the transfer of technology and other innovations to banana farms. These are also considered to be the source of St. Lucia's more general political fractiousness, as the rural population—almost inevitably described as "illiterate" and "ignorant" by many educated urban residents—is thought to be especially volatile and easily swayed by demagogues in politics and the media.[14] Interestingly, such views appear to mimic those of the island's administrators during the colonial period, who, as seen in Chapter Two, regarded the rural poor as irrational, easily duped, and incapable of self-government.

Bernard Cornibert, a St. Lucian economist who presently serves as chairman of WIBDECO, has repeatedly laid the industry's problems squarely at the feet of farmers' educational and cultural limitations. In an assessment written long before the end of market preferences, Cornibert asserts: "One of the problems associated with low productivity in the banana industry ... is the high frequency of poorly educated or uneducated farmers. The capacity and willingness of those farmers to absorb and to accept advice is severely limited" (1980: 8). Like many other assessments of the "farmer problem," however, his analysis soon takes on a moral dimension, implying that the farmer's underlying failures are his improvidence and laziness: "How one gets that farmer to forgo present consumption of, say, a bottle of rum, for future productivity is still a very serious problem that probably stretches beyond normal economic considerations ... Effectively, what happens is that inefficient and indiscipline [sic] farmers, many of whom should be out of the industry, are being subsidized by the efforts of the more diligent and committed farmer." Claiming that uneducated farmers will "naturally resist" the shift to a more open market, he concludes that "changes are necessary and, painful as they may be, they must be implemented" (Cornibert 1980: 8). The WIBDECO chairman, whose salary of EC $35,000 per month is derived entirely from the sale of Windwards bananas, apparently sees little irony in lecturing the economically stressed producers of that fruit about the need for greater discipline and austerity.

Other, more contextualized assessments of the role that farmers play in questions of quality and yield point out that for most of its existence, the preferential market produced little incentive for either. A St. Lucian journalist observes that "while much of [farmers'] ignorance has a deep correlation to illiteracy, the root cause seems to be the culture of dependence forged from the evolution of the industry into an indirect welfare system from the British" (Vitalis 1999: 5). Peter Serieux, a veteran grower who chairs one of the local banana buying companies, amplified this point:

> [T]he era of preferential treatment was also an era of neglect ... it's like a parent who never prepared a child for the world. If you are constantly holding a child's hands for fear it will fall, it will never learn to walk. Same thing with bananas. A simple thing like product standardization, [Geest] never allowed the Wind-

wards to achieve that. They would buy all of the product at bargain basement prices, sell the 70 percent that was good at premium prices and make a huge profit and dump all the rest [on wholesale markets]. If a farmer gets the same price regardless of what kind of fruit he produces, why should he bother? It's only since '96 that they started working on this, and today our quality is second to none. The old system was another form of colonialism; they never allowed our development to where we could stand on our own. (Pers. comm. 2000)

That the structure of the banana industry, beginning with Geest's producer prices, has long fostered a kind of dependence among growers and disincentive for quality seems indisputable. Criticisms of the former St. Lucia Banana Growers' Association often focused on this point, and on the association's economic inefficiency and high levels of indebtedness. "Cross-subsidization," in which the BGA used cess collected from profitable farmers in order to make inputs, loans, and price supports available to less profitable operations, is among the practices most often cited by those seeking greater efficiency in the banana industry. Until its privatization in 1998, the BGA regularly subsidized the producer price of bananas from its own coffers during periods of low prices, or even contracted debts in order to do so. Such practices enabled many farmers to remain in business when they otherwise would have dropped out of production, and had the effect of stabilizing the island's aggregate output of fruit. Of course, this approach took a toll in ever-growing indebtedness. By the time the BGA was replaced by the privatized St. Lucia Banana Corporation, its debts had grown to EC $42 million (US $15.6 million), all of which was absorbed by the St. Lucian government (Jn Pierre, pers. comm. 2000). Similarly, during the period of the industry's expansion the BGA became a significant employer in its own right, swelling to over 800 staff members on the eve of privatization. According to former employees, many BGA staffers were minimally qualified and had obtained their jobs through their party political ties or nepotism, resulting in a great deal of overstaffing and underperformance.

A succession of government-supported reviews characterized the BGA's cross-subsidization and overstaffing as anomalies that interfered with the business functions of the association (see, e.g., St. Lucia 1990). In the same vein, St. Lucian journalists during the 1980s and 1990s seemed simultaneously obsessed with and appalled by the political infighting among the BGA's board members and government. Yet far from being unexpected, these practices were very much rooted in the guiding if unstated objectives of the association. When initially organized in the 1950s, the BGA had been a democratically operated producers' association, but given its growing island-wide membership and the expansion of the electoral franchise, it quickly become a stepping stone for those with political ambitions. Having used the BGA to acquire power during the 1960s, Premier and later Prime Minister John Compton moved to make the association an arm of the state. At first this was achieved by adding minority representation of the government to the BGA board, a move that was strengthened in 1967 by Compton's UWP-sponsored legislation to change the BGA from a private entity to a government-affiliated statutory board. The ensuing decades saw repeated conflict between growers' representatives and government-appointed board members, with periodic shifts in power between the two segments. When growers' representatives became too politically independent, the government passed legislation allowing it to dissolve the board and appoint all new officers of its choosing. Such dissolutions occurred in 1979, when a newly elected St. Lucia Labour Party government purged the board of UWP supporters, and again just three years later, when a reelected UWP government reversed the SLP's appointments (Jn Pierre, pers. comm. 2000). In 1993, when the BGA became too closely associated with growers' protests and thereby with the opposition SLP, Compton's UWP government responded by dissolving the board once again.

In its transformation from producers' association to a contested branch of government, the BGA's operating objectives, as opposed to its discursive statements, are revealed as primarily political rather than economic. When considering the Banana Act of 1986, which technically lent the force of law to BGA agronomic recommendations, it is understandable how previous analyses might identify the association as a mechanism enforcing the demands made by Geest and the world banana market on island growers (Trouillot 1988; Slocum 1996). Geest's officials no doubt welcomed the new legal provision, as they were probably its intended audience. If so, there is also little doubt that they were eventually disappointed at the government-controlled BGA's reluctance to legally impose its own policies with regard to agricultural production.

However, if analysis shifts from discourse to actual practice, a different picture emerges of the relationship between the BGA, growers, and the general public, one informed by the agency model of the state. In practice, the association's central operating features—its cross-subsidization and overstaffing—served not the interests of Geest but the goals of party politicians eager to cultivate and retain new constituencies. No governing party wishing to remain in power of any of the islands could ignore the number of active voters who were banana growers; nor could it allow periods of low prices to enflame those voters' indignation. Hence, by transferring earnings from productive farmers to more marginal operations, the BGA's cross-subsidization ensured a minimal livelihood for many rural voters who would otherwise have been unemployed. Non-farmers too benefited from BGA policies, for the association's bureaucracy provided a ready source of patronage employment for hundreds of St. Lucian party loyalists, many of whom could claim little involvement with or knowledge of agriculture.

In sum, since its inception the banana industry in the Windwards has served primarily political rather than economic aims. Initially, these were the priorities of an imperial power seeking to stabilize an impoverished and restive colony, an objective later co-opted by ambitious local politicians. To attempt to put the industry on a "competitive business footing," as the newly elected SLP government described its task in 1997, was to alter the industry's entire raison d'etre.

Notes

1. These accounts are derived from working-life histories given by a Honduran banana worker in Belize in 1995 and a St. Lucian grower in 2004. Their experiences are recounted here as representative of those who work in each region's banana industry. Both individuals are referred to by pseudonyms. The description of working conditions on "Boca del Tigre" are based on the Honduran informant's account of his prior work experiences on a Dole-affiliated contract farm in Atlántida. It is drawn as well from the author's 1993–95 ethnographic research in Cowpen, Belize, where large-scale mechanized farms are patterned after their Honduran counterparts. About 92 percent of the farm labor force on Belizean banana farms consists of immigrants from Honduras, Guatemala, and El Salvador (Moberg 1997: 118). In Belize, banana workers encounter working conditions resembling those on farms in Hispanic Central America, albeit with a complete absence of unionization.

2. The prevalence of daily violence has formed a continuous theme in literature on Central American banana plantations ever since the first scholarly accounts were compiled in the 1930s. See Kepner (1936: 164ff.), McCann (1976: 144ff.), Bourgois (1989: 5), and Moberg (1997: 102ff.).

3. Untold numbers of the bags wash downstream and end up in the Caribbean. Inshore fishermen along the Caribbean coast report that the bags ensnare their gear and marine life alike. Manatees and sea turtles that mistake the floating bags for jellyfish, an important prey species, often die after consuming them.

4. Keith originally planted bananas as a source of cheap food for his railroad workers, turning only later to the crop's commercial potential in North American markets when the anticipated passenger traffic failed to materialize.

5. In 1910–11, United Fruit engineered Miguel Dávila's removal from the presidency of Honduras and his replacement by Manuel Bonilla, who extended valuable land and railroad concessions to the company. Twenty years after fomenting a coup against Arbenz in Guatemala, the company bribed the president of Honduras to remove an export tax to which the company objected (McCann 1976).

6. As Clegg (2002: 65) notes, Britain's promotion of banana production in its colonies following the war was also spurred by the central government's lack of hard currency reserves after 1945, which prevented the country from importing sufficient amounts of Dollar Area fruit to satisfy domestic demand.

7. An externality common to all export agriculture, regardless of the conditions of production, is the "carbon footprint" left by the transportation of agricultural goods to distant markets. While the cost of long-distance shipping or jet transport is reflected in the price of such goods, the environmental cost of carbon emissions from ships, trucks, and cargo jets is not. Winter demand for fruits and vegetables grown in tropical latitudes or the southern hemisphere contributes in this fashion to global warming and is a major factor behind contemporary movements to promote consumption of locally grown foods.

8. The ECU was the common unit of value adopted by the European Community in 1979 and was replaced by the Euro of equal value in 1999.

9. Chiquita's abrupt decision to sell Fyffes was widely regarded as an inexplicably bad business decision at the time, given the provisions of access to the European market under Lomé.

10. Although Chiquita's sales in Europe had been affected by the EU provisions, financial analysts argue that many of the company's woes in the EU and elsewhere, such as the sale of its Fyffes subsidiary, were self-inflicted. The company's exaggerated forecasts of market demand in the late 1980s led it to engage in a costly expansion of production in Central America. The resulting oversupply of the market drove down its profits and, indirectly, those of other banana companies. In 1998, from total sales of US $45 billion, the company posted profits of only $44 million, the equivalent of a 65 cent return on a $10,000 investment. By 2000, the company's stock was trading at less than five dollars a share (Barlett and Steele 2000).

11. The same principle could conceivably challenge the US Endangered Species Act, which prohibits the importation of shrimp harvested by foreign trawlers that fail to protect endangered sea turtles, or US farm policy, which subsidizes exports by American farmers. Despite the US government's generous support for exports and its numerous restrictions on imports, however, the United States has rarely had to defend its trade policies before the WTO. Critics point out that few nations are willing to risk the political and economic consequences likely to result from challenging the US in multilateral bodies such as the WTO.

12. In addition to being a major shareholder in the company, John Foster Dulles, Eisenhower's secretary of state, had formerly represented Chiquita as a lawyer. His brother Allen Dulles, formerly a member of Chiquita's board of directors, served as director of the CIA under Eisenhower.

13. The specific products targeted for tariff retaliation are decided by the US trade representative, although tariffs often have unintended consequences that may be self-defeating. US government tariffs on Scottish wool sweaters prompted a UK-wide consumer boycott of Chiquita bananas, leading to the ironic result that the company asked the US government to suspend the sweater tariffs that had been imposed on its behalf. Other tariffs, however, remained in place.

14. Admittedly, St. Lucia's airwaves are filled with incendiary commentary aimed at working-class and rural listeners. The daily radio program "What Makes Me Mad" usually focuses on the foibles of bureaucracy and political leaders, while Sam Flood, an immensely popular satirist who broadcasts mostly in Kwèyól under the pseudonym Juk Bois, is the primary source of national and international news for many rural listeners.

— Chapter Five —

BANANA POLITICS

Growers responded enthusiastically to their new voice in local and national affairs and meetings were attended by virtually every grower ... For
the first time everyone felt influential in the operation of the industry.
> —Rochelle Romalis (1975) on St. Lucia's BGA before reorganization
> in 1968

Democracy and Disenfranchisement in the BGA

Long before the WTO issued its ruling on EU trade policy, changes in the
European market had created economic and political repercussions of seismic proportions in the Eastern Caribbean. How these changes were experienced in St. Lucia's Mabouya Valley, and their dramatic political consequences at the national level, are considered at some length in this chapter.
While banana farmers throughout the Windwards encountered common
adversity in the global economy during the 1990s, local responses to these
conditions were nowhere as dramatic as in St. Lucia. There the impact of
declining prices lay bare societal fault lines of class and culture arguably
more acute than on other islands. By the time the conflicts engendered by
global economic changes finally drew to a close toward the end of the decade, they had swept away a political dynasty built on the banana industry and laid the foundation for its thorough institutional transformation.

The event that triggered these changes was the flood of cheap Dollar
Area fruit onto the newly unified European market in 1992. From September of that year until the following October, banana prices in St. Lucia plunged more than 70 percent. As months passed and prices fell ever
further below farmers' costs of production, rural communities across the
island grew increasingly restive. John Compton's UWP government and

the Banana Growers' Association informed growers that the price collapse reflected market changes beyond their control, both noting that producers throughout the Windward Islands were experiencing similar tends. In contrast to the other islands, however, on St. Lucia the fall in prices prompted an explosive confrontation between many farmers and the island's BGA and government. The stated cause of these grievances was the perceived wastefulness and corruption of the BGA's board of directors at a time when farmers struggled with the lowest returns to production they had ever experienced. Yet underlying their anger was a phenomenon especially pronounced in St. Lucia; that is, the profound cultural and social class distance separating them from their ostensible representatives in the BGA and government. The long-simmering indignities that Kwéyòl-speaking farmers had experienced at the hands of the English-speaking elite of town compounded the sense that they alone bore the brunt of low prices. Indeed, these grievances probably account for why rural St. Lucians, unlike other Windward Islands growers, reacted to the fall in prices with a near insurrection in some areas.

At their lowest point in August 1993, banana prices in St. Lucia dropped to EC $0.18 per pound (US $0.07), or about EC $0.10 less than most farmers' break-even point. Yet during this time BGA officials continued to engage in business as usual, appearing virtually oblivious to the distress of farmers. In 1993, the association was spending EC $10,000 per month for the members of its board of directors to attend meetings, a sum reportedly greater than the meeting reimbursement budget for the St. Lucian government as a whole (Reynolds 2004: 26). Reports circulated of board members who billed the BGA up to $600 for several meetings attended on the same day, and of one who received $200 in reimbursement for claiming to attend a cocktail party in an official capacity. Upper-level staff positions, paid at salaries six to seven times greater than the average farmer's gross earnings, were openly awarded as favors to board members' family and friends, while lower-level positions were packed with appointees given jobs in exchange for loyalty to the governing party. Farmers noted that the BGA's executive secretary had been appointed to his position after campaigning for the election of the association's chairman. While voting down a proposed pension scheme for farmers, the board approved tens of thousands of dollars as compensation for laid-off staff members. Then, in a decision many farmers viewed as a calculated provocation, the BGA directors voted to award themselves a bonus. The bonuses came after the board had transformed an EC $16 million surplus in 1990 into an EC $23 million deficit three years later (Reynolds 2004: 26).[1] In the eyes of many farmers, such actions suggested that the association had become self-serving and remote from the interests of rural residents on whose production the BGA depended.

The anger that many growers expressed at BGA practices was compounded by their inability to remove or censure members of the board of directors. Originally established as a democratically operated producers' association, during the 1960s the BGA was reorganized in ways that disenfranchised the large majority of banana growers. Until 1968, when it was restructured as a statutory organization, the BGA held annual conferences of delegates comprised of representatives elected at its branch levels. A total of forty branches were organized on a regional basis around the island, and each was allowed to elect one delegate for every thirty members. By 1967 the number of banana growers in St. Lucia had risen to approximately 17,000, meaning that more than 500 delegates were eligible to participate in the BGA's annual conference. According to a 1978 government inquiry into the BGA, "It was felt that, apart from providing for a cumbersome meeting, the preponderance of small farmers at the Conference provided the risk of domination by those farmers in the management of the Association" (St. Lucia 1980: 11). A later report was even more candid in disclosing the government's desire to limit small farmer representation: "[T]he industry was too important to Saint Lucia's economy to tolerate threats of instability (defined as small grower active participation) ... and therefore [the BGA] should be made a statutory body with government power to dissolve the board of directors" (St. Lucia 1990: 8).

When the Compton government introduced the Banana Growers' Association Act of 1967, it redefined the BGA as a statutory board and created four categories of growers for purposes of representation on the association's board of directors. "Under Small Growers" were defined in the legislation as those who produced fewer than 500 pounds of bananas per week, while "Small," "Medium" and "Large" growers produced increments of up to 12,000 pounds or more per week.[2] Only farmers belonging to the latter three categories were eligible for election to the annual conference of delegates. Each of these categories was also to be represented by two elected members on the BGA board of directors. Companion legislation limited the number of elected delegates to one per branch, regardless of the size of the branch's membership. In addition, an English literacy requirement was introduced for all elected delegates. After reorganization, which took effect in 1968, the BGA's annual conferences were pared down from often-boisterous meetings of 500 farmers representing all industry participants to just 40 delegates drawn from the largest producers of each community.

In 1978, "Under Small Growers" producing 500 pounds or less of fruit per week comprised nearly 90 percent of all banana farmers on the island, all of whom were denied representation or voting rights in the annual conference and board of directors. Such restrictions proved wildly unpopular with the newly excluded farmers, leading district branches around the island to introduce annual resolutions throughout the 1970s challenging the allocation of BGA directorships. In 1977, the UWP minister of agriculture rejected such challenges, noting that "[t]he reason for stipulating the minimum was no doubt to ensure that persons eligible for election as Delegates should have a reasonable stake and involvement in the Industry" (St. Lucia 1980: 12). The 1978 Commission of Inquiry concluded that "[i]t is clearly an injustice to exorcise 90 percent of the producers in an industry contributing 35 percent of total output from the decision making process of that industry" (St. Lucia 1980: 14) and recommended that the government establish two new directors' positions to represent Under Small growers. These positions were duly created and occupied by small-scale producers. Yet, leaving nothing to chance, the government ensured that these positions were held by official appointees rather than directly elected from the ranks of farmers as larger growers' representatives were.

As the participation of small farmers in the BGA was progressively restricted, their economic and political disenfranchisement acquired a cultural dimension as well. Although the official language of the annual conferences had always been English, the earlier predominance of small-scale Kwéyòl-speaking farmers meant that in practice meetings had been run on a bilingual basis, with a good deal of simultaneous translation taking place for delegates who were less than fully fluent in English. After the BGA's 1967 reorganization excluded such delegates, annual conferences and board meetings were conducted exclusively in English at BGA headquarters in Castries. The BGA Communications Office continued to perform much of its public education and extension work in Kwéyòl, notably through its weekly radio program *Bon Kalité*, which provided agronomic and fruit handling recommendations as well as information about shipment days.[3] Now, however, farmers who were predominately Kwéyòl speakers had become simply the objects of BGA decisions rather than participants in them. Given that John Compton, who claimed personal credit for the BGA's reorganization, had built his political career upon channeling the grievances of Kwéyòl-speaking wage laborers and farmers, it is surprising that he overlooked the volatility inherent in policies that disenfranchised so much of the rural population. The collapse in banana prices and deepening discontent among farmers in 1993 created a prime opportunity for other would-be leaders to occupy the political vacuum that Compton and the BGA had opened.

The Banana Salvation Committee

At the May 1993 meeting of the BGA branch in the eastern village of Mon Repos, Abel Wilson and Patrick Joseph, two moderately large-scale growers and branch delegates, raised the issue of the price situation before local farmers. Recalling the events that led to that discussion, Joseph recalled years later,

> It come about because the prices for bananas didn't even cover the costs of harvesting bananas. If you harvested, say, a hundred cartons of bananas, it would cost you maybe $400 to do so, and you would get about $260 when you sold them. By the time you pay for the cartons and pay your workers you had nothing to live on. You had to subsidize your own operation. So in other words, you was paying them to take your bananas (Joseph, pers. comm. 2004)

At the BGA branch meeting, Wilson and Joseph presented resolutions calling for the association to reduce its operating expenses and guarantee farmers a price of EC $0.30 per pound for their fruit. The resolutions passed handily in voting by the branch membership, but received belated and perfunctory replies from the BGA Communications Office in Castries. Dissatisfied with the association's response, Wilson and Joseph invoked a rarely used clause in the BGA Act to call for an island-wide extraordinary conference of delegates. At that conference, held in August, board members found themselves on the defensive as delegates attributed responsibility for low fruit prices in part to the association's waste and corruption. The delegates passed a unanimous resolution calling on the BGA to guarantee a minimum price for bananas, and to reduce its operating expenses by 35 percent and its contributions to WINBAN by 40 percent. In addition, the BGA was called upon to convene a committee to report within sixty days on specific measures that would be adopted to reduce association expenses and inefficiencies.

The review committee's deadline passed without the promised report, while fruit prices inched upward by only one cent per pound. At that point Wilson, Joseph, and three other BGA delegates broke with the association and began separately organizing meetings with farmers around the island. From an initial meeting with farmers in Mon Repos, the dissident gatherings were soon attracting hundreds of angry farmers island-wide in communities reeling from the effects of low prices. "It was a grassroots movement and because everybody was being affected in the same way, it was not hard to mobilize," Joseph recalled years later. "The media houses came out and were attracted by the crowd, so that really spread the word. The only set of people who didn't pay attention was government. And you know they just took it to mean that there was a set of dumb farmers out there, illiterates, and that if you just ignore them they'll go away" (Joseph, pers. comm. 2004).

By September, the breakaway delegates had formally registered their organization as the Banana Salvation Committee (BSC) and apportioned official responsibilities among themselves. As secretary, Joseph quickly emerged as the most publicly prominent leader of the BSC, and he rather than Wilson, the group's chairman, was usually identified in print as its spokesman. In their mass meetings, BSC leaders cultivated a populist style intended to contrast sharply with the formal bureaucratic procedures adopted in BGA meetings. Whereas the BGA board and annual conferences of delegates met behind closed doors in the association's headquarters in Castries, Joseph and other BSC leaders addressed mass crowds gathering on short notice in banana-growing communities around the island. BSC leaders traveled through rural areas with PA systems mounted on the roofs of their cars to announce, in both Kwéyòl and English, the time and location of their next rallies. In banana-growing communities, fliers were distributed exhorting farmers to attend the rallies to "help put the G back in the SLBGA!" (Slocum 2006: 147).

Such populist strategies, while well rooted in the St. Lucian labor movement, had long been absent from official functions of the now highly bureaucratic Banana Growers' Association. Most conspicuously different was the use of language in the two organizations. Most BGA board members and delegates never deviated from formal English in meetings, while BSC leaders addressed farmers' rallies predominately in Kwéyòl. When the leaders directed a rhetorical question to (absent) BGA or government officials during such events, they invariably shifted to English for emphasis. As Slocum observed at these gatherings (2006: 180ff.), the leaders' strategic and extensive use of Kwéyòl when addressing farmers proclaimed the BSC's identification with them. Code-switching to English, as she further noted, implied that those officeholders in the BGA and government—to whom the questions in English were addressed—lacked familiarity with the language used by most of the rural population. In this fashion, the BSC drew skillfully upon both the economic and cultural grievances of banana farmers, deriving a degree of legitimacy from their shared cultural and linguistic identity that many farmers denied the association and government.

Yet for all its deliberate scripting as a populist grassroots movement, the BSC proved no less hierarchical than the BGA and government in the breadth of its decision making. The group's executive committee (composed of its five founders, all from the vicinity of Mon Repos) met weekly at the home of either Joseph or another committee member to plan strategies. These private meetings served to set the time and place of rallies and to draft press releases. The participation of the broader farming population was actually solicited only in the mass rallies that the BSC staged in farming communities, the timing and agenda of which had already been determined by the executive committee. At the rallies themselves, decisions made by the executive committee were presented as proposed courses of

action and farmers were asked to ratify those decisions by verbally affirming them. No mechanism existed to elicit alternate strategies or sets of
demands from farmers or to widen decision-making beyond the executive
committee. Indeed, BSC supporters who advocated broader participation
in the committee's decision-making found their proposals flatly rejected
by its leaders, as one early supporter, then an officer in the National Farmers' Association, quickly learned:

> I said [to Wilson] that what we need to do is to call elections and elect offic-
> ers who represent a wide cross section of the island. And these people who
> are part of the Executive, can come to meet and so when they go back home
> they would have meetings with their branches and everybody would speak the
> same language. What I hoped was that this thing would be like the BGA in the
> old days, before government interfere in it. But they told me, no, this is a Mon
> Repos issue because [Joseph] is from Mon Repos. And then I told him, well if
> this is about him rather than we, then I am going to back out. (Celestine, pers.
> comm. 2004)

In addition to the structural parallels between the BSC and BGA, the
leaders who founded the breakaway movement were much more similar
in background to their counterparts in the BGA than the small-scale farmers they claimed to represent. All were fluent in English, had lived for
a period of time and been educated in the US or UK, and had achieved
some measure of business success either at home or abroad. Wilson himself had previously served on the board of directors of the BGA. For his
part, Joseph attributes his involvement in the BSC to the political sensibilities gained in the United States when he participated in the civil rights
movement: "I didn't choose this work, it chose me ... I believe you are put
here for something, and a lot of things that I learned in the States when I
lived there for 16 years I had no reason to learn them, but I did. It was an
opportune time to learn how to lead protests. I marched with King and
Abernathy and Jesse Jackson. I was in Washington with Stokley Carmi-
chael ... somehow, I did all of it, and I learned from that and applied it to
the Salvation Committee." In this respect, Joseph's experience reflects that
of many activists throughout the Caribbean who returned from abroad
with political sensibilities gained in the US civil rights and Black Power
movements of the 1960s.

While Joseph may have looked to the US civil rights movement for in-
spiration, he was also following a well-trodden St. Lucian path of drawing
upon rural discontent and social injustice for his own political advance-
ment. Having been a supporter of the UWP until the mid 1980s, he switched
his allegiance to the St. Lucia Labour Party after a falling-out with John
Compton. Although not officially aligned with the SLP, the BSC's leaders
openly campaigned for SLP candidates and mobilized farmers by tapping

their discontent with the Compton government. Indeed, Joseph and his allies are usually credited with ushering the SLP into power by mobilizing rural votes against the UWP government in the 1997 elections. As will be seen in Chapter 6, and as an earlier generation of political anthropologists might have predicted (e.g., Barth 1959, 1966; Bailey 1969), his decisive contribution to the SLP's electoral success was not without a reciprocal expectation on his part.

By late September 1993, the BSC and the UWP government were headed for a direct confrontation. Addressing a meeting of over 1,000 farmers in the Cul de Sac Valley on October 4, BSC leaders issued an ultimatum: the BGA was to respond to the demands raised in the August conference or face a no-cut strike the following day. At public meetings around the island over the previous week, BSC leaders had hinted at a possible strike. Now a stoppage was imminent, barring an immediate concession on the part of the BGA. Strikes by wage laborers on large sugar and banana farms had been commonplace in the 1970s and 80s, and they had been a major factor in the decision of the remaining large-scale planters and Geest itself to abandon estate production. For own-account farmers to refuse to harvest the fruit from their own farms was unprecedented, however. The BGA and government warned that the planned no-cut strike was a threat to the very survival of the industry. While on a state visit to Washington, D.C., Prime Minister Compton had earlier learned of the strike threat and hastily addressed the nation via satellite television in an attempt to ward it off. In his comments, broadcast live on October 3, he warned that if Geest's ship failed to obtain its expected consignment of fruit from the island, the farmers themselves would pay heavily for "dead freight," a charge incurred when ships return home with empty cargo space. Moreover, he predicted that Geest would increasingly source its bananas from elsewhere after having lost confidence in St. Lucian farmers' willingness to produce fruit on a reliable weekly basis. In short, Compton warned, if farmers struck they would only be hurting themselves and jeopardizing their own standard of living.

While outlining the dire economic consequences of a strike, Compton failed to comprehend the depth of farmers' anger at the BGA and government, and his efforts to remind growers of his efforts on their behalf clearly backfired. Joseph recounted that many farmers, instead of being persuaded not to strike by Compton's televised remarks, were incensed by his attempt to claim credit for their past economic well-being: "[T]he prime minister had made that famous statement that … when we met them, they were poor, they only had a cutlass and they live in a straw hut, and now they live in a big house and have TV and refrigerators and vehicles. That enraged the people even more, because if they have these things it's not because the prime minister got them and handed them to them; it's because they work hard and they get it" (pers. comm. 2004). Joseph recalled that at the rally on October 4, held the night after Compton's televised speech, he had posed an alternative strategy to farmers, suggesting that they wait until the prime minister returned to the country to raise their concerns directly with him. Joseph said he was almost driven from the platform by the catcalls and jeers of angry farmers determined to stage the strike the following day, regardless of the prime minister's response.

The Strike

Tuesday, October 5 1993, was to be a cutting day, the first of two days during the week that farmers on the eastern half of the island could deliver their fruit for sale. Geest's ship was docked at Vieux Fort awaiting delivery of bananas from the Mabouya Valley and farming communities to the south. Yet farmers who attempted to harvest their fruit in defiance of the BSC's strike call found the road to Vieux Fort impassable. During the night, barricades of felled trees, burning tires, derelict cars, and even several semi-trailer trucks had sprung up across the entire course of the road. Officially, the BSC denied any knowledge of or involvement in the traffic stoppage, stating that it had been a spontaneous act. "Nobody actually planned that we were going to block roads and stop vehicles and such," Joseph stated years later. "There was no planned anything. People went to sleep Monday night and somehow they decide, boy if we going to strike, we need to do something. They take a page out of Martinique's book, because in Martinique, no traffic moves when there's a strike. And so by morning, trees were across the road that people had cut overnight. By that first night, the Barre d'Isle was just a bed of trees from one end to the other" (pers. comm. 2004).

Police were dispatched to dismantle the barriers, but some were deterred by stone-throwing crowds and everywhere they were forced to withdraw by the tenacity of those who constructed the barricades. Even when onlookers allowed the police to clear a stretch of road for traffic, no sooner had they removed a barricade than others were erected elsewhere. By Wednesday, the government and BGA conceded that the country had in effect been cut in two by the roadblocks. Tourists arriving at the international airport in Vieux Fort were told to take air shuttles instead of the customary taxis to Castries, and the BGA was forced, reluctantly, to warn non-striking farmers not to challenge the strikers' blockades.

Strikers' anger was not only directed at officials and police, but often at their own neighbors. Dozens of farmers who had earlier vowed that they would harvest fruit during the strike awoke on Tuesday to find that their packing sheds had been burned to the ground, the boxes and fertilizer stored in the sheds having made for particularly incendiary conditions. On the farms of those who had objected to the strike or advocated conciliation with the government, harvestable stems of fruit hanging from banana plants had been ruined by strikers wielding two-by-fours bristling with nails. Much of the anger acquired a distinctly partisan quality, as farmers known to be strong UWP supporters were most often targeted for such sabotage, whether they intended to harvest their fruit or not. A former BSC supporter who had broken with the organization over its increasingly overt ties to the SLP found almost all of his personal and farm assets destroyed by arsonists. Anticipating that his shed might be attacked if he stored banana boxes in it in preparation for harvest, he instead stored the boxes in his home. That, however, did not deter the attackers: "Not just my shed, but the house was burned, everything, my truck, my equipment. I have not been able to recover from that up to now," he noted eleven years later.[4] The farmer enumerated twelve growers personally known to him in the Mabouya Valley alone whose sheds had been destroyed, including four who he said left banana farming permanently as a result. The exact number of farms damaged over the entire island during the three days of the strike in October is unknown, probably because the magnitude and severity of the government response were soon to dominate all local reporting about the strike.

On Wednesday afternoon Prime Minister Compton, having just returned from the US, entered the fray by maneuvering his pickup truck through a gauntlet of barricades from his home in the eastern village of Micoud to Riche Fond in the Mabouya Valley, where throngs of strikers were engaged in a tense stand-off with police. Compton had hoped to appeal to them to end their blockade, go home, and allow harvested fruit to pass. Instead he was greeted with curses, his vehicle was pelted with stones, and he was forced to withdraw. An aide driving immediately behind Compton was less fortunate: his vehicle was set on fire and he was forced to flee with the prime minister in his pickup. Later proclaiming that the dispute between farmers and the BGA had been taken over by "certain criminal elements who had been particularly active in the Mabouya Valley," Compton dispatched police reinforcements to the valley with instructions to "take all necessary measures to restore law and order" (Reynolds 2004: 12).

The reinforcements who arrived at Riche Fond shortly after dawn on Thursday were in fact not ordinary police, but elite US-trained Special Services Unit (SSU) troops. The SSU, which had been formed by Compton in the 1970s in response to rumors of a leftist conspiracy to seize power, was derided by the prime minister's opponents as a "goon squad."[5] The SSU troops were notorious among labor activists and Compton's opponents for their heavy-handed disruption of public protests with tear gas and billy clubs. On Thursday morning they arrived in the valley equipped with shields, riot gear, and, unknown to the protesters, live ammunition.

Confrontations between police and strikers were by no means unknown during the 1970s and 1980s, but St. Lucian police had never before employed deadly force to disperse crowds (Wayne 2002). Writing of the events of October 7 from secondary sources, St. Lucian journalist Anderson Reynolds states that the SSU troops fired on the crowd after one of the soldiers had been struck and felled by a rock (2004: 77). Former BSC Secretary Patrick Joseph recalls it differently, stating that the troops began firing while still a great distance away, without any provocation or warning. Regardless of what triggered the shooting, all accounts agree that it continued long after the panicked crowd had dispersed and sought shelter in nearby homes and businesses, and behind vehicles and trees. The armor-piercing ammunition used in the assault penetrated cement walls and car doors, wounding several people who believed they had fled to safety. When the smoke cleared, two young farmers, Randy and Julius Joseph, lay dead on the highway, having been shot in the back as they fled. Another twenty-five strikers and bystanders were wounded, among them a woman critically injured by an errant bullet while shielding her child in the closet of a nearby house. According to Slocum (1996), who resided in the area at the time, a stunned and uneasy silence descended over the valley's banana growers, who rarely ventured far from their homes in the weeks following the killings.

End of an Era

After the 1993 shootings at Riche Fond, Prime Minister Compton dissolved the BGA board of directors and announced that the government would run the association itself. Its actions would ostensibly ensure that "all areas of waste, extravagance, and fraud are eliminated and the farmer gets his fair share which is not nibbled away by rats along the way" (Reynolds 2004: 135). The BSC leaders could claim a kind of victory when Compton echoed the charges of corruption and wastefulness that they themselves had earlier leveled at the BGA. Yet the prime minister displayed little contrition over his actions leading up to the strike and his order to suppress it by force. His televised address to the nation after the military action again antagonized farmers by continuing to claim credit for the social and economic progress experienced in their communities. For many of Compton's critics, his self-proclaimed martyrdom by the events of the previous days, during which his own farm was attacked, verged on megalomania:

> I have had my country house set on fire. I have had my banana sheds burnt and my property destroyed. I have cried to no one. I have picked up my broken tools and started over again. They may destroy my property but they will never break my spirit. I have seen this industry transform St. Lucia and its people. The grass huts ... have given way to beautiful homes with water, electricity, television, and now telephone. For this I seek no honor, no glory, no financial reward. My only reward is the advancement and progress of this country ... These are some of the things which sustained me when I faced alone the angry mob at Riche Fond, an area which has benefited so much from my work and sacrifice. About 36 years ago near the very spot, I looked down the barrel of the gun of the Barbadian police during the sugar strike. On Wednesday I looked into the faces of hatred, heard the curses from the very same throats of the people to whom but a few weeks ago I was Daddy Compton, so great was the hostile propaganda against me. But I remember the lessons of history and the Bible that the same voices which shouted Hallelujah will shout "crucify him" without pausing for breath. (In Reynolds 2004: 136–137)

Although the BSC remained active through the 1997 elections, it never again amassed the visible support at its public events that it had prior to the October 1993 strike. An understandable fear of government retaliation in the wake of the shootings inhibited some participation at BSC rallies. Years later, however, many farmers—even those who remained sympathetic to the BSC agenda—say that they were also repelled by the ferocity that strike participants had shown to their non-striking neighbors. "The BSC gang unleashed a poison here," one Mabouya Valley farmer observed in 2003. "I supported them, until all the shed burnings and mischief like that. There is still so much anger because of what happened during those days." Other strikes were called by the BSC in early 1994 and again in 1996, but turnout was much lower and they were accompanied by none of the attempted disruption of roads. The burning of sheds and destruction of harvestable fruit continued, however, despite the BSC's official disavowal of such strategies.

Following the first no-harvest strike, the UWP government went on the offensive to prevent further stoppages, including a concerted attempt to undermine the credibility of BSC leaders among rank-and-file farmers. The UWP minister of agriculture presented credible evidence that the BSC leaders called strikes during weeks when their own farms were not harvesting fruit, and thereby avoided making the sacrifices that they demanded of other farmers (Slocum 1996: 149). Even more seriously, the prime minister attacked the BSC's claim to be a grassroots movement, alleging that its leaders were funded and supported by Chiquita to serve as a front group for the US multinational. According to Compton, Chiquita regarded the BSC as a means to ultimately seize control of the island's fruit from Geest, in the process remaking itself as an ACP importer and gaining a favored position in the unified European market. Recalling the events prior to the 1993 strike, Compton claimed years later that Chiquita "started the same things [it] has been doing all over the world. They start trying to get in here. And they financed the problems, the people who created the problems. I would get a fax making certain demands from the Banana Salvation people, you need to do so and so within such a time, and the fax number when I look at it is area code 305!" (Compton, pers. comm. 2004).

There is no independent corroboration of Compton's claims that BSC faxes originated in Miami, source of the 305 area code, nor does his claim clearly demonstrate Chiquita's financial backing for the BSC.[6] Nonetheless, statements by the BSC and the subsequent actions of its secretary lend some credibility to the claim that Chiquita retained an active interest in the conflicts within the St. Lucian banana industry. As BSC secretary, Joseph frequently proposed bypassing St. Lucia's traditional marketing outlets in favor of a negotiated contract with Chiquita. In 1998, when he became chairman of the BGA's successor, the St. Lucia Banana Corporation (SLBC), Joseph entered into marketing negotiations with the US banana company. Ultimately he was prevented from finalizing these contracts by the St. Lucian government, ironically the same one that he had helped to elect in 1997 by mobilizing he votes of banana farmers for the SLP.[7] To this day, however, Joseph defends his relationship with Chiquita, claiming that had the island negotiated contracts with it instead of Geest, the US company would have had a sufficient stake in the EU trading regime to not challenge it several years later.

The UWP government's efforts against the Banana Salvation Committee in the wake of the strike included additional heavy-handed measures, the most notable being the 1995 passage of Section 651 of the St. Lucian Criminal Code. This law made it a criminal offense for any person to urge another to "desist from … the carrying out of any lawful activity on his property" (in Francois 2004: 13). Although phrased in broad terms that could theoretically prohibit any work stoppage, the law was passed specifically to prevent further no-harvest strikes in the banana fields. Realizing that Section 651 was unenforceable, if not unconstitutional, the government used it mostly as an instrument of intimidation rather than actual prosecution.[8] Joseph asserts, for example, that farmers were warned if they were arrested under the law, as a condition of parole they would have to report to a police station every Tuesday for a year. He claims that authorities selected Tuesdays (shipping days) for reporting to prevent farmers from selling bananas for the length of their probation. Ultimately, there were never any convictions under Section 651. Yet warnings to farming communities about the tough parole requirements, together with a few high-profile arrests in 1996 (with subsequently dropped charges), may have dampened broader participation in no-harvest strikes after 1995.

Apart from measures to discredit the BSC and threaten prospective strikers, the threat of no-harvest strikes soon dissipated in the wake of external events. At the end of 1993, the reformulated BGA temporarily guaranteed farmers a price of EC $0.30 per pound, essentially granting the demand that had led to the strikes in the first place. Price pressures on growers were also alleviated by adjustments made in the Caribbean's favor to the Single European Market banana protocol after 1993, although these arrangements were soon to come under attack by Chiquita in the WTO. Yet slightly improved conditions in the mid 1990s did not win back allies for the UWP government among growers, many of whom had come to see Randy and Julius Joseph rather than John Compton as the real banana industry martyrs. Their funerals at the Catholic Church at La Ressource in the Mabouya Valley and an Adventist church nearby had attracted thousands of mourners from around the island, many of whom carried placards demanding the prime minister's resignation. On the roadside near the site of their deaths, the BSC constructed a shrine in 1994 containing a memorial plaque commemorating the "two banana farmers killed by police ... during protest action for a better price for *our* bananas" (emphasis in original).

The more Compton and his ministers attacked Patrick Joseph and the BSC after the killings, the more the government's standing seemed to sink among growers. This fact was not lost on the opposition SLP, whose candidates increasingly accompanied Joseph in his public appearances around the island. Public opposition to the draconian Section 651 swept beyond the banana fields to encompass most of the country's unions, members of its legal profession, and even the understandably cautious civil service. Having decisively lost support among banana growers and organized labor, and unwilling to call early elections that he would most certainly lose, Compton resigned as prime minister and relinquished the office to his UWP protégé Dr. Vaughn Lewis in 1995. This political newcomer was entrusted with the responsibility for bringing the party through the next round of elections, a charge that proved formidable beyond Compton's expectations. In June 1997, the island's electorate meted out a punishing defeat to the UWP, which lost all but one of its seats in the seventeen-seat national assembly. Significantly, in the two districts comprising the Mabouya Valley, once a Compton stronghold, the opposition SLP candidates received up to two-thirds of all votes cast.

In summarizing the calamitous end of the UWP's nearly uninterrupted twenty-seven–year tenure as St. Lucia's governing party, Reynolds notes, "[b]ananas had again decided the fate of the island's political leadership. Bananas had helped to cause the downfall of Mr. George Charles, bananas had helped usher Mr. John Compton into power, and bananas brought his legacy to a close." Yet the end of that era had not dissolved the close association between the banana industry and partisan politics. The very promises that the newly installed Labour government of Dr. Kenny Anthony had made in exchange for the BSC's crucial electoral support unleashed a new period of fragmentation, instability, and infighting within the banana industry. It is to that phase that we next turn.

Notes

1. BGA directors pointed out that some EC $10.7 million of this had been used by the association to subsidize banana prices during their decline in 1992 and 1993 (Reynolds 2004: 139).
2. Production was not measured in cartons until the shift to in-field packing in 1980.
3. The radio program *Bon Kalité*, or "Good Quality," formerly served as the primary broadcast medium for transmitting agricultural information and harvesting recommendations to rural St. Lucians. An English-language program entitled *Spotlight* tended to focus on market and business-related aspects of the banana industry, perhaps reflecting and reinforcing the cultural and linguistic divide between banana producers and those who administered the industry. In the late 1990s, *Zafa Fig* ("Banana Affairs") replaced *Bon Kalité*, although the emphasis remained on agronomic and post-harvest handling information. *Spotlight* continues to be broadcast in English, but is now televised.
4. Like several other Valley residents who experienced retaliation from BSC supporters during the strike, he requested that his name not be used in publications from this research.
5. Compton's fears were driven both by domestic concerns and the rise in nearby Grenada of the overtly socialist New Jewel Movement, which came to power after overthrowing the government of Eric Gairy. The New Jewel government attracted support from some segments of the St. Lucia Labour Party, some of whom in turn received weapons training on Grenada. Compton later strongly supported the Reagan administration's effort to isolate and topple the NJM government.
6. Area code 305 is indeed in Miami, but Chiquita is headquartered in Cincinnati.
7. As a further irony, the SLP government ultimately orchestrated Joseph's fall from grace in the eyes of most farmers by bringing criminal charges against him for embezzlement while he served as SLBC chairman.
8. The unenforceable breadth of the law is suggested by the fact that several island religious leaders speculated in the local press whether they would be subject to prosecution if they urged their congregations to rest, rather than work, on the Sabbath.

— Chapter Six —

PRIVATIZATION AND FRAGMENTATION

[A]llegiance is regarded not as something which is given to groups, but as something which is bartered between individuals against a return in other advantages. The system of authority and the alignment of persons in groups is thus in a sense built by the leaders through a systematic series of exchanges ... Political action, in this setting, is the art of manipulating these various dyadic relations so as to create effective and viable bodies of supporters.

—Frederik Barth, *Political Leadership Among Swat Pathans* (1959)

The Twists and Turns of Political Calculus

The strategies employed by the Banana Salvation Committee to win the allegiance of St. Lucia's banana growers were by no means novel, rooted as they were in the proven political tactics of John Compton and George Charles in the 1950s. Since the origins of mass electoral politics in that decade, populist leaders have routinely appealed to rural wage workers and small-scale farmers by inveighing against the island's "full belly, big money men." Under this label they have, at various times, subsumed merchants, employers, large-scale planters, Geest and other foreign companies, "industry bureaucrats," and government officials. Initially representing themselves as independent agents of humble origins (or at least affinity), all of St. Lucia's populist leaders have eventually aligned themselves with a political party and sought votes from their rural supporters, either on their own behalf or for their party's candidates.

During its long absence from power, the St. Lucia Labour Party sought repeatedly to employ this strategy to bring down the Compton government, which had used similar tactics to build its power base of loyal banana farmers. Here we examine how the political calculus of BSC leaders and the SLP candidates they supported led ultimately to the BGA's demise and fragmented the industry into competing private businesses. As will be seen, this fragmentation was actually abetted by the new SLP government, which aimed to deny potential opponents a single platform for challenging its rule, much in the way Compton had reined in the BGA thirty years earlier.

The SLP's electoral strategy might have succeeded decades before its 1997 triumph over the UWP, had not the private ambitions of the party's most formidable and charismatic populist leaders, George Odlum and Peter Josie, outweighed their party loyalty. The political strategies of these erstwhile allies not only led to their repeated estrangement from and rapprochement with the SLP, but occasionally placed them in adversarial positions vis-à-vis one another. Among observers of island politics, their overt maneuvering within and between the country's two major political parties provoked little comment and virtually no censure. Indeed, apart from the central role that rural voter mobilization plays in St. Lucian politics, perhaps the most notable feature of the country's political landscape is the opportunistic, rapidly shifting allegiances of aspiring officeholders. In this respect, the island's power seekers exhibit the same pragmatism and transactional strategizing documented in anthropological studies of political leaders elsewhere, among them Swat Pathans warlords (Barth 1959), leaders of Maltese religious factions (Boissevain 1968) and Mafia kingpins (Bailey 1969).

The major precedent for the Banana Salvation Committee during the 1990s was a series of rural social movements against low wages and poor working conditions led by Odlum and Josie twenty years earlier. Like many West Indian activists of the time, and not unlike the BSC's Patrick Joseph, the English-educated Odlum was inspired by the civil rights movement of Martin Luther King and the black nationalism of Malcolm X, as well as the socialist and non-aligned movements then sweeping the postcolonial world. As a founding member of the St. Lucia Forum, a group of intellectuals seeking a radical alternative to the island's two primary political parties, Odlum emerged on the political scene as a scathing critic of Compton and the governing UWP.[1] Together with his colleague Peter Josie, Odlum conducted nighttime "consciousness raising" rallies with workers on Geest's plantation in the Roseau Valley and the Barnard estate in the Mabouya Valley. The ensuing strikes and confrontations with police led by Odlum and Josie during the mid 1970s were critical events in the decisions of the Barnard family and Geest Industries to abandon plantation production, factors that eventually led to their lands being turned over to own-account farmers via the UWP's land settlement programs. Much like

Compton in the late 1950s, Odlum and Josie cultivated an intensely loyal following among rural workers by personally bearing the brunt of police assaults at the head of the marches and picket lines that they organized.

By the late 1970s, the men had joined the SLP in an alliance of convenience against the governing UWP. In defiance of the SLP's centrist leader Allan Louisy, the leftist "Odlumite" faction of the party, as it became known, advocated close ties with Cuba and the People's Revolutionary Government of Maurice Bishop in nearby Grenada. With their ability to mobilize poor rural voters, Odlum and Josie helped the SLP sweep into power in the 1979 elections. Their organizing and electoral work on behalf of the SLP came with a price, however. Prior to the elections Odlum had secured a private agreement that Louisy would initially take over as prime minister, but then would step aside, within six months at most, to vacate the position for Odlum. As the deadline came and passed without any indication that he intended to fulfill his promise, Louisy's determination to stay in office set off a factional fight within the party that threatened to undermine the government.

Louisy responded with the venerable strategy of divide and rule, by which he sowed divisions within the Odlumite faction to prevent unified action against him in his cabinet. Josie, then serving as the minister of agriculture, was publicly praised by Louisy as the more "responsible" member of the SLP left wing.[2] He was secretly told he would be made prime minister instead of Odlum if he severed ties with his longstanding ally. Soon Josie was seen socializing with members of the Louisy faction and avoiding public identification with his former allies, the party's radicals. Like Odlum before him, Josie was encouraged by Louisy to wait some months for the transfer of power to take place, only to find that the offer was eventually withdrawn. Embittered and feeling used by those he had helped put in power, Josie rejoined with Odlum to vote in the national assembly with the UWP against his own party's budget, and the SLP government fell as a result of Odlum and Josie's decisive votes. Thus, the activists who had paved the way for the UWP's 1979 defeat played a critical role in the UWP's reentry to power in early elections. More remarkably, by playing the two allies against each other, Allan Louisy had managed to extend what was supposed to be a few months as prime minister into a tenure of three years.

After heading the short-lived Progressive Labor Party during the mid 1980s, Odlum gravitated to the UWP. In exchange for Odlum's mobilization of rural voters for the party in the 1992 elections, Prime Minister Compton appointed him the country's UN ambassador. Seeking to win back the support of disaffected banana farmers after the 1993 shootings, Compton also named Josie to a new ministerial post overseeing government policy toward the banana industry. In this manner, St. Lucia's most overt revolutionaries of the 1970s—who during that time had been given to wearing fatigues à la Castro and Guevara—now became suit and tie–clad members of the conservative government they had formerly denounced as corrupt and oppressive. When Compton stepped down as prime minister in 1996, Odlum returned to St. Lucia from his UN post. Sensing the UWP's weakness and a new electoral opportunity, he again changed parties, this time to challenge the UWP's Vaughn Lewis as the SLP candidate in a special by-election. He narrowly lost that effort but, with Pat Joseph, campaigned vigorously among banana growers for the SLP in the 1997 elections.

In exchange for his campaign efforts, Odlum was appointed foreign minister in the newly elected SLP government of Kenny Anthony. Before long, however, he grew increasingly critical of Anthony's policies toward the banana industry, home to most of his natural constituency. For his open dissension, Anthony fired Odlum from the cabinet, an unpopular decision with banana growers that probably cost the SLP both of its assembly seats in the Mabouya Valley in the 2001 general elections. At the time of his death from cancer in 2003, "Brother George," as Odlum was eulogized by his followers among the rural poor, was in the midst of reconciling (for a second time) with Compton and the UWP. His funeral was attended by St. Lucian politicians of all persuasions, as indeed he had at one time or another been allied with many of them. Notwithstanding the ease with which he adopted and shed party affiliations and his notable lack of success as an actual candidate, Odlum was always taken seriously by the island's political establishment, a testament to the size of the rural constituencies that he could deliver to the party of his choosing.

Privatization and Payback

By 1996, with general elections impending in less than a year, the UWP government was under intense pressure to mend relations with the country's alienated banana growers. Peter Josie, Compton's specially appointed "banana minister," announced in October that grower representation would be restored to the BGA, three years after the government had dissolved its board. Soon thereafter, BSC-supported candidates swept all six elected positions on the board of directors. Anticipating this result, before he turned the BGA board back to growers Josie had amended association policies to require that the board's chairman receive the votes of all five government-appointed members. In this way, even if Patrick Joseph were elected to the board, he would surely be blocked from the powerful position of chair. As a former BSC supporter explained, "with the change in by-laws, the government guaranteed that Joseph would be shut out. Josie wanted to leave the chairman's position to a board member who might be more open to persuasion." As it turned out, Joseph did not run for a board position but secured for himself an appointment as chairman of the BGA's Finance Committee. Even then, he was helping to lay the groundwork with his allies in the opposition SLP for an eventual dissolution of the BGA and its replacement by a private company, one that he himself would head.

Much as Odlum had been rewarded by both the SLP and UWP for the favors he performed on their behalf, Patrick Joseph's decisive contribution to the SLP's 1997 victory was soon repaid as well. Viewed by many small-scale banana growers as a "messiah" for his blunt challenges to the entrenched elites in the Compton government and BGA, Joseph commanded a devoted following that delivered solid majorities to the SLP over most of the eastern half of the island. The lone exception to the SLP sweep of banana-growing regions was in former Prime Minister Compton's home district of Micoud. There longstanding government largesse and personal loyalties had returned Compton's successor to the assembly as the sole remaining representative of his party. Garnering nearly two-thirds of all votes cast nationwide, Kenny Anthony's newly elected government clearly owed a great debt to the BSC secretary. The manner in which this debt was repaid, as well as the ensuing infighting between Joseph and his former BSC allies, largely account for the complex and highly fragmented structure of the island's banana industry today.

Shortly after the May 1997 elections that brought to SLP to power, Anthony announced that the government would absorb the EC $42 million debt of the BGA, reorganize it as a private company, and hand it over with a "clean slate" to control by banana growers. Upon privatization in the following year, all BGA assets were transferred from the government to the newly created St. Lucia Banana Corporation (SLBC), with one share provided to every farmer who sold 2,000 pounds of bananas between 1993 and 1997 (or about twenty boxes per year). When the government introduced its privatization proposal, it presented two scenarios to farmers: the SLBC could be organized as a cooperative, with policy determined on the basis of "one member, one vote," or it could become a corporation in which voting power was based on the number of shares held. The large majority of growers favored the former proposition, which, like the pre-1967 BGA, would make the organization more representative of small farmers.

Realizing that this arrangement would secure his election as chairman, Joseph also strongly favored this policy. His opponents in the industry, seeking to bar him from an executive role in the new shareholding company, advocated voting rights proportional to production. Large growers, long accustomed to their prevailing influence in the association, objected to the "one member, one vote" proposal, prompting a compromise in which they could buy an additional share at EC $2,500 in exchange for greater voting power. This arrangement still left them in a minority position, and championing the cause of small farmers, Patrick Joseph easily won election as the SLBC's chairman. To his critics, and those of the SLP, the manner in which privatization was carried out suggested that the government had simply handed control of the newly privatized company over to Joseph. As further acknowledgement of his services to the party, the SLP had named Joseph to the Senate, the largely ceremonial, if honorific, "upper house" of the St. Lucian parliament.

As chairman of the SLBC, Joseph wasted little time in challenging entrenched practices in the industry. Among the first of his targets was WIBDECO, the company responsible for the distribution and marketing of Windwards bananas. Created in 1994 to replace WINBAN, WIBDECO is jointly owned by the producers' groups of each of the Windward Islands (which collectively control half of the company's shares) as well as the island governments (which control the other half). Shares were apportioned among the producers' groups based on production, so as the largest contributor of Windwards bananas, St. Lucia also has the greatest number of shares allotted to producer groups. Despite this fact, the SLBC has no greater voice in WIBDECO's policies than do the producers' groups on the other islands. In 1997, WIBDECO entered into a joint partnership with the Irish banana company Fyffes (now independent of Chiquita) to buy out Geest's wholesaling business in England, a venture formally registered as WIBDECO UK but still known in the islands as Geest.[3]

Upon taking control of the SLBC, Joseph engaged in a high-profile battle with WIBDECO both in the islands and in the UK over its returns to producers, its sale of import licenses that belonged to the island producers' groups, and the costs of its shipping. Joseph lobbied unsuccessfully for a shift in WIBDECO policy to make representation on the corporation's board proportionate to island production, a position seemingly at odds with his advocacy of a "one member, one vote" policy within the SLBC. Failing to significantly alter the corporation's policies, the SLBC began selling its fruit directly to Geest, ostensibly to cut out WIBDECO's administrative costs and deliver a higher fruit price to its growers.[4] In addition, the SLBC forced Geest to remove the "dead freight" provision in its contract, under which it had charged farmers for shortfalls in the number of boxes that made up each shipment. It did this by negotiating openly with a Chiquita subsidiary that employed containerized shipping of bananas. When the SLBC delivered a "trial shipment" of containerized fruit to the UK, WIBDECO's and Geest's officials were infuriated that Joseph had dealt with the US multinational, but had little choice but to surrender the dead freight provision, which had been a feature of banana marketing from St. Lucia since the 1950s.

For Joseph's longstanding critics in the UWP and the banana industry, his willingness to bypass a West Indian–owned company in favor of Chiquita confirmed their suspicions that he, if not the entire BSC, had been bankrolled by the US multinational. For both the government and Joseph's allies in the BSC, several of whom held executive positions in the SLBC, the chairman's dealings with Chiquita soon after the company's successful suit before the WTO was seen as a blatant betrayal of the national interest. In 1998, Chiquita acknowledged that it had hired G. Philip Hughes four years earlier to quietly promote an expansion of the company's interests in the Eastern Caribbean. Hughes, who had been US ambassador to the region under the first Bush presidency, was to meet on behalf of the company with government and banana industry officials in the islands (Gallagher and McWhirter 1998b). His goal was to persuade them to establish a joint venture with Chiquita and transfer the island's lucrative banana import licenses to the US company, allowing it to ship up to 2.5 million additional tons of bananas to the European market. In exchange, Chiquita said that it would offer a slightly higher producer price to the islands' farmers and the benefits of its technical expertise in handling and shipping.

Hughes later stated in an interview with the Cincinnati Enquirer that "Chiquita was offering a terrific deal. But they had one problem: the mindset of the Caribbean leaders … The leaders really had a negative mind-set about Chiquita. They considered it almost their enemy" (Gallagher and McWhirter 1998b). After being turned down by the Windward Islands governments, Chiquita approached farmers' associations and representatives on each of the islands. Of these, only the BSC seemed responsive to the company's overtures. At least one former BSC executive committee member quoted in the same article believed that the BSC was covertly funded by Chiquita, a charged denied by Joseph notwithstanding his acknowledged support of Chiquita's proposed joint venture. If most island leaders and growers were distrustful of the US multinational, it is likely that they were better aware of the company's regional history of broken promises and strong-arm tactics than was the lobbyist it sent to the Caribbean. Once the multinational controlled the region's lucrative banana import licenses, many growers believed, it would have no reason to purchase any fruit from the islands, much less at a higher than prevailing price.

At the same time that Joseph's dealings with Chiquita were generating concern among industry participants, the SLBC succumbed to internal factionalism that cost it its monopoly over the island's banana sales. In 1998, a group of relatively-large scale farmers who had been longstanding opponents of Joseph broke away from the SLBC and organized the Total Quality Fruit Company (TQFC). Joseph's choice of Englishman Tony Smith as the SLBC's general manager over a BSC founder who had expected the job triggered a contentious leadership struggle within the company. By 2000, Joseph had become estranged from all of the former BSC leadership, who then abandoned the SLBC to establish another rival marketing firm, the Banana Salvation Marketing Company.

With the creation of each new fruit company, the industry's limited and declining revenue was further divided. The result was a continuing financial weakening of the SLBC and its ability to provide inputs and services to farmers on a cost-effective basis. The companies were further undermined by growers themselves, who quickly learned that by procuring inputs and supplies from one company on credit and then selling their fruit to a rival firm, they could avoid repaying their debts. The SLBC's response to fragmentation was to raise its fruit prices to growers in an attempt to win them back as suppliers and to drive the rival companies out of business, echoing the tactics Chiquita had used to secure monopolies over producers. Unlike Chiquita, however, the SLBC had no other profitable operations to subsidize higher prices in the short term. This strategy enabled it to retain the largest share of the island's growers as suppliers, but caused it to sell much of its fruit at a loss and to accrue debts that by 2000 were estimated at between EC $4.5 and 12.5 million.

By 2003, the banana industry on St. Lucia had become fragmented into five rival companies, all originating from the personal animosities of their directors and all competing for the island's steadily declining output of fruit.[5] All but one of the companies was operating at a loss. The direst consequence of fragmentation was each company's abandonment of responsibility for pest control, which had earlier been uniformly administered by the BGA over the entire island. The SLBC contended that such matters as aerial spraying were the responsibility of WIBDECO, which, for its part, claimed that the companies, as the successors to the BGA, retained that responsibility. As a result, by 2002 leafspot (or Yellow Sigatoka, caused by the fungus *Mycosphaerella musicola*) had reappeared on St. Lucian farms after having been under control for several decades. Yet even then, the companies and WIBDECO could not agree among themselves on a disease control strategy.[6]

Although fragmentation of the industry was threatening banana production itself, there were also those who regarded it as politically useful. Officially, the SLP government lamented the divisions within the industry and called for cooperation among the various firms that purchased the island's bananas. In actuality, a director of one of the companies that split from the SLBC, himself a close acquaintance of Kenny Anthony, stated that the prime minister feared Joseph's influence among banana growers and privately welcomed any division within the industry that might reduce it. Although he owed the election of the Labour government to Joseph, and had publicly supported Joseph's leadership of the SLBC, behind the scenes the prime minister encouraged the creation of other fruit companies. Joseph called time and again for regulation of the industry to prevent growers who received SLBC inputs from selling to rival firms, but whereas the SLP government acknowledged the need for such measures, it never got around to the necessary legislation. Similarly, a director of the TQFC confidentially recalled one conversation with Prime Minister Anthony: "He even told me, 'We need balance; we can't have everything in the hands of one man.' So they gave us a lot of support, because they saw us as the last opportunity to have an open industry." According to this informant, Anthony feared that if Joseph headed the sole company handling the island's fruit, then the SLP would hold power "at his mercy" and most likely force the government to withdraw from WIBDECO.

Given the intensifying feud between the SLBC and WIBDECO, it was inevitable that the St. Lucian government would find itself caught in the middle. In response to criticisms from Joseph as well as the BGAs on St. Vincent and Dominica[7] that WIBDECO constituted an unnecessary and expensive additional layer of bureaucracy, WIBDECO asserted that it was the local banana companies and producers' groups that were ineffectual and redundant. It pointedly claimed that the industry as a whole would be better off without them. In June 2001, WIBDECO's "Proposal for Restructuring the Banana Industry" was formally presented to a meeting of the heads of government of the Windward Islands and EU representatives. The proposal emphasized the need for a "streamlined management and operation structure to reduce cost and improve efficiency, … a streamlined, restructured and targeted grower base, [and] significant investment in farm inputs, rehabilitation and replanting, and both off-farm and on-farm infrastructure" (Campbell, Olney, and Mulraine 2001: 9). The company proposed that it directly purchase bananas from "targeted" growers, so that "further reduction in the current grower numbers is inevitable" (Campbell, Olney, and Mulraine 2001: 10). This arrangement would not only reduce the number of commercially active growers to those satisfying WIBDECO's specifications, but would also eliminate any need "for the respective BGAs as they exist in their current state" (Campbell, Olney, and Mulraine 2001: 10). The furor that WIBDECO's proposal set off among growers in St. Lucia (many of whom believed they would have no future as commercial farmers under its recommendations) forced the SLP government to not only disavow the proposal, but to block WIBDECO from any future direct purchases from growers. As a local WIBDECO official commented confidentially in 2004, "Anthony knew he would have to face growers in the next election, but he would never have to face us."

Although in this instance the SLP government sided with farmers against WIBDECO, there were signs of increasing estrangement between the SLBC chairman and the prime minister. During much of 2001, Joseph and Anthony feuded publicly over the distribution of dividends from WIBDECO's profits, which were paid by the company to the government but formally were intended for producers' associations. Joseph claims that the government initially denied the existence of the dividends, then de-layed paying them until it calculated the share destined for each com-pany, and finally refused to pay the SLBC's share until Joseph signed an agreement that all of the dividends would be returned directly to farmers. Joseph refused this condition, saying that a portion of the dividend should be invested in the recently privatized Bank of St. Lucia to earn interest income for the SLBC. Yet the government's demand strategically drove a wedge between Joseph and the thousands of small-scale farmers who un-til then had remained staunch supporters. In person and on his weekly radio call-in program, the SLBC chairman was besieged by rural residents who felt that his refusal to meet the government's condition was delay-ing a badly needed supplement to their incomes. The government finally relented and paid the dividend without precondition, but accusations of corruption and embezzlement were soon swirling around the SLBC chair-man. The charges originated with the financial comptroller of the SLBC, who in 2001 forwarded documentation of supposed financial irregulari-ties at the company to the director of public prosecution. One of the claims made by the comptroller was that sales from the SLBC-run Ranju Farm[8] were credited to Joseph's personal bank account. Soon after the accusa-tions were made public, Joseph abruptly resigned his position at the SLBC and left the country for several months. Curiously, neither criminal nor civil charges were subsequently forthcoming, and by 2003 it had emerged that the original "documentation" of his alleged wrongdoing was of ques-tionable authenticity.

For his part, Joseph claims that the accusations against him were or-chestrated by his former allies in the SLP government, who were deter-mined to derail his overtures to Chiquita. By pitting farmers against him, he said, the government sought to eliminate a potential opponent by strip-ping away a rural constituency that was more loyal to him than to the SLP. If these were indeed the government's objectives, in large measure they succeeded in severely damaging Joseph's reputation among grow-ers. Like the UWP's efforts to tarnish the BSC's credibility a decade before, however, government criticisms of Joseph did not translate into increased grower support for the SLP. In rural St. Lucia, where newspapers are rare and a still sizeable segment of the population is functionally illiterate, innuendo and rumor often pass as the primary sources of information. Further, actual or de facto government control of the broadcast media heavily colors most radio and television reporting on the country's political figures, to the inevitable detriment of those who have incurred the ruling party's disfavor. Given these factors, it is perhaps not surprising that many of Joseph's most ardent past supporters regard him as a disgraced and fallen figure today.

Although definitive proof of Joseph's alleged embezzlement was never established, many remain convinced that he was guilty of corruption, citing as evidence his sudden resignation and departure from the country. Some even adamantly maintain, against all evidence to the contrary, that he was tried, convicted, and imprisoned for a time. In the Mabouya Valley, where little more than a decade ago many farming residents regarded him as a "savior" (even if he was also opposed by a substantial minority), there are few farmers today who express much support for the former BSC leader. Meanwhile, the passions of the 1993 strike he led have steadily receded, a fact evidenced by the now neglected and overgrown appearance of the BSC shrine to the victims of the police shootings. As memories of those events faded, many valley residents appeared ready to invite back the political figure most associated with Green Gold to salvage what remains of the banana industry.

Saving the Industry, or Saving the Government?

In 2001, the SLP government convened a Banana Industry Task Force to devise strategies to reverse the industry's decline. A central recommendation of the task force was the creation within the Ministry of Agriculture of the Banana Emergency Recovery Unit (BERU), an agency intended to stanch high rates of attrition among farmers by coordinating extension services and disseminating technical innovations. To head the agency the government selected neither a farmer nor a politician, but a no-nonsense leader in the country's banking sector, a gesture intended to show that the industry would now be established on principles of efficiency and productivity rather than "cross-subsidization" between profitable and more marginal farmers.

The costliest of the innovations planned by BERU is drip-line irrigation, to be introduced in five major river valleys throughout the country. Financial support for these efforts comes primarily from the European Union, which during 1993 and 1994 utilized its STABEX[9] and Special Fund for Assistance initiatives to enhance the global competitiveness of the Windward Islands banana industries. In the "agro-ecological" zones targeted by BERU for irrigation, the agency has also promoted the introduction of meristem tissue culture bananas. Tiny, uniform-sized shoots of this high-yielding variety (HYV) are imported in test tubes from a plant-breeding firm in Israel and "acclimatized" for the first twelve weeks of growth in shade houses at the Ministry of Agriculture's extension farm, from which they are then shipped out to eligible farmers across the island.

As is the case for many HYV crops, tissue culture bananas offer the possibility of improved productivity but are more susceptible to climatic variation and pests than are traditional varieties. In addition, they require a technical "package" including mechanical land preparation, irrigation, and the administration of inputs at precise intervals. According to BERU's director, tissue culture and irrigation alone, if used optimally, could increase the per acre productivity of the average St. Lucian farm from eight to twenty tons per year. For farmers that qualify for BERU assistance, land preparation and tissue culture plants are heavily subsidized, and farmers' payments for irrigation are deferred until after the plants begin bearing. BERU employs thirteen extension officers and assistants to advise farmers and to monitor their use of the technical package. One of the extension agents' first tasks was to survey each of the country's banana farmers and classify them as "fully commercial," "semi-commercial," and "subsistence" farmers. Only farmers in the first two categories were to be eligible for any BERU assistance. According to BERU's data, at least 30 percent of the country's farms are automatically excluded from the irrigation and tissue culture programs because they lie outside the zones scheduled for irrigation, largely because of their topography and hydrology (La Force, pers. comm. 2003).

Like other programs introducing technical innovations to traditional agriculture, such as South Asia's infamous "Green Revolution," these changes have the potential to widen socioeconomic disparities within banana-producing communities. This fact has not been lost on critics of BERU, many of whom claim that the actual distribution of irrigation is likely to be far narrower than the agency predicts. By 2004, the third year of its operation, BERU had succeeded in irrigating just 7.5 percent of the country's acreage under bananas and introducing tissue culture plants on a total of 500 acres island-wide. At this rate, with most of its funding derived from limited European Union sources and a mandate to continue its work only until 2006, BERU would be unable to irrigate more than a tiny fraction of the area it had originally foreseen.

The prospect of growing inequity in banana-farming communities because of the differential distribution of services was seized on by the opposition party. The UWP's Vaughn Lewis claimed that "the incentives being provided to a limited number of farmers are ... directed at creating a small elite group of farmers, rather than servicing the many. This marks a return to the old model of the now deceased St. Lucian sugar industry and the big estates, where many labored but few benefited" (*The Voice* 2003d: 5). For his part, John Compton, who emerged from retirement to replace Lewis as the UWP's leader in 2005, charged that only growers who were prominent government supporters were benefiting from the SLP's investments in the banana industry. Compton's charges of bias in the distribution of government assistance to the industry mirror those of UWP supporters on the ground. In the Mabouya Valley, land from the Ranju farm, which was declared insolvent in 2003, was to be formally distributed to squatters who occupied the land after the SLBC abandoned the farm. Some residents allege that SLP partisans received land titles from the Ministry of Agriculture, while squatters known to be UWP supporters were evicted.

By 2004, as some farms were being quarantined because of their leafspot infestations, farmers' anger at the industry's fragmentation, partisan distribution of benefits, and ineffectual government response to the disease was widely reported in the country's several independent and opposition newspapers. A new round of meetings and rallies in rural communities over the industry's decline coincided with the emergence of new political alignments that attempted to appeal to dissatisfied growers. One of these, the Organization for National Empowerment (ONE), was headed by the indefatigable Peter Josie, who threatened a no-cut strike and denounced the SLP for treating farmers "like a prostitute" (*The Voice* 2004b: 1). Ausbert d'Auvergne, spokesman for the newly created National Development Movement (NDM), sarcastically responded to Prime Minister Anthony's call for opposition groups to "stop playing politics with the banana industry." Writing in the country's leading opposition paper, the NDM leader noted, "We all know who played politics with the Banana Industry prior to 1997. We also know who must take responsibility for the disastrous 'restructuring` of the Industry after 1997" (*The Voice* 2004a: 3). Ignatius Jean, the SLP minister of agriculture, responded by labeling d'Auvergne and other government critics as opportunists scheming to launch "yet another political party [that] will seek to ride the backs of our farmers, lying to them, deceiving them, and promising all sorts of unattainable goals" (Jean 2004: 24).[10] Enumerating over EC $106 million in expenditures from domestic and international sources on behalf of the industry since 1997, including the SLP's write-off of the BGA's debt, Jean claimed that "no other Government in the Windward Islands can be said to have done so much to save the livelihood of its farmers" (Jean 2004: 29). Indeed, the government calculated in 2001 that it had contributed EC $32,000 on a per farmer basis to the industry, which it characterized as "a staggering financial sacrifice" (St. Lucia 2001a: 4).

Noting that most of the funding for BERU is derived from EU grants, the SLP's critics, such as Patrick Joseph, claim that such high-profile expenditures represent "public relations" rather than concrete government investment. Joseph asserts that more mundane services provided from the general fund that are critical to the industry's day-to-day operations, such as the maintenance of feeder roads, have been allowed to atrophy, a claim seconded by many farmers. Like the UWP's Compton, Joseph argues that the SLP government has cultivated support from private foreign investors, primarily in the tourism sector, to the neglect of the banana industry. Government ministers regularly observe that by 1995, tourism had surpassed agriculture as a contributor to the island's GDP and by 2003 generated more than twice the foreign exchange revenue of bananas (Anderson, Taylor, and Josling 2003: 133). In 2004, the SLP government's minister for tourism provoked a storm of controversy—as well as a later disavowal by Prime Minister Anthony—when he suggested that the week-long annual St. Lucian Jazz Festival was of greater economic importance to the island than all of the annual receipts of the banana industry. Such statements were taken by the opposition UWP to reflect the government's actual economic preference for tourism-led development, notwithstanding the SLP's rhetorical commitment to banana producers.

Tourism: Last Legal Pillar of the Economy

As St. Lucia shifts from an equitable and environmentally sustainable economic strategy built on smallholding banana farms to a heavier reliance on tourism, it is almost certain to incur the social and environmental costs experienced elsewhere (Conway 2002). It is instructive, then, to consider the experience of other Caribbean islands as St. Lucia embarks upon a similar pattern of development.

On islands that have relied longer and more heavily on tourism, such as Barbados and Antigua, environmental damage from tourist development has degraded the very resources that once attracted hundreds of thousands of visitors per year to each destination (Patullo 1996b). The construction of beachfront resorts has decimated mangrove swamps and coastal wetlands throughout the region. Antigua, for example, witnessed the loss of 50 percent of its mangrove coastline over a fifteen-year period beginning in 1980 (Patullo 1996b). Coastal wetlands are essential for mitigating water pollution and rainwater runoff, especially in places lacking modern sewage treatment facilities. Further, they are critical to the tourist industry itself in providing nurseries for the reef fish and lobsters that island-based hotels and restaurants rely upon for much of their sales (Sasidharan and Thapa 2002). Divers and marine biologists working in Antigua and Barbados confirm that the effect of coastal tourist development has been siltation of once-pristine inshore waters, dying coral reefs, and dwindling fish stocks.

The Caribbean's heavy involvement in cruise ship–based tourism has also aggravated problems of water quality and waste disposal while contributing little to the islands with regard to employment and revenue. In every year since the mid 1990s, cruise ships have accounted for the majority of all tourist arrivals on St. Lucia, yet have generated less than 10 percent of all tourism revenues on the island (*The Voice* 2003b: 2). When the former head of the St. Lucia Hotel and Tourism Authority publicly deplored the low net contributions of cruise ship tourism to the local economy and advocated an increase in docking fees, cruise operators threatened to boycott the island. Attempts by other governments in the region to capture the revenue potential of cruise ship tourism by imposing head taxes and environmental levies have usually led cruise operators to simply remove the offending islands from their itineraries. Often constructed with substantial subsidies from the governments of their home countries, luxury cruise ships offer travel packages that significantly undercut land-based operations in terms of price. Their employment contributions to island economies are limited to the several thousand Caribbean residents employed on the ships themselves, as well as vendors who hawk handicrafts and t-shirts to cruise passengers at each port of call. Mabouya Valley residents employed on cruise ships describe an apartheid-like division between themselves and the lighter-skinned, usually European employees who work in higher-paid and tipped positions.

While almost all profits on cruise ship tourism are repatriated, the ships leave in their wake a host of environmental and waste disposal problems. Worldwide, cruise ships discharge 20 million gallons of raw sewage into the seas every day (Ioannides 2002), and leave behind huge volumes of solid waste. Waste disposal from cruise ships and land-based hotels has joined coastal water quality as the most significant environmental problem on the densely populated islands of the Caribbean, where landfill space is at a premium. On Barbados, the government created a new landfill in the mid 1990s largely to deal with the waste generated by the 400,000 or more visitors to the island each year (Beckles 1996). Ironically, the dump is situated in the middle of one of the few remaining forested places on the island, a national park that the government has also promoted as a significant ecotourism attraction. In these older sites of Caribbean tourism, the economic effects of environmental degradation were already being felt by the late 1980s, when growing numbers of tourists abandoned both islands for less environmentally spoiled destinations.

In recent decades, both UWP and SLP governments have attempted to capitalize on the shift in tourist interest away from the more developed and environmentally compromised islands. The dawn of mass tourism on St. Lucia began in 1989 with the construction of the Jalousie Plantation Resort and Spa. This foreign-owned US $60 million resort was to be built on a 320-acre site between the two peaks of the Gros and Petit Pitons (France 1998). The development plans at what was considered a treasured national landmark triggered opposition among many St. Lucians as well as the Organization of American States, which recommended preservation of the site as a national park. Notwithstanding public protests and international appeals, including those by Nobel Laureate Derek Walcott, the UWP government of the time authorized the project as a means of generating foreign exchange and employment. Some environmental costs of the resort were apparent even before its opening, as rainwater runoff damaged a nearby reef and artifacts from an Amerindian burial site were destroyed in the building of tennis courts.

Jalousie is an all-inclusive resort, following a model pioneered by Club Med in which tourists prepay for their rooms, meals, drinks, and entertainment before arriving on the island and are encouraged, in the words of the Sandals resort chain, to "leave [their] wallets at home." Because the entire travel package is purchased in the tourist's home country, all-inclusives generate few of the economic linkages to the local community that are present in traditional tourist operations (Patullo 1996a). In St. Lucia, eight of the country's twelve major hotels are foreign-owned all-inclusives that repatriate virtually all of their profits, generating palpable resentment among local restaurant owners, tour guides, cab drivers, and vendors (Patullo 1996a). These sentiments are compounded by the enclave-like nature of most all-inclusive operations. Almost all such operations virtually seal off their guests from any contact with local people and strictly regulate whatever contact does occur between them. At Jalousie, local fishermen are no longer permitted to work in coastal waters within sight of sunbathing guests, and non-guests can only enter the resort or use an ostensibly public beach after having purchased an expensive pass. Restrictions on local access to all-inclusives provoked widespread indignation in the Caribbean after an incident in 1994 when Prime Minister Lester Bird of Antigua was barred from entering a resort on that island because he lacked a pass (Patullo 1996a: 82).

During the course of a year, approximately twice as many people visit St. Lucia as reside on the island. Land values have soared from a boom in resort and condominium construction in the northern tourism-dependent areas of the island, which has further accelerated the exodus from agriculture. Meanwhile, many of the problems of sewage and waste disposal experienced in "mature" tourist destinations such as Barbados and Antigua are repeating themselves on St. Lucia. During a conference on water management in October 2002, foreign technicians toured several projects designed to address these problems on the island. Among them is the Deglos landfill, a site designed in part to accommodate the solid waste from hotels and cruise ships. There were audible gasps from the group of geologists and engineers when they learned that the landfill sat atop a pressure point on the island's largest aquifer, which provides drinking water for the 45,000 residents of Castries and many surrounding villages.

As agriculture recedes in the wake of the WTO ruling, tourism is left standing as one of the few legal sources of economic activity available to the Eastern Caribbean. The shift from smallholder farming to tourism seems likely to reverse a century-long trend of greater equity in resource use. On Barbados, where tourists use four times as much electricity and ten times as much fresh water as local residents, as well as producing 1.5 times as much solid waste, the foreign exchange and employment benefits of tourism have clearly come at high cost with regard to resource use (Moberg 2006: 150). There, much of the tourist infrastructure remains in the hands of Barbadians, but on St. Lucia the foreign-owned, hermetically sealed enclaves of all-inclusive resorts compound profligate resource use with an exceptionally limited distribution of economic benefits. As will be seen in the next chapter, the number of jobs and amount of income generated in St. Lucia's tourism sector fall far short of the livelihoods formerly created in the banana sector.

At one time, claims that the government neglected the banana industry in favor of foreign-controlled investment could ignite grower indignation island-wide and provide a platform for launching a successful political career. Some of the SLP government's critics offer the conspiratorial view that the industry's loss of importance was by design, in effect displacing banana farmers to enable the SLP to cater to other, more affluent constituencies associated with tourism. Peter Josie, one such critic, has charged that the "Labour [Party] set about to deliberately sabotage the banana industry, thereby greatly reducing the strength and clout of local banana farmers" (2003: 4). Whether by default or design, banana growers are a mere shadow of their former significance as a political constituency. Since the strikes that paralyzed the country in 1993, more than 80 percent of the island's growers have dropped out of production as a result of low prices, anxiety about the future, and demoralization. The remaining banana growers, for all their sporadic anger at government policy and national elites, are now too few in number to be either feared or reckoned with as a political force. Yet their plight, and the continued demise of the banana industry during the tenure of the SLP government, symbolized for many voters the failure of Anthony's privatization initiative. By 2006, the white haired 81-year-old but still politically active "Daddy" Compton had emerged as one of the most vocal critics of SLP policies toward the banana industry and the economy in general. Compton surprised numerous political observers, who had written him off as a spent force, by leading the UWP to an election victory in that December's general elections. By year's end, he once again occupied the prime minister's office that he had held for the large majority of the previous forty-five years.[11] How much of his political support stemmed from nostalgia for the relatively prosperous days of Green Gold may not be known. For his part, following his election, the returning prime minister attributed his winning margins in rural districts to banana growers disillusioned with nearly a decade of privatization under SLP rule.

Notes

1. Odlum's political clashes with Compton are notable given the widespread belief that in private, the two men were friends and often conferred on political matters. As a St. Lucian journalist observed, "there were members of Compton's party who were convinced that their leader took advice from one man only: George Odlum—who had a degree in political science" (Wayne 2002: 34). Their private relationship may account for the periodic political reconciliations between them.
2. In addition, Louisy may have taken advantage of Josie's indignation that his more charismatic ally had become the de facto head of the party's left wing. "Why is it always Odlum and Josie," the latter was heard to ask, "and not Josie and Odlum?" (Da Breo 1981: 59).
3 The venture continues to be referred to informally in the islands as Geest, mainly because the Geest label is still attached to much Windwards fruit sold in Britain.
4. In response, WIBDECO began contracting directly with large-scale farmers to purchase their bananas so as to deprive the SLBC of some of its sales.
5. By late 2006, only the SLBC and the TQFC remained in business, the island's other banana companies having been liquidated.
6. Leafspot remains under control on the other Windward Islands, where a comparable fragmentation of the industry into competing companies has not occurred.
7. In 2002, the Dominican banana industry underwent a process of privatization like that of St. Lucia, but it has averted the fragmentation experienced by St. Lucia's industry. St. Vincent's BGA continues to operate as a government statutory board.
8. The Ranju Farm comprised a portion of the former government-owned Dennery Farmco Estate, which was acquired by the SLBC and named after the two farmers slain at Riche Fond in 1993.
9. STABEX, an acronym from the French Système de Stabilisation des Recettes d'Exporta-

tion, was established in 1975 as a European Commission (later EU) initiative to offset the unstable prices faced by ACP producers. By the early 1990s, STABEX resources were being used in the Windwards to enhance the productivity and competitiveness of the region's banana farms.

10. D'Auvergne subsequently became Compton's campaign manager in 2006, and claimed credit for the UWP's return to power in December of that year.

11. Compton's return to power was short-lived. In May 2007, he suffered a series of strokes from which he never fully recovered. Still serving as prime minister but pledging to resign from office for health reasons before the end of the year, Compton died on September 7.

— Chapter Seven —

SURVIVORS

The new rural poor are mainly men and women displaced by structural changes in banana farming … All the poor cope with decreasing incomes by eating less. The rural poor will "gather from the land," reaching a stage when they will "cook and eat boiled bananas with a little salt" … [I]nformants complained that stealing produce from people has become a frequent coping mechanism of the needy.

> —*Poverty Reduction Fund Social Assessment Study*, St. Lucia (Cowater 2000)

"Power Hungry People"

Any observer of the Windward Islands banana industry cannot help but be struck by its complex bureaucracy and redundant layers of administration. As seen in the previous chapter, this administrative redundancy arises less from the functional requirements of production and marketing than from the myriad political and economic interests that permeate the industry. These interests and the conflicts that they have spawned show no sign of waning, even as the productive base on which the entire superstructure rests has shrunk to a fraction of its former size (see Figures 7.1 and 7.2). While the number of commercially active growers on every one of the Windward Islands declined 80 percent or more in the decade after 1992 (Figure 7.3), there has been little reduction in the industry's administrative bureaucracy.[1]

This chapter examines the livelihoods of the Mabouya Valley residents who remain in banana production, with particular attention to the effects of globalization and fragmentation of the industry on farming households.

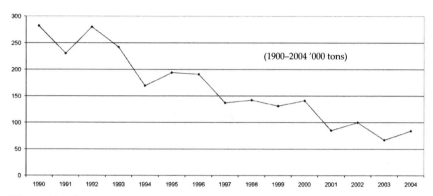

Figure 7.1 | Banana Production in the Windward Islands

The strategies by which the politically ambitious seek to entrench themselves in positions of power—whether in the industry or government—have direct and largely negative consequences for the remaining banana producers. At each link in the chain from grower to consumer, a portion of the value of all exported bananas is claimed by those who govern that particular segment of the industry. As the last to be paid from this commodity chain, farmers receive whatever is left after each level of the bureaucracy has sated itself on the fruits of their labor. Of all Windwards bananas sold in the United Kingdom, WIBDECO claims a 31 percent share of the retail price, UK supermarkets receive 40 percent, and just 11.5 percent of the retail value is returned to the growers themselves (van de Kasteele and van der Stichele 2005: 32). Historically, most grower resentment has centered on the fact that they incur all of the risks and costs of production, while most of the benefits of their labor accrue to others. An officer in the Mabouya Valley Fair Trade Group raised a similar point in what could

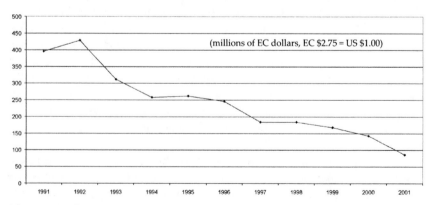

Figure 7.2 | Real Value of Windward Island Banana Exports

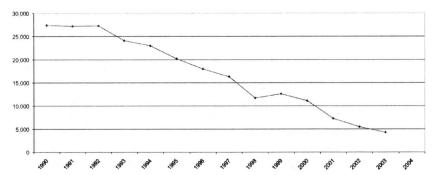

Figure 7.3 | Number of Active Growers in the Windward Islands, 1990–2004

pass as a direct adaptation of Michels' Iron Law of Oligarchy to the banana industry:

> Once a person gets a position of power, they are very reluctant to give it up. This is exactly how island politics works, whether you're talking party politics or banana politics. For politicians, the banana farmer is a means to an end; the end being how he gets elected and holds office. That's how the present [SLP] government came to power in '97, and that's how the opposition and people like Peter Josie are trying to replace it. For the banana companies and WIBDECO and even the Fair Trade people in WINFA[2] the banana farmer is also a means to an end; the way they collect their salary. It's the farmer who's carrying all these power hungry people on his shoulders. (Lynch, pers. comm. 2003)

Earnings from the industry trickle up to higher-level administrators, who formulate most of the decisions about production and post-harvest handling that growers must implement. The ever-increasing requirements to which growers have been subjected since the early 1990s have made it difficult for all but a fraction to remain economically viable, once all the levels above the farmers have taken a cut from their production. A cost-accounting study of the St. Vincent banana industry found that the shift from in-field Crown Pad packing to the mini–wet pack system increased labor costs alone by 215 percent between 1992 and 1998 (Kairi 2000: 91). Premium fruit prices associated with the farm certification program introduced by WIBDECO at the end of the decade increased best-case scenario anual profits slightly, from EC \$3,426 to \$3,821 per acre. However, for farmers who relied on hired labor, the added input and labor requirements of mini-wet packing more than doubled per-acre production costs, from EC \$7,753 to \$16,757. Not surprisingly, the average St. Vincent farmer employing wage labor saw his or her per-acre profit of EC \$1,626 in 1992 transformed into a loss of EC \$1,132 per acre six years later. Although many farmers racked up deepening losses after 1998, both the island-owned WIBDECO and WIBDECO UK have posted annual profits in the tens of millions of US dollars since then.[3]

Since the introduction of the mini–wet pack process and the farm certification program, costs of production have continued to rise as farmers are subjected to new demands in export markets. In 2002, the remaining Windward Island farmers learned of additional impending increases in their costs when the European Retailers Working Group, a continent-wide organization representing retailers and national governments, formulated a set of Good Agricultural Practices (known as EUREP-GAP). All growers of agricultural commodities exported to the European Union were expected to implement the EUREP-GAP regulations by January 1, 2004. According to a publication explaining the new requirements to Windwards farmers, the forty-one criteria required for EUREP-GAP compliance "are designed to meet the European consumers' demands for safe food, safe working conditions, fair worker treatment, and minimal environmental impact" (Noel 2004: 5). Many growers in the Windwards appeared puzzled and angered that their ostensible allies in the European Union, after having failed to preserve the tariff-quota system in the WTO, went on to impose new, expensive preconditions on their exports. Several industry leaders interviewed in St. Lucia said that island growers had become unwitting victims of protectionist policies in Europe whose real beneficiaries were the continent's farmers rather than its consumers. These individuals view the new requirements as a manifestation of what one British analyst calls "Europe's monstrous common agricultural policy, which coddles rich farmers and prices those in the poor world out of the European markets" (*The Economist* 2006: 12).

Some EUREP-GAP specifications, such as recording the amounts and frequency of all farm chemical use and construction of packing sheds with cement floors, had already been required of island banana growers under WIBDECO's farm certification program. In another instance of initially voluntary innovations that eventually become obligatory, these requirements now must be observed by all growers under EUREP-GAP. EUREP-GAP's new specifications for working conditions, such as the provision of first aid kits, potable water, lockable chemical storage areas, and toilets[4] on all farms, pose additional expenses ranging well above EC $3,000 for most growers. On St. Lucia, the costs of EUREP-GAP compliance for many farmers were partially offset by subsidies from BERU (which in turn receives much of its funding from the European Union) or their local Fair Trade associations. For non–Fair Trade growers or "subsistence" category farmers who are ineligible for BERU assistance, however, the costs of compliance had to be met entirely out of pocket. Farmers who failed to pass EUREP-GAP certification audits (performed by WIBDECO) by the end of 2004 were barred from the export of fruit to the European Union, unless certifying agents had granted extensions in specific cases to rectify minor points of noncompliance.

Farmers determined to remain in the industry have devised a wide array of survival strategies to offset the increasing costs of production. Given the generally similar external economic pressures placed upon all banana-growing households in the Windwards, some of these strategies are consistent across the region. Farmers on all of the islands complain of the growing scarcity of farm labor, due largely to the out migration of young men and women, at the same time that the labor requirements of banana production have increased. As noted earlier, some St. Lucian farmers have reacted to these pressures by reinstituting past practices of labor reciprocity (*koudeman*). Similar labor sharing practices have been revived among farmers on Dominica and St. Vincent. Still other responses are rooted in the particular institutional and cultural features of individual islands, raising distinct economic opportunities for growers as well as those who abandon production.

Although today's banana industry administrators deplore the "cross-subsidization" by which island BGAs underwrote farmers' production costs in the past, without such assistance even larger numbers of farmers would have abandoned production. The distinctive institutional structure of each island's banana sector has provided farmers with differing opportunities for manipulating industry rules to their benefit. On St. Vincent, where anyone tending thirty banana plants can be registered as a grower with the island BGA (which remains a public statutory board), family members utilizing a single plot usually hold multiple registrations. While most of the inputs and credit employed on the family farm might be charged to a son's registration, for example, farm sales would be credited to his mother's. Because each registration is ostensibly a separate farming operation, it is difficult for the BGA to recover debts from many banana-growing households. The privatization of the industry on St. Lucia was intended, in part, to prevent such occurrences, although as seen earlier, the resultant fragmentation of the industry into rival companies afforded farmers new opportunities for cross-subsidization. By purchasing packaging materials on credit from one company while selling fruit to its rival, farmers attempted to gain some breathing space, albeit temporary, in an industry where their costs of production and packaging were rapidly outpacing their returns. Despite their recognition that such practices collectively harmed the industry, the upstart banana companies that arose to

challenge the SLBC quietly encouraged such practices in the hope of garnering for themselves a larger share of the island's productive base.

Household Subsidies to Banana Production

For most households that continue to rely on bananas as an income source,
the increasing costs of production mean that banana sales must be sup-
plemented with other activities. Most farmers have reached back to a
longstanding Caribbean tradition of "occupational multiplicity" by diver-
sifying household economic activities or deploying the labor of household members off the family farm. Island BGAs and extension agents,
including those of St. Lucia's BERU, have long recommended that farmers
concentrate their livelihoods on "pure stands" of bananas. These recommendations arise from the assumption that farmers will maximize their
production of bananas by exclusively allocating all of their land and labor
to the crop. In addition, extension agents recognize that farmers who in-
terplant food crops with bananas are reluctant to apply farm chemicals at
recommended levels, as many of these would prove toxic on food crops.[5]

Against such advice, most farmers have responded to the increasing
costs of banana production by actually cultivating a wider range of crops
than before, many of which are intercropped with bananas. Nearly 80 percent of all surveyed banana growers cultivate other crops as well, and 64
percent sell some of those crops for additional income. The most commonly cultivated subsistence crops are "ground provisions," including
sweet potatoes, yams, sweet cassava, dasheen (taro, or *Colocasia esculenta*),
and tannia (cocoyam, or *Xanthosoma sagittifolium*), one or more of which
are grown by 53 percent of all surveyed households and sold by 32 percent. Other locally grown crops include coconuts, plantains, hot peppers,
mangos, tomatoes, okra, cacao, spices, and peanuts, all of which are sold
in small amounts locally or in Castries. Because island markets tend to
be easily glutted with produce, the supply of which often outstrips local
demand, the earnings from local crop sales are highly variable from week
to week. Other than bananas, Scotch bonnet peppers are the only crop
with a non-local market; they are sold fresh to a firm that exports them by
air to Miami. Despite the unpredictable nature of local markets, sales of
subsistence crops average EC $4,329 annually for Mabouya Valley banana
farmers, more than one-half the average net annual income derived from
bananas (EC $7,864).

Data from the 2004 survey on labor and input expenditures versus returns from sales indicate that some 27 percent of Mabouya Valley banana-
growing households actually generate a net negative income from the pro-

duction of bananas. In these cases, farmers report that earnings derived from activities other than banana production are not only essential to their survival, but subsidize their banana farms by enabling them to pay farm workers or purchase inputs during periods of low fruit prices.[6] Evidence from previous studies of the Mabouya Valley suggests that the diversification of banana farmers' economic activities has increased dramatically in recent years. Slocum found that 74 percent of the farming households in her 1994 survey of valley residents contained at least one member who worked off the farm during that year (1996: 122). According to her informants, more than half of these households had sought off-farm income only within the previous five years, a period corresponding to the emergence of the Single European Market and the dramatic decline in banana prices. By 2004, 121 (91 percent) of the 133 surveyed Mabouya Valley banana farming households contained at least one member who worked off the farm. This figure is all the more striking considering the recent closure of a nearby apparel factory that had formerly provided the largest share of local wage opportunities, at least for women.

Taken together, the two surveys suggest that involvement in off-farm employment for the valley's banana-growing households increased by at least 250 percent between 1989 and 2004. Correspondingly, there has been a marked decline in the number of households relying exclusively on banana farming as a livelihood. A 1997 survey made under contract to the St. Lucian government determined that, on average, Mabouya Valley farmers derived 63 percent of their assets from banana sales. In that year, nearly a third of all growers reported that banana farming was responsible for all of their assets (Cargill 1998). The 133 Mabouya Valley farmers surveyed in this project in 2004 reported that on average 51 percent of their assets were derived from banana farming, but by then only 4 percent of the farmers could claim that they relied exclusively on bananas for all of their assets. Clearly, to the extent that many farmers remain commercially active banana growers, it is income generated outside the banana industry that makes this possible. In this sense, households increasingly subsidize banana production with other income-earning and subsistence activities.

Although most banana farming households rely heavily on family members' off-farm earnings to support themselves, the large majority of their heads of household (81 percent) remain full-time farmers. This is not surprising given the day-to-day demands of banana production, which would require them to hire additional farm labor or even a full-time farm manager, were they to seek work elsewhere. Indeed, this is the case for half—thirteen out of twenty-six—of the owner-operators who work full-time off the farm. These individuals are employed in professional or skilled trades and include an air traffic controller, a manager for WIB-

DECO, and a teacher (all three of whom have college degrees), as well as several semi-trailer truck drivers or heavy equipment operators. These farm owners, whose annual off-farm incomes range from EC $9,600 to $60,000 per year (with a mean of $20,976), represent a small remnant of the many salaried or relatively highly paid skilled workers who invested in banana farms as a supplement to their incomes during the industry's heyday in the 1980s. By their own accounts and those of extension agents, the majority of full-time professional or skilled workers who invested in banana farming as a supplemental income source during the 1980s have since dropped out of production. Among the few who remain, farming is at most a part-time activity that for much of the week is entrusted to a full-time paid farm manager. The other thirteen farmers who generate some off-farm income work sporadically in unskilled construction or other manual labor, or in small-scale trading. Their off-farm incomes are considerably less than those of their counterparts engaged in professional or skilled employment, varying from EC $1,000 to $7,200 per year (with a mean of $2,534).

Apart from a small number of people with professional credentials, such as nurses, accountants, and teachers, regular employment opportunities for Mabouya Valley residents are severely limited in both their number and earnings potential. Some manufacturing jobs are available in textile and other light industries in the free trade zone near Vieux Fort, at the southern tip of the island. As is widely reported concerning apparel manufacturers worldwide, managers strongly prefer to hire women for such employment, ostensibly because of the greater manual dexterity and patience of female workers.[7] From the sample of 133 Mabouya Valley farming households, only ten women work in such facilities, probably because the round-trip cost of transportation to Vieux Fort consumes nearly half of their average piecework wages from a nine-hour shift (EC $35–40). Formerly, a US-owned apparel factory in the nearby town of Dennery had employed about 600 area residents, among them many young women from the Mabouya Valley, in manufacturing lingerie for the Victoria's Secret chain. Its abrupt closure in 2000 after more than twenty years of operation sent the local unemployment and out migration rates spiraling upward.

Although the St. Lucian government has heavily promoted tourism as a replacement for agricultural employment, in practice earnings from the tourist industry have proven a poor substitute for farm earnings. Most tourist hotels are located well to the north of Castries, far from the island's main agricultural zones. Tourist facilities pay domestics and unskilled workers wages of about EC $40 (about US $15) per day. Like the earnings at the Vieux Fort factories, these wages are substantially reduced (by about a third) due to the cost of the 1–1½ hour trip each way by minibus from the Mabouya Valley. Hotel positions involving closer interaction with tourists, such as receptionists, wait staff, and bartenders, generate considerably higher base earnings as well as the opportunity to augment one's wages with tips. Such positions are coveted but few in number, and demand a degree of fluency in standard English and a level of urbanity, if not formal education, beyond the range of many rural St. Lucians.

The greatest share of male members of banana farming households who work off the farm identify their employment as some form of construction, although in almost all cases such work is sporadic and temporary. Given the decline in the banana industry since the early 1990s and the resulting rise in criminal behavior on the island, it may come as little surprise that the most commonly mentioned full-time off-farm work for male members of valley households is "security." Virtually all hotels, banks, and most Castries businesses employ security details. Uniformed guards constantly patrol beaches in front of tourist facilities to ward off panhandlers as well as itinerant vendors, much to the chagrin of those who wish to sell souvenirs to tourists. Among Mabouya Valley men, security employment is considered prestigious for its regular wages and benefits as well as the fact that it offers physically undemanding work in comfortable surroundings. Unarmed security guards earn a little more than farm workers (about EC \$45 per day), but unlike most farm or construction workers they can count on full-time permanent employment. Further, security guards who receive training in firearms or dog handling may earn as much as \$75–90 per day.

Perpetua James, a community development officer from the government's Ministry of Social Transformation office in nearby Dennery, pointed out that recent economic trends have generated a related employment boom, even if it has failed to completely offset the closure of the local textile factory. With an escalation in drug trafficking, theft, and violent crime in the 1990s, the St. Lucian government found its existing prison facilities sorely inadequate to house the number of people convicted of or awaiting trial for such crimes. On a bluff high above the town of Dennery, the government broke ground on the state-of-the-art Bordelais Correctional Facility in 2002. In addition to the approximately 200 men engaged on a short-term basis in its construction, the prison employs a permanent staff of about sixty, most of whom work as prison guards, cooks, and kitchen help. "These days, it seem that the only growth industry here is locking people up, mostly for drugs," James noted as she squinted up at the gleaming new prison perched 150 yards above the community development office. Sunlight glinted off of the razor wire that topped the prison fences. "In the time of banana, we used to talk about 'green gold.' These young men locked up there use the same expression, but for them it's a different kind of green they talk about."

Chayanov in the Caribbean

In 1993, thousands of farmers and rural residents gathered in front of St. Michael's Catholic church in La Ressource, a hamlet in the Mabouya Valley, to mourn the death of parishioner Randy Joseph and protest the Compton government's suppression of the banana strike. On a weekday afternoon in September 2004, the site is occupied by just a dozen or so children playing after school in the parish's well-swept yard. A forty-foot container trailer is perched incongruously on blocks in front of the church entrance. Fr. Raymond Laurent, the parish priest at St. Michael's, explains that he and the local St. Vincent de Paul Society use the trailer to store and distribute food and other necessities for the valley's indigent residents. Many of these items are purchased from a second collection that he takes up at Sunday Masses, but most are contributed by Food for the Poor, a US-based Catholic relief organization. Donated by Caritas, a worldwide Church-affiliated charity, the trailers have sprung up in all of the island's rural parishes in response to the deepening economic distress of their surrounding communities. Having gone on record in support of Caribbean farmers during the WTO dispute, the island's Catholic Church has since taken a leading role in dispensing help to those displaced from the industry.

The concerns that the religious organizations and relief agencies express about deepening rural poverty are amply borne out by government and Church records. In 1996, a year of record low banana prices, the Caribbean Development Bank found that 18.7 percent of all St. Lucian households lived in poverty, defined by World Bank criteria in terms of reported expenditures on food and non-food items. In comparison, the two Mabouya Valley banana-growing communities included in the island-wide study registered household poverty rates of 63.3 percent (Kairi 1996). During 2003, Food for the Poor provided more than US $2 million for indigent relief on St. Lucia, with the largest share of it directed to La Ressource, Micoud, and Babonneau parishes, all of which were heavily dependent on banana production and have witnessed a sharp decline in farming incomes (Boxill, pers. comm. 2004). Working with the teachers in a neighboring school to identify the children most in need, Fr. Laurent attempts to provide their families with packages of food and other necessities at least once per month. St. Michael's parish makes charity avail-

Figure 7.4 | Parish priest of Mabouya Valley, in front of a trailer used to store charitable aid to families displaced from the banana industry.

able to all indigent residents, regardless of denomination, but Fr. Laurent's is only one of several charitable initiatives active in the Mabouya Valley. ADRA, the Adventist Development Relief Association, dispenses clothing and food through most of the Seventh-day Adventist churches on the island, including the 200-member Adventist congregation in nearby Belmont. For its part, the St. Lucian government has also launched a number of World Bank– and EU-funded anti-poverty initiatives, although publicly disbursed aid under these programs is frequently alleged to be a form of patronage for the party loyalty of valley residents.[8]

On the second floor of his rectory, looking out over a sea of banana plants, Fr. Laurent described the local conditions when he was first posted from his native Castries to La Ressource in 1980. "I had seen a lot of development in those days," Fr. Laurent recalled. "Banana was very prosperous then; it brought in a lot of money. And you saw that people were buying vehicles. The size of the houses and the vehicles, these things indicated that things were not too bad. And the children were very happy, they were properly clothed and they were not missing school because their relatives in the banana industry were able to support them and give them everything they needed."

After protracted assignments in Trinidad and West Africa, Laurent returned to St. Michael's at the end of the 1990s. The community's transformation in the interim shocked him upon his return:

> There was a dramatic decline in the ease that the people had. You know, they lived happily before, but they have to struggle much more now than they used to. People work harder now than ever and they get next to nothing from their toils. Sometimes an entire harvest is rejected and the farmer still has to pay his workers and feed his family. And the tragic thing is, you see it mostly with the small children now, the ones who are the least among us.[9] They are always the last in the family to eat, the last to get new clothes or shoes. I know a lot of them are not going to school just because the parents can't afford uniforms or supplies. And some of these farmers who supported their families so well in the past, well, they are too proud to ask for help.

Like Fr. Laurent, all longstanding residents of the Mabouya Valley are able to point out the visible symptoms of the banana industry's decline. For grower Mary Baptiste, who opposed the 1993 strikes and whose packing shed was burned as a result, the drop in banana prices and ensuing political conflicts signaled a loss in mutual trust from which the community has yet to recover. "Sometimes you hail them, the people who was on the other side [of the strike], and they just look at you hard. Or sometimes they give you a plastic [insincere] smile, but then they shush [gossip] plenty when you pass them by." On the way to her farm, Baptiste called out to some neighbors, pointedly ignored others, and identified numerous abandoned parcels in which weeds were overtaking neglected banana plants. First to go out of production were the steepest hillside farms, established in the 1980s when all available lands in the valley itself had already been brought under cultivation. Now, as the hillsides are gradually reforested with lush secondary growth, even some farms on prime bottomlands with well-drained top soils are being abandoned. What happened to their owners? Have they sold their lands to other, more prosperous farmers? "Nobody sells their land here," Baptiste shook her head. "We Caribbean people always keep our little plot, even if we're living in another country. Sometimes their family members take it over and use it for groundfood or what have you, but not another banana farmer. The reason is that banana just don't pay enough for somebody to hire more labor. Nobody's growing more bananas than they used to. Nobody. Now where the owners are, I can tell you that. Some are in New York, some in London, Antigua, St. Croix, and many, many of them gone to Martinique. But not me. I'm staying here. I'm a survivor."

Baptiste's seemingly prosaic commentary in fact touches on one of the more heated debates to arise in economic anthropology since the rediscovery of Chayanov's *Theory of Peasant Economy* in 1966. Prior to the school of agricultural economics associated with Chayanov, social differentiation theorists assumed that in a situation of low prices or other economic adversity, most farmers are forced out of production into landlessness, becoming wage laborers as a result. A small number of comparatively wealthy farmers, who are better able to withstand periods of low earnings, in turn appropriate the land of their heavily indebted neighbors and expand the scale of their production. Yet as Mary Baptiste indicates, there is little evidence of this trend toward class differentiation the Mabouya Valley. Of the 133 surveyed farmers, 25 reported that they had obtained new lands in the past ten years, with the average size of the new parcel being 2.3 acres. Only two of these farmers reported that they had purchased the land, all the others stating that they had obtained additional land through rental or "share."[10] However, the area under bananas cultivated by farmers who had expanded their control of land was virtually no greater, at a mean acreage of 4.6 acres, than that farmed by those who did not obtain additional land, at a mean of 4.2 acres—a statistically insignificant difference.[11] While the average net annual earnings from banana sales on expanded farms were somewhat greater than those reported by growers who did not acquire new lands (EC $10,032 vs. $7,358), this difference was also not statistically significant. One notable difference between the groups was the age of the farmer, with those acquiring additional land being nearly seven years younger on average than those who did not (39.8 years versus 46).[12]

The age difference, combined with the fact that those who acquired land had been farming in the area for an average of four years less than those who did not add new land, suggests that land transfers in the valley reflect underlying demographic processes instead of socioeconomic differentiation. In other words, individuals who have acquired land within the past decade have done so because they are entering farming on their own (often taking over from an elderly parent) or are seeking additional land to support young but growing families. Indeed, the 2004 survey of Mabouya Valley farmers reveals that the average farm size in that year (4.3 acres) was almost unchanged from that of previous surveys of the same region during the 1990s (Cargill 1998, Slocum 1996), despite massive attrition over the past decade. In contrast to social differentiation theory, which would predict increasing average farm sizes from consolidation among fewer owners, these land distribution trends correspond more closely with the predictions of Chayanov, who asserted that much of the apparent "inequality" in landholdings in peasant communities resulted from families having different needs for land over various stages of their life cycles (1966: 56). Absent the complexities of family land tenure and the reluctance of migrants to sell land to those who remain back home, of course it is likely that some consolidation in the hands of wealthier farmers would in fact occur.

For social differentiation to take place, however, there must be both a profitable potential use for land and a readily available source of wage labor to farm it. As Mary Baptiste recognized, the availability of workers, rather than land, largely sets the maximum size limit on an economically viable banana farm in the Windwards today. Simply put, even if large-scale farmers were able to overcome daunting institutional and cultural factors to permanently procure land from neighbors who have abandoned production, they would be hard pressed to find enough farm labor to cultivate it. Mabouya Valley residents, BERU officials, and company extension agents concur that the largest farmers (those who cultivated ten or more acres in bananas before 1993) have all either dramatically scaled back or ceased banana production entirely as supplies of wage labor have dried up. This is a major reason for the withdrawal from the industry of professional and other non-farming full-time workers who invested in banana production during the 1980s, when absentee-owned farms employing full-time managers could still generate a sizable profit.

In contrast, the smallest farms, which rely more heavily on household labor than outside hired workers, might appear to have an advantage in cost-accounting terms, especially since the shift to the labor-intensive mini-wet pack system. Yet these entities too have experienced severe difficulties in recent years as the costs of WIBDECO farm certification, and more recently EUREP-GAP requirements, have exceeded the amount of revenue they are able to generate. As a result of the twin processes of increasing production costs and diminishing labor supplies, there has been a tendency for both the largest and the smallest-scale farms to drop out of banana production. Indeed, one notable feature of the graph (figure 7.5) depicting the distribution of farm acreage under bananas is how little dispersion is evident from the mean of 4.3 acres. Presently, 71.8 percent of all Mabouya Valley households recorded in the 2004 survey cultivate between 2.5 and 5 acres of bananas, a range that falls within an optimal balance between the minimum revenues and available labor supplies required to remain in production.

One subset of farming households that may be at a particular disadvantage because of the increasing costs of production and growing scarcity of labor is those headed by women. Compared to other regions and

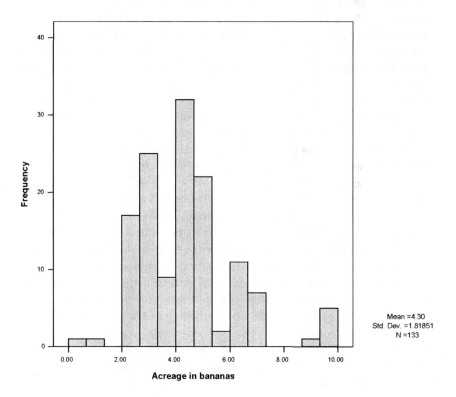

Figure 7.5 | Distribution of Land under Banana Cultivation: Mabouya Valley, 2004

Source: Author's survey data

industries associated with commercial agriculture, banana farming in the Windward Islands has long been characterized by an exceptionally high level of female proprietorship. Women make up 30.1 percent of the 133 farmers surveyed in 2004, a figure closely corresponding to their representation in previous surveys of the valley. On average, female farmers are significantly older than their male counterparts (48.6 years versus 43.2 years).[13] Overall, advancing age is strongly associated with less involvement in farming, as reflected in farmers' annual incomes from banana sales.[14] In addition, among other statistically significant differences along gender lines, women cultivate smaller areas of land in bananas (3.8 acres versus 4.5), earn less from other crops (EC $2,157 versus $5,263), and generate far lower net annual earnings from banana sales (EC $4,504 versus $9,325). Women are also significantly more likely than men to state that they grow fewer bananas presently than they did five years ago.[15] Given that their labor costs are only slightly lower (and not statistically so) than those of male farmers (EC $296 per fortnight versus $358), it may appear that female-headed operations are increasingly caught in the squeeze between rising production costs and increased labor scarcity. Offsetting such trends is the fact that female-headed households are more likely to derive income from household members working off the farm and remittances from abroad. To the extent that many women like Mary Baptiste remain "survivors" in commercial banana production, it may be such off-farm income sources, especially including foreign remittances, which make it possible for them to retain a foothold in agriculture.

"The Least among Us"

The abandonment of banana production and banana-growing communities that Baptiste noted for the Mabouya Valley is a story that could be repeated throughout the Eastern Caribbean. All available evidence indicates that migration from banana-producing areas has skyrocketed since the early 1990s. The most dramatic instance of this is Dominica, an island far less economically diversified than any of the other Windwards. On a per capita basis, Dominica was formerly three times more dependent on bananas as a source of export earnings than St. Lucia. When the island's birth rate is measured against its death rate, Dominica exhibits a natural population growth rate of 2.9 percent per year, one of the highest in the Anglophone Caribbean. Yet between 1990 and 2000, the island actually witnessed a 10 percent decline in population, indicating a massive level of out migration (Fontaine 2007: 5). In contrast, St. Lucia's population as a whole grew by

11.1 percent during the same period, from 133,308 to 151,143 (St. Lucia 1991, 2001b). Yet despite a high level of natural population growth (2.4 percent per year) and population growth at the national level, most banana-growing settlements in the Mabouya Valley declined in size during the 1990s. If town dwellers are excluded from Dennery Quarter's census figures, the resulting count indicates that the Mabouya Valley's population grew by just 1 percent between 1990 and 2000 (St. Lucia 2001b). The difference between the valley's population growth rate and that of St. Lucia as a whole would suggest high levels of emigration, albeit not as great as Dominica's.

The 2004 survey of banana farmers registered 679 people presently living in 133 households scattered throughout the Mabouya Valley. Collectively, farmers identified another 168 members of their households as living abroad, or 19.8 percent of the total household members accounted for in the survey (Table 7.1). The mainland US (generally New York City) is the most common destination for St. Lucians who emigrate, claiming 66 of the 168 known migrants (39.3 percent of the total migrant population). The US is followed by Martinique (37 migrants, or 22 percent), the UK (36, or 21.4 percent), Antigua, Barbados, or other former British West Indies (10, or 5.9 percent), the US Virgin Islands (9, or 5.7 percent), Guadalupe (3, or 1.8 percent), and "sailing," that is, cruise ship or other maritime employment (1, or .6 percent). Of all surveyed farmers, only 28 out of 133

Table 7.1 | Destination of Household Members Living Abroad: Banana-Growing Households (n = 105)*

	Frequency	Percent of Total
US mainland	66	39.3
Martinique	37	22.0
United Kingdom	36	21.4
Anglophone Caribbean	10	5.9
US Virgin Islands	9	5.7
Canada	6	3.5
Other Francophone Caribbean	3	1.7
"Sailing"	1	0.6
TOTAL	168	100.1%

*28 out of 133 households reported no members living in other countries.

Source: Author's survey data

(21.1 percent) indicated that they had no household members or immediate family living abroad.

The distance over which migration takes place and the legal status of migrants in their new places of residence heavily affect the frequency of contact and strength of ties that they maintain with the communities and family they left behind. Migrants to the US typically enter the country on short-term tourist visas, but most do so with the intention of long-term residence, work, and study. It is believed that most St. Lucian migrants in the US have overstayed their visitors' permits and are residing and working there illegally. St. Lucians who return from the US attest to a brisk underground trade in fake social security cards, which can be obtained for about US $200 in the Caribbean émigré neighborhoods of Brooklyn. The quality of these documents suffices to obtain work, especially from employers who ask few questions about a worker's origins, but few migrants dare to travel on falsified documents that would not withstand scrutiny by immigration officers. Some migrants are able to eventually obtain legitimate green cards through marriage, service in the US military, or other means. Absent such documentation of legal status, however, it is extremely risky for migrants to return to the island to visit as they then find it difficult or impossible to return to their new homes in the US. As citizens of the British Commonwealth, St. Lucians formerly encountered fewer work or residence restrictions in the UK and Canada, although both countries have heightened entry and work criteria for Caribbean residents since the early 1980s. The heavy traffic between St. Lucia and Toronto or London testifies to the sizeable migrant communities established in those places before the tightening of restrictions.

Most first-time migrants are in their mid twenties to early thirties, with a very slender predominance of men over women. This slight gender imbalance is reflected in a somewhat lower number of men in the remaining island population, where the male to female ratio is about 1:1.08. However, what is notable about the Windward Islands, compared to other countries with high rates of emigration, such as Mexico, is the relatively large number of women as well as men who do migrate internationally, whether singly or in marital or common-law relationships. Because many people who migrate have already established households with children in St. Lucia, life in the United States as an illegal immigrant entails prolonged and even indefinite family separation. Few would-be migrants have sufficient resources to bring children with them, and in any case US consular officials are reluctant to provide visitors' visas for entire families at a time, at least for families from nonprofessional backgrounds.

The increasing rate of migration in recent years has dramatically intensified a trend, known as the "barrel child" syndrome and first noted more than a generation ago in the West Indies (Clarke 1966), of young children being left behind by their parents to reside with grandparents or other senior relatives. The name refers to what is often the only tangible contact between parents and their children—the barrels of clothing and other goods sent by absentee parents to partially provide for their families in the islands. The barrels are standard-sized cylindrical fiberboard or plastic shipping containers measuring about four feet high and two feet in diameter. Any and all items that can be stuffed into the barrels are shipped back to the islands from ports in the US, Canada, the Virgin Islands, and the UK. These material goods supplement the earnings that are periodically returned home as remittances in the form of Western Union money transfers, bank drafts, money orders, and cash. Somewhat fewer than half of the farmers with family members abroad stated that they received cash remittances (46 out of 105), with female heads of households statistically more likely to report remittances than males.[16] Yet virtually all farmers with family members in the United States or Great Britain (97 out of 102) acknowledged that they periodically received material goods, including barrels, at least once per year. Rare indeed is the rural household that does not have at least one spare barrel on its premises. What may now serve as a storage or waste receptacle once contained an eagerly awaited shipment of goods from family members abroad.

A major share of all the cargo that freighters bring from other countries into the Port of Castries consists of barrels from St. Lucians living elsewhere. On each barrel, the recipient's name, island address, and phone number are written in heavy marker. One of the six warehouses at the port is entirely allocated for barrels, which are stacked two or three high on pallets reaching to the ceiling. The number of barrels brought into the country increases significantly during the Christmas season, when the customs department affords incoming barrels some preferential treatment: usual import duties are waived in favor of a 5 percent "service charge" on the barrel's insurance and freight costs, as long as the items it contains are limited to clothing and food. Customary duties are imposed on any appliances, electronic goods, or other "luxury" consumer items. In practice, this means that the recipient of a barrel of clothing and food during the Christmas season pays a service charge of about EC $20–25 instead of the customary $70–80 duty applied during the rest of the year. Importation of barrels also increases around Easter, but the customs department does not relax import duties at that time of year.

According to Earl Blanchard, docks manager for the St. Lucia Air, Sea and Ports Authority, about 75 percent of the barrels imported to St. Lucia enter at Castries, with the remainder offloaded in Vieux Fort. Based on monthly import figures obtained from the Castries Ports Authority, and

Figure 7.6 | Barrels from St. Lucians abroad destined for home. For many children, these are their only contact with absent parents.

allowing for a 25 percent extrapolation for Vieux Fort, an estimated 12,000 barrels or more were imported to St. Lucia in 2003. This amounts to about one barrel per every thirteen island residents per year. Sheds 6a and 6b at the Port of Castries, where barrels are inspected and stored until they can be retrieved by their recipients, are busy at all times of the year. From the beginning of December until the end of January, when the port handles more than 4,000 barrels and processes their accompanying paperwork, the sheds become frenzied, even chaotic sites of activity. Recipients jostle for position in queues to pay fees and collect barrels, while lines of hired pickup trucks snake out of the Ports Authority parking lot and wind down the adjacent highway for several blocks.

Mr. Blanchard, who has worked with the Ports Authority for thirty years, has long been familiar with the practice of migrants supporting their families by sending barrels of necessities back home. Since the mid 1990s, however, he has seen a dramatic increase in the number of barrels arriving on the island. "I would say, at least a 300, maybe 400 percent increase since 1995. We used to get between 2,000 and 2,500 barrels each year. Now we get more than that just in the first three weeks of December. We operate here with about the same staffing as ten years ago, so sometimes things slow down with the processing and sometimes tempers get short." Pointing out the addresses printed on the sides of the barrels lining both sides of a corridor in Shed 6a, Blanchard notes that not even one in five is destined for people living in Castries, a striking discrepancy given that the city is home to almost 40 percent of the island's population. Instead, the large majority are bound for the small rural settlements that have lost so much of their population to foreign migration.

It is relatively easy to identify the numbers and destinations of barrels imported into St. Lucia, but less easily quantified is the social dimension of the barrel phenomenon; that is, how children fare when they are raised apart from either parent. Jacinta Henry, a twenty-year veteran teacher of the La Ressource primary school who now serves as its principal, estimates that 30 percent of the children in the area live with neither parent.[17] "Before 1992, 93, when things got bad in the industry, it was down in the single digits. Migration has never had such a great impact on our student population." In terms of the disruptions caused by foreign migration, the families of banana farmers are considerably more stable than those of former banana workers. To the extent that farming households continue in banana production, at least one of the parents will remain in the area to work on and manage the farm. Indeed, of the 133 farmers surveyed, only 30 (22.5 percent) were not in a more or less continuous co-residential conjugal relationship.[18] Among a similar number (31, or 23.3 percent), either the farmer or, more commonly, his or her partner periodically migrates to Martinique on a short-term (fifteen-day) basis for work.

In contrast, with the contraction of local banana production and wage-earning potential, nonfarming households formerly reliant on wage labor have seen an indefinite long-distance exodus of both parents. Because many farm workers' brothers and sisters are similarly stressed in economic terms or equally likely to migrate, the most common candidate for caregiver under such circumstances is a grandparent or, in many cases, an older teen-aged child. Teachers and social workers concur that the barrel phenomenon has had long-term negative effects on the children who grow up under such arrangements. Henry notes that what might initially appear to be a tenable if temporary arrangement, when young children are placed in the care of still middle-aged grandparents, becomes unmanageable as children and their caregivers grow older. "Can you imagine being 70, 75 years old and having to provide guidance to a 16-year-old girl or boy who is starting to experiment with sex and drugs?" she asked.

> Grandparents don't have the energy for raising teenagers, and teenagers don't respect grandparents for their experience. So these children end up raising themselves or worse, being raised by their friends. Now what 75- year-old man or woman can stand up to a rude 18-year-old boy? For the first time in our history, we're seeing elder abuse. It's the grandparents who get what little money is coming in from the outside, but once these older teens get into drugs, some of them will threaten the old people or even beat them to get control of the money. Sometimes we see the grandparents going without anything to eat while the teens are out drinking and smoking weed. (Henry, pers. comm. 2004)

When teenagers are the de facto caregivers for their younger siblings, or when they effectively control the funds intended to support their charges, the younger children's maintenance and education usually suffer. Most of the primary schools in St. Lucia are under joint Church-state governance. Under this arrangement a religious institution (to this day, usually the Catholic Church) constructs local schools and controls many aspects of their curriculum, while the government pays teachers' salaries. Although tuition is not charged, even primary school students must be provided with uniforms, shoes, and books and supplies, the costs of which range from EC $200 (about US $75) per year in Infant One to $500 (about US $185) in Standard Six (respectively, the equivalent of first grade and eighth grade in the US). Henry estimates that close to 25 percent of the students who are legally required to attend her school today are chronically truant, compared to fewer than 5 percent in the early 1990s. Further, many of those who do attend school lack shoes, textbooks, or appropriate uniforms. "Now you know, we are supposed to enforce the policies island-wide. But what if I turn these children away for want of a uniform? It's better that they are here under any circumstances, even if we have to bend the rules." For his part, Fr. Laurent noted an ironic aspect to the deprivation experienced by many small children raised by siblings: "It's pitiful to see the way they are dressed and cared for, because it's obvious they are neglected. But then you see their older brothers and sisters are well-dressed, you look at them and sometimes they are better dressed than people in the States. You ask them, where do you get the money, how do you get the means to maintain yourselves so well? Because there's no visible income." For some younger men who have grown up in barrel households, aspiring to a lifestyle informed by satellite TV and globalized standards of consumption requires a great deal of income, the sources of which they cannot allow to remain visible. It is those "invisible," usually illegal activities to which we next turn.

Notes

1. The exception to this among the four Windward Islands is Grenada, which has ceased exporting bananas altogether and whose BGA is inoperative. On St. Lucia, the transition from the BGA to the SLBC was accompanied by a staff reduction of about 20 percent, but this was more than offset by the subsequent creation of other banana companies.
2. WINFA, the Windward Islands Farmers Association, is a region-wide umbrella group based in Kingstown, St. Vincent. A relatively inactive organization during the 1980s and early 1990s, WINFA later positioned itself as the regional coordinator for Fair Trade marketing. It now derives almost all its budget from a portion of the sale of all Fair Trade fruit grown in the Windwards.
3. WIBDECO officials claim that their profits reflect the sale of highly lucrative licenses for the importation of fruit into the EU rather than the earnings from Windwards fruit itself. Nonetheless, as seen in Chapter 5, the companies were forced through concerted action by the SLBC to share these returns with growers.
4. This was widely misunderstood to mean that farmers would have to install septic tanks. Said one indignant grower, "I have to have a flush toilet on my farm and I don't even have one in my house!" Pit toilets satisfy this requirement, but on tiny Caribbean farms they still represent a costly reduction in the amount of land available for farming.
5. Mabouya Valley farmers acknowledge that they use chemical inputs at lower than recommended levels when bananas are intercropped with food crops. Grossman (1998) provided quantitative evidence to this effect for St. Vincent.
6. Banana prices fluctuate considerably during the year, with lowest prices generally occurring during the winter months, when demand for the fruit is lowest. At these times, off-farm incomes are especially critical.
7. Many critics of textile and other light industrial manufacturers point out that young women are preferred for such employment because they are less likely to challenge male managers or to form unions and strike (Collins 2003: 145).
8. Since 1999, the government has allocated funds from the European Union for poverty reduction in rural communities. Among these is STEP, the Short Term Employment Programme, which provides temporary public works jobs. Consideration for STEP

requires applicants to request such assistance from their member of the National Assembly, causing some to allege that it has become a form of political patronage. In 2004, when the SLP still held a large majority of assembly seats, a valley resident described how the program worked:

> Mainly you find a person who is of the same political persuasion as the Parliamentarian, as you know most of them are Labour ... [I]f you're visible [as a UWP supporter], they'll say, "c'est che Labour dusei." This is Patwa. It means, you must be Labour through and through. They ask you what party you support. And if you don't answer Labour, you don't get the job. (Henry, pers. comm. 2004)

9. In referring to indigent children, Fr. Laurent is paraphrasing Jesus' admonition to his disciples to aid the poor: "I was naked and you clothed me, I was hungry and you fed me ... whatsoever you do to the least of these, you do also to me" (Matthew 25:31–46).

10.. Whereas rental implies an annual fixed payment in exchange for access to land, "share" is an equally common arrangement in which individuals gain access to land (usually on a family member's parcel) in exchange for a share of their production.

11. One tailed t-test not significant at $p \leq .05$.

12. Two tailed t-test significant at $p \leq .05$.

13. Two tailed t-test significant at $p \leq .05$.

14. Pearson's $r = -.227$, significant at $p \leq .05$.

15. Chi-square = 6.28, significant at $p \leq .05$ with 2 df.

16. Chi-Square = 8.9, significant at $p \leq .05$ with 1 df.

17. Henry's estimate almost exactly matched that of a census enumerator for the Mabouya Valley. In compiling data for the 2001 census, she found that about 28 percent of the children aged twelve and younger were living in households not headed by a parent, either with grandparents, an older teenaged sibling, or much less commonly, an aunt, uncle, or friend of the parents.

18. Formal marriage relationships among couples are less frequent than in the US. More than half (57 percent) of the farmers in conjugal relationships describe their partners as "common-law" spouses or "boyfriend" or "girlfriend." Usually, marriage is not formalized until after about the age of forty, although even some elderly couples remain in common-law unions.

Chapter Eight

DESPERATE TIMES, DESPERATE MEASURES

Illegal enterprise ... embroils most of its participants in lifestyles of violence, substance abuse, and internalized rage. Contradictorily, therefore, the street culture of resistance is predicated on the destruction of its participants and the community harboring them.
—Philippe Bourgois, *In Search of Respect* (1995)

The destruction of the poor is their poverty.
—Old Testament (Proverbs 10:15)

A Legacy of Smuggling

The histories of the Caribbean and Europe are inextricably bound with a nefarious if profitable triangle trade. Throughout the seventeenth and eighteenth centuries, a continuous circuit of goods, labor, and capital linked Africa with the West Indies and England in ways that generated much of the wealth for the industrialization of the North Atlantic world. Slaves taken from Africa were deposited in the Americas to produce sugar, rum, tobacco, and cotton for export to England. Profits from the sale of these commodities provided the investment capital required for the English factory system. In turn, England's West Indian and African colonies—part of an empire over which the sun never set—offered a potential market for her manufactured goods. The creation of such markets required first the displacement or suppression of local artisan production, a process resting on a flood of cheap English manufactured goods and colonial administrative policies that pushed native people into a cash economy. Such parasitic relationships between regions were widely acknowledged in their time, even if the human suffering that fueled Europe's development is rarely mentioned in development discourse today. Quoted in Eric Williams's seminal study of West Indian slavery and English capitalism, an early industrialist in Bristol, England, coolly observed that "there is not a brick in the city that is not cemented with the blood of a slave" (1944: 61). Ironically, the anti-colonial intensity of Williams' study was such that, decades later, when the radical historian turned conservative prime minister of Trinidad was confronted by a nationalist Black Power movement, he attempted to limit the circulation of his own book.

The Caribbean is notable as well for the actions of those who challenged the prerogatives of empire. With their intricate, unguarded coastlines and many secluded inlets, the Windward Islands appear tailor-made for piracy. Well into the nineteenth century, brigands thrived on the seizure of merchant and Crown vessels carrying the wealth of the New World to the Old, and relied on island geography and treacherous reefs to deftly avoid detection and capture. Similarly, their seizure of shipping outbound from Europe allowed them to circumvent Crown monopolies on commerce and to supply settlers hungry for goods otherwise available only in the colonies of rival powers. The features of island geography that proved so amenable to concealment and smuggling are unchanged to this day, and have facilitated a new triangle trade linking St. Lucia with its closest neighbors, Martinique and St. Vincent. In the Windwards, the loss of livelihood for both banana growers and their former workers has triggered an explosive growth in inter-island trafficking of illegal drugs. The smuggling that ties these islands together carries formidable penalties for those who are apprehended as well as greater physical dangers at the hands of other traffickers. Yet the potential for great rewards tempts many islanders today, like their predecessors centuries ago, to engage in illicit commerce between the islands.

These practices are less novel than they might initially appear, for smuggling has always been a fact of island life. For much of the Caribbean population, smuggling provides either a necessary supplement to regular earnings from "legitimate" economic activity or goods that would be otherwise prohibitively expensive. More than that, however, smuggling is rooted in Caribbean culture as an integral part of Creole identity. That identity, dichotomized within the master symbols of "reputation" and "respectability" (Wilson 1995), draws heavily from activities and values that challenge European-derived conventions. While "respectability" flows from conformity with European and upper-class expectations of behavior, for the large majority of island residents not belonging to local elites one's "reputation" among peers derives from skill, cleverness, and wordplay that deviate from, if not openly mock, the conventions of respectability (Wilson 1995). Making the most of opportunities, taking maximum advantage of available resources, strategically cultivating useful relationships, and above all avoiding detection and punishment for skirting the law, are the hallmarks of both a successful smuggler and someone who rises in the esteem of others (Browne 2005).

The basis for trafficking was laid long ago in the extensive travel and contact between islands. Since slavery's abolition, the Caribbean has been a place of out migration for purposes of employment, whether for durations of days or decades. Beginning in the late nineteenth century, thousands of Afro-Caribbean residents were dispersed widely throughout coastal Central America as workers on banana plantations and the Panama Canal (Frederick 2005). Although St. Lucians figured as well in this hemispheric diaspora, these days they engage in a greater degree of continuous inter-island traffic on a short-term basis than do their neighbors in the other Anglophone Windwards. As mentioned earlier, St. Lucians nurture especially close historical, cultural, and linguistic ties to Martinique. Lying across just nineteen miles of ocean from St. Lucia's northwest coast, the island's mountainous silhouette is easily visible from beaches north of Castries. Yet for all its proximity, Martinique, because of its comparative affluence as a French overseas department, seems a world apart from the other Windward Islands. As French citizens, Martinicans enjoy all of the legal and social welfare benefits of their metropolitan compatriots, so their living standards and wage levels are appreciably higher than those on St. Lucia. As in many relatively prosperous societies, jobs considered too low-paying, dangerous, or humiliating for nationals to occupy are instead held by immigrants, usually St. Lucians and, to a lesser extent, Dominicans. Most St. Lucians do not speak French, but their command of Kwéyòl, which is virtually identical to the first language of most Afro-Martinicans, enables them to seek informal employment and other opportunities on the island. For obvious linguistic reasons, such opportunities are foreclosed to residents of monolingual Anglophone islands such as St. Vincent and Grenada.

Legally, St. Lucians are allowed to visit Martinique for up to fifteen days without a French visa, and many take advantage of that time to seek temporary employment on the island. Indeed, given the close distance between the islands, thousands of St. Lucians work more or less continuously on Martinique, coming home every fifteen days on crowded ferries in order to retain their legal eligibility to return. Others seek to blend inconspicuously into Martinican society as long-term, if illegal, residents. Shantytowns on the outskirts of Fort-de-France are populated mostly by St. Lucians and Dominicans, as well as some Martinican migrants from the countryside. In Fort-de-France, many migrants seek construction jobs in the city's more or less continuous building boom or work as domestics with wealthy Martinican families. Many others gravitate to the country-side, where they work in the island's banana industry. Although many Martinicans empathize with St. Lucians and abet their efforts to reside and work illegally on the island, migrants must assiduously avoid contact with *gendarmes* and other authority figures to escape deportation or imprisonment. Much of the Martinican police force consists of whites from metropolitan France, few of whom exhibit much sympathy for Caribbean migrants who circumvent the country's residence and employment laws. An inability to answer a *gendarme's* question in standard French—for police, a shorthand indicator of immigrant status—is likely to result in lengthy questioning, confinement, and, according to many return migrants, beating and other forms of physical mistreatment. Notwithstanding such risks, it is estimated that as many as 40,000 St. Lucians work and live for at least part of the year in this French Caribbean enclave, a testament to the island's reliance on the comparatively low-wage labor that migrants provide (Compton 2004: 7).

For St. Lucians displaced from banana industry employment, Martinican banana farms offer wages considered far superior to those at home. Because Martinican bananas are shipped to France not as exports but technically as French produce, the French government has been able to skirt the dictates of the Single European Market and retain protectionist measures for the island's banana industry since 1993. As a result, bananas produced in the country's Caribbean overseas departments have historically enjoyed guaranteed markets in France and high prevailing retail prices. Most banana farmers in Martinique are small- and medium-sized investors from mainland France who were originally attracted to the island's industry in part because of the protected French market. Compared to the Windwards banana industry, Martinican farms are much larger (with an average size of about 30 acres), more heavily mechanized (trucks, rather than workers' backs, are used to transport fruit from field to packing shed), and employ considerably larger numbers of workers. The conditions under which banana workers are employed reflect the generous provisions of French labor law. Full-time Martinican banana workers receive a minimum salary of US $1,800 per month and benefits for a 35-hour work week, plus four weeks of annual vacation.

Competition from Dollar Area imports to the French market has increased in recent years, and as the 1997 WTO ruling challenges France's guaranteed market for its producers, banana growers in Martinique are faced with growing retail price pressures. In response, they rely upon larger numbers of temporary workers to avoid paying the minimum wages and benefits specified for full-time employees under French law. Many of these temporary workers are migrants who left banana-producing areas of St. Lucia and Dominica for the daily wages of €40 (US $55 as of August 2004) offered to day laborers on Martinican farms. These wages are more than thrice those paid in the Mabouya Valley, an attraction that, according to many St. Lucian farmers, has drained away their most experienced workers.

Indeed, the wages paid on Martinican farms have attracted many members of St. Lucian banana growers' households as well. Among the 133 banana growers surveyed in 2004, 35 (26.3 percent) reported that one or more members of their households worked regularly in Martinique, with those individuals having spent an average of 18.8 weeks there during the previous year. Reportedly, the number of migrants among nonfarming valley households is even greater. According to a former census enumerator for the La Ressource area, about 65 percent of non-landholding households in the Mabouya Valley contained at least one member who had visited Martinique during 2000–01 in search of employment.[1] Once on the island, some of these migrants discovered that, for all the earnings to be gained as banana workers, even more lucrative opportunities awaited them in a society with such high levels of disposable income. Martinique's metropolitan sensibilities and living standards and the presence of a sizable population from mainland France generate an effective demand for recreational drugs far exceeding that of any of the surrounding islands. A gram of cocaine purchased in Vieux Fort for US $18 can be sold to a French businessman or tourist in Fort-de-France for US $80. For banana workers displaced from St. Lucia, a few seemingly quick and easy transactions of this sort bring within reach the exalted standards of living that islanders associate with the United States and Europe, which are never remotely attainable by any other means in the islands themselves.

Schadenfreude

Virtually all segments of Caribbean society reacted furiously when the United States government announced its plan to challenge EU preferences for ACP bananas before the World Trade Organization. Most of this anger arose from the perceived injustice of the world's wealthiest country and remaining superpower acting with so little regard for its much poorer neighbors. While the US government zealously supported Chiquita's effort to take over the 2 percent of the world's banana market reserved for Windward Islands producers, it appeared wholly indifferent to the tens of thousands of islanders whose livelihood relied on that market. "When you are powerful and you use your wealth and influence to benefit others, you're a humanitarian," a teacher in Dennery opined, "but when you use it to grind the poor and the weak farther down into poverty, you're nothing more than a bully." Most in the Caribbean predicted that people displaced from the banana industry would have no where to turn but the illegal drug trade or emigration, options that would affect the United States in ways that its government seemingly failed to anticipate when it took its case to the WTO. Rhetorically, these predictions often assume the form of warnings made to visiting US officials and other US nationals who casually inquire into the ongoing banana wars. The exasperated, even vaguely threatening comments of a Vincentian agronomist that we met in 2000 are typical in this regard: "The people here are not about to go away. If they can't live by shipping bananas to the UK, they'll live by shipping marijuana to you." The agronomist's field assistant, who had been silent until that point, added simply, "Desperate times call for desperate measures."

The intensity of the emotions expressed by many residents of the Caribbean during the banana wars and their aftermath often shocks visitors from the United States, particularly when contrasted with the soft-spoken politeness with which islanders routinely greet visitors. Yet their anger finds a ready counterpart in much of the world, especially given most Americans' apparent indifference to preemptive wars and human rights violations committed by a government that claims to act in their name. US citizens who fail to critically inquire into the actions of their government abroad are often puzzled and hurt by the hostility directed toward the United States in other countries. To avoid asking difficult questions about their role in the world, many US nationals simply chalk such attitudes up to envy.[2] Lacking a precise equivalent, English has borrowed the term *Schadenfreude* from the German to refer to the secret pleasure that one feels at the misfortune experienced by an adversary. This aptly describes the response of Caribbean residents whose livelihoods have been destroyed by the American government's neoliberal trade policies when they learn of its simultaneous inability to cope with the drug trade and illegal immigration. Many displaced banana growers and workers hold these to be the just desserts of unjust actions.

All available evidence points to a significant escalation in drug trafficking and drug production in the Eastern Caribbean coinciding with a decline in banana production and banana-related incomes in the region. In 1989, about 29 percent of all cocaine entering the US was transshipped through the Caribbean, but by 2001 that figure had jumped to 48 percent (UN 2003: 4). Regional earnings from the drug trade in the Caribbean are now estimated at US $3.3 billion, nearly equaling the value of all of the region's legal export products taken together and far exceeding that of its agricultural exports (UN 2003: 7). Presently, about half of all South American cocaine entering the US does so via the Eastern Caribbean, where chains of smugglers move parcels of the drug from island to island in speed-boats and across land until it reaches US territory in Puerto Rico. From San Juan, small quantities are transported by paid "mules" on domestic flights to Miami, New York, and other mainland destinations, averting the intense scrutiny that passengers on international flights receive from customs agents and drug-sniffing dogs. According to a 2003 US government report, St. Lucia has emerged as the leading Eastern Caribbean link in the cocaine trade (*The Voice* 2003a: 1). In that year, police seized 152 kilograms of cocaine and 230 kilograms of marijuana on St. Lucia or in its waters, more than twice the amounts intercepted on any other Eastern Caribbean island (*The Voice* 2003a: 1). During the first eight months of 2003, St. Lucian police also destroyed a record EC $73.3 million (US $28 million) worth of marijuana plants found growing on islanders' farms (Radio St. Lucia 2003). Most startling to drug enforcement agents was the fact that St. Lucia had become the focal point of a smuggling ring in which banana growers and UK banana inspectors colluded to convey illegal drugs to the UK. At Southampton in 2002, three people were arrested after eight kilograms of cocaine with a street value of US $1.2 million were found in a box containing bananas from St. Lucia. One of those arrested was a fruit quality assessor employed with WIBDECO UK, and the other two were St. Lucians who had traveled to Britain to receive the drugs on arrival (*The Voice* 2002: 1). Previously, other boxes containing cocaine had arrived on banana ships from the Caribbean, but the drugs were detected and confiscated without leading to arrests.

Most cocaine passing through the region en route to the US enters St. Lucia at Vieux Fort, is moved across the island to secluded inlets on the leeward shore, and is then transported by speedboat to other islands. By virtue of their fluency in both English and Kwéyòl, St. Lucian smugglers are uniquely well-suited to moving drugs from St. Vincent northward through Martinique. Farther to the north, in Dominica, a Kwéyòl dialect closely related to St. Lucia's is widely understood, although English is more widely spoken among Dominicans on an everyday basis. Nonetheless, Kwéyòl serves as the medium in which that island's traffickers communicate with drug buyers in the nearby French department of Guadeloupe. Cocaine brings a higher street-level price in Miami and New York (approximately US $90–100 per gram), but street prices in the French overseas departments are not far behind. These nearby markets offer St. Lucian and Dominican traffickers the possibility of quick profits.

The situation with regard to marijuana in the Windwards is in some ways opposite that of cocaine, but ironically, the effect is the same—relatively low local retail prices on the English-speaking islands. Apart from a brief but virulent crack epidemic in the 1990s, little cocaine is used in the Windwards. Marijuana, on the other hand, is widely used and extensively grown in both "Rastafarian" and non-Rasta circles, and hence readily available at low prices.[3] Thus, because of either limited demand (in the case of cocaine) or abundant supply (in the case of marijuana) neither drug fetches a particularly high price in most of the Anglophone West Indies.[4] On the other hand, laws prohibiting the cultivation, possession, and sale of marijuana are much more heavily enforced on Martinique than on their counterparts in the former British West Indies. The effect of this is to raise the Martinican street price for the drug far above that on the Anglophone islands. Hence, while there is relatively little profit to be made by selling marijuana on the Windward Islands themselves, the drugs grown and transhipped through them fetch much higher prices on Martinique and Guadeloupe.

Lawrence "Spice" T., currently a small hotelier on Dominica, was engaged in the drug trade between that island and Guadeloupe for about three years. For the first two years of his trafficking career, he purchased marijuana from farmers in the hills east of the town of Roseau and sold it to upper-class Guadeloupans, earning profits that enabled him to eventually move into the more lucrative cocaine trade. A pound of marijuana purchased for EC $500 (US $188) on Dominica would clear US $1,000 on Guadeloupe after his expenses were covered, a profit of more than 500 percent. Spice prided himself in wrapping and concealing his parcels so thoroughly that they were virtually impossible for drug enforcement agents to locate. He claims that on one occasion when his skiff was boarded by US drug enforcement personnel with drug-sniffing dogs, they were unable to detect nearly five pounds of marijuana in a hidden parcel wrapped with citrus peels, onions, and cinnamon bark. Over time, his frequent absences from the island and construction of a new home and tourist lodge aroused local authorities' suspicions. Whereas the marijuana trade relies almost entirely on small-scale island growers and local sellers, the cocaine trade involves contacts and transactions with much larger-scale international suppliers. Spice discovered too late that his phone—with which he arranged purchases with cocaine dealers in Trinidad and Colombia—had been tapped. Arrested on Guadeloupe by French officers operating jointly with the Dominican police, Spice spent nearly a year in an island prison awaiting trial (no bail is permitted under the country's drug laws) and served another three years after being sentenced as a first-time offender. He was able to shorten his sentence by three months by virtue of good behavior and his completion of a prison course in the French language, in which he is now fluent. Out of the total prison population of about 250 in Guadeloupe, Spice estimated that about 50 were Dominicans convicted of drug trafficking. His relatively light sentence, and the prospect of a much more severe penalty for a second conviction, prompted him to find another livelihood upon his release.

"I see my time in jail as a chance that God gave me to turn my life around. Three years isn't too bad a price to pay for that," Spice concluded. "Some of these guys, though, as soon as they get out they're back to making deals. And the second time you're caught, it's no joke. They're going to lock you up in France for ten or fifteen years, and that's the last you'll see of your family that whole time." Ironically, Spice noted that the French language course for which he received time off his sentence was especially popular among convicted smugglers who planned to go back to trafficking after their release. "They think if they can speak good French, maybe not perfect but good enough, they'll blend in better ... enough to fool the police into thinking they're from the countryside and not another island."

Eradicating Eradication

Twenty miles south of the St. Lucian town of Vieux Fort lies the north coast of St. Vincent, a rugged zone of steep volcanic slopes that is entirely inaccessible by road from the rest of the island. Apart from the much larger island of Jamaica, this isolated region between the villages of Chateaubelair and Georgetown produces more marijuana than any other place in the Caribbean. Although most who are casually acquainted with the West Indies associate marijuana with the region's Rastafarians, it was actually introduced to the islands in the nineteenth century by Indian indentured laborers, most of whom were brought by the British to Trinidad and Jamaica as plantation workers.[5] Both countries became the region's major producers of the drug and exported growing quantities of it to the United States and other developed nations in the 1960s. By the following decade, the US had embarked on the course of drug eradication by which it has attempted to stem domestic consumption ever since. Although Jamaica has proved an elusive target in this regard, Trinidad's much higher population densities and the absence of significant forest cover or rugged landscapes provided few places of refuge for marijuana producers. Displaced from Trinidad by the mid 1970s, commercial marijuana production shifted northward, to the mountainous, inaccessible north coast of St. Vincent (Cottle, pers. comm. 2004).

According to island residents involved in the marijuana trade, the average marijuana grower in the northern region of St. Vincent cultivates about two acres of crop. Cultivation is usually dispersed among several parcels as a sort of "risk insurance." Smaller parcels are more difficult to identify by authorities, and the eradication of one will still leave the grower free to harvest the other, undetected parcels. On the other hand, dispersal of plots also increases the cost of surveillance (usually with hired watchmen) to protect harvestable plants from theft by other islanders. In 2004, costs of establishing an acre of marijuana were about EC $1,000 (US $375), which included the use of some herbicides in the land clearing stages and nitrogen fertilizer after planting. Because weeding following the establishment of a cannabis field cannot easily be performed with chemical herbicides, marijuana is almost as labor-intensive as banana growing. A farm of two acres is likely to employ two or three full-time wage workers, who are typically paid about twice the prevailing rate of banana farm labor. Fields are cleared and planted in July for a September harvest. A second crop is later planted for an April harvest. Well-tended farms on relatively level lands can produce about 100 pounds of saleable marijuana leaves per acre per harvest. While marijuana sells on the street in Kingstown, St. Vincent, for about EC $400 (about US $150) per pound, it can fetch as much as US $1,500 per pound when sold in Martinique.

Experiencing a demise in banana production as great as that on St. Lucia, large numbers of displaced Vincentian banana farm workers, and to a lesser extent farmers themselves, established marijuana farms in the sparsely populated northern region of the island during the 1990s.[6] During this time, a series of events ultimately relating to US-supported drug eradication policies caused this formerly shadowy population to emerge as a cohesive and increasingly mobilized political constituency. Increased drug interdiction efforts by the US government raised the street price of drugs in the United States by the late 1980s, but this did not translate into lasting higher prices and profits for Caribbean producers. Rather, where marijuana was concerned, the primary effect of drug eradication in the Caribbean was to stimulate domestic production in the US. From being a net importer of marijuana until 1992, the United States has gone to being a net exporter, with production in California alone exceeding that of the entire Caribbean (Gettman 2006; NDIC 2005). By the early 1990s Caribbean marijuana growers had lost their most lucrative market, less from the successful interception of their drugs than from home-grown US competition. The demise of the US as a destination for the region's marijuana production was reflected in how St. Vincent's growers disposed of their harvests. By the end of the decade, an estimated 60 percent of the marijuana grown on St. Vincent was sold to buyers from other West Indian islands or European visitors, with most of the remainder consumed locally (Rubenstein 1999: 243). At present, almost no marijuana grown on the island leaves the Caribbean region, except for small amounts smuggled abroad by the occasional tourist returning home.

Much to the chagrin of Vincentian marijuana producers, throughout the 1990s Prime Minister James Mitchell and his New Democratic Party (NDP) closely collaborated with the US government in seeking to eradicate marijuana cultivation on the island. The last and most ambitious of these efforts, launched in November 1998 as "Operation Weedeater," allowed armed US personnel (among them Marines, drug enforcement agents, and Coast Guard members) free rein over the island, its airspace, and its adjacent waters. The operation also involved 122 military or police personnel from six other Caribbean nations (*The News* 1998c: 1). The primary method of eradication involved raids on marijuana-growing areas of the north, where teams of soldiers in Coast Guard Sea Knight helicopters were deployed to spray, uproot, or incinerate fields. By official reports, the three-month operation resulted in the destruction of over one million marijuana plants. The Vincentian government observed that few suspects were apprehended during the operation as the sound of approaching helicopters gave early warning, enabling growers to flee to safety. Other observers assert that the government was in fact reluctant to arrest growers because it feared the political fallout that would result from large numbers of prosecutions.[7]

Considering the thousands of Vincentians believed to be directly dependent on marijuana cultivation and sales for their livelihood, and the many more relying indirectly on their earnings, Mitchell's reasons for sponsoring three large-scale eradication efforts during the 1990s remain a matter of speculation. Rubenstein (1999: 234), an anthropologist residing on St. Vincent, argues that the upper middle-class and professional circles on which the prime minister counted for much of his political support seek to control marijuana use as a means of broader social control. The lighter-skinned, educated elites, whose influence in politics and the press is disproportionate to their actual numbers, regularly inveigh against marijuana use and its alleged psychological and social hazards, despite the equivocal nature of the evidence for their claims. Behind their promotion of greater penalties for its use, Rubenstein argues, is a desire to control a darker-skinned working-class segment of the population that they regard as shiftless, lazy, and criminally inclined. In short, the anti-marijuana crusade in which the prime minister took part was one with strong racial and social class overtones.

Mitchell's zeal for eradication was probably intended as well to placate an even more powerful constituency, the US government. In part to quell the anger of the Black Congressional Caucus and critical Caribbean émigré voter bases in New York and Florida over its WTO action, the Clinton administration promised increased economic aid to the region to offset its loss of EU banana preferences. Such aid was conditional on governmental cooperation in US anti-drug efforts. Hence, to qualify for the promised assistance for island residents displaced from banana production, all four Windward governments were compelled to take action against many of those who had been displaced. Perhaps sensing an opportunity to claim an increased share of economic assistance, Mitchell collaborated with the US drug eradication efforts more ardently than most regional leaders. Yet satisfying the demands of his upper-class supporters and the US government came at a steep political cost for the Vincentian prime minister.

Not all influential segments of the island's population supported eradication. Many of the island's business owners, including the president of the St. Vincent Chamber of Commerce, recognized that a large part of their retail sales depended on the earnings of those who grew and sold marijuana (Rubenstein 1999: 246). Virtually alone among members of the press, the publisher of *The Vincentian* newspaper excoriated the government for destroying livelihoods without providing even part-time jobs as alternatives, arguing that in the vacuum created by marijuana eradication residents were turning to cocaine trafficking instead (Rubenstein 1999: 233). Even more unprecedented were direct lobbying and public protests by marijuana growers themselves, who had previously been hesitant to identify themselves in public. When Operation Weedeater was announced, hundreds of island residents organized a coalition calling itself the Committee of Concerned Citizens and Ganja Farmers to oppose the eradication plan (*The News* 1998a: 1). In a letter addressed to President Clinton, the committee called for a cessation of the US-sponsored program, "which will only bring added hardship and endless miseries on our people" (*The News* 1998b: 4). Years later, Junior "Spirit" Cottle, a former leader of the movement, recalled that the committee received a great deal of support from an island population weary of anti-drug efforts that seemed to bring more problems in their wake. According to Cottle, after each of three major eradication drives during the 1990s the island experienced a spike in criminality and cocaine use. "People still have to make a living, and if they can't grow marijuana and sell it, some of them start to sell cocaine," Cottle asserted.

> And then, there are persons who use marijuana as their recreation, when that becomes more scarce, they may experiment with another drug. And normally with harder drugs there's more craving, you know crack cocaine is much more addictive and much more expensive than marijuana, and so you find there's more stealing. It becomes a vicious cycle. So we wrote a letter to the prime minister and tried to meet with him, but he wouldn't meet with us, because we were involved in illegal activities. But mainly, yes we were opposed to eradication, but we were also looking for legal alternatives. And the public responded very well. You'll find there were people in the business community, in the Chamber

of Commerce, who supported us. They provided some funding for our move-ment, they provided food and transportation for meetings. Because they know that marijuana provided a lot of their livelihood indirectly. And they saw what happened each time there was eradication. (Cottle, pers. comm. 2004)

Alongside the social problems that arose in the wake of eradication, newer environmental issues were also becoming apparent. Although some growers whose fields were destroyed by eradication were permanently dissuaded from drug production, most planned to resume after the pres-ent cycle of eradication drew to a close. When growers reestablished their fields, they deliberately planted on steep slopes where helicopters would find it impossible to touch down during future raids. These areas were prone to soil erosion after clearing and planting, which was in turn aggra-vated by later eradication efforts. By the time of Operation Weedeater in 1998, the relocation of marijuana farms to steep hillsides had indeed made helicopters less effective in directly delivering troops to marijuana farms. Eradication personnel were inconvenienced but not entirely impeded by these planting practices. When military personnel ultimately did de-stroy farms on steep hillsides, severe sheet erosion resulted. One discern-ible effect of this was siltation of streams and degradation of watersheds throughout the northern third of the island.

The committee's concerns about the untold costs of eradication policy were conveyed in print by a few sympathetic reporters and editors at the island's newspapers. Juxtaposed with these concerns, the prime minister's continued unwillingness to meet with the committee made him appear oblivious to a looming social and environmental crisis. Moreover, Mitchell's rebuff had the unintended effect of turning the eradication efforts into a partisan political issue. Opposition politicians with the United Labour Party (ULP) were quick to fill this void by meeting with committee repre-sentatives and endorsing an end to marijuana eradication. The ULP leader Dr. Ralph Gonsalves, a white Vincentian of upper middle-class Portuguese background, publicly expressed his empathy for the "ganja men" affected by eradication efforts. He even addressed committee rallies clad in dashikis and the red, green, black, and gold colors by which Rastafarians identify themselves. As Gonsalves cultivated a close working relationship with the coalition representing the island's marijuana growers, small businesspeo-ple, and others disenchanted with Mitchell's pro-US policies, it became apparent that the tide was shifting against the NDP government. Few islanders were surprised when Gonsalves and the ULP swept to power in the 2001 elections. Notwithstanding the multifaceted makeup of the anti-NDP vote, most observers on and off the island credit the organized efforts of marijuana growers against the US-supported eradication effort as the catalyst that forced Mitchell's pro-US government out of office.

Since the election of the ULP government, the Committee of Concerned Citizens and Ganja Farmers has seen some of its recommendations incorporated into public policy. Although marijuana cultivation and possession remain nominally illegal on St. Vincent, the ULP government has ended eradication programs in the northern part of the island and ceased to enforce laws barring marijuana possession for personal use. Incorporating former committee leader Junior Cottle into a government post as its liaison with marijuana growers, the ULP administration developed an integrated forest management program designed to shift cultivation away from easily eroded hillsides and critical watershed areas. Marijuana growers were thus officially recognized by the new government as "stakeholders" in the crafting of agricultural and conservation policy, an unprecedented position for illegal drug producers to hold in any Caribbean society. Cottle describes part of his charge as the promotion of alternative (legal) livelihoods among marijuana growers, in large part because of the increasing dangers to which participants in the drug trade are exposed and the violence with which it has become associated. But in an interview he was somewhat short on specific alternatives available to island drug producers seeking other options.

For its part, the Gonsalves government has won some admiration among nationalists throughout the region for its assertiveness vis-à-vis the US government and the Bush administration in particular. Among its first actions was an order indefinitely suspending all government cooperation with United States military anti-drug operations on the island. St. Vincent also made headlines as one of a handful of regional governments that rejected the Bush administration's effort to exempt US soldiers and other nationals from the jurisdiction of the International Criminal Court, despite considerable pressure placed on Latin American and Caribbean leaders by the US State Department and even Bush himself.[8] The US administration was quick to retaliate for this decision by cutting off all "security" assistance for the St. Vincent government, a figure amounting to about US $300,000 per year (*The Mirror* 2003: 1). In a gesture that must have triggered a gratifying spell of schadenfreude throughout the region, the Gonsalves government responded that US security assistance had been formerly used for anti-drug enforcement programs on the island, most of which would now be suspended as a result of Washington's decision.

The Triangle Trade

With their linguistic ability to straddle the British and French West Indies, St. Lucians are culturally well-positioned to engage in smuggling between the regions. Geographically they occupy a similarly optimal space between drug growers in St. Vincent and buyers in Martinique. With favorable seas, St. Vincent can be reached within two hours by speedboat from Vieux Fort, and by the following afternoon a trafficker can dispose of his inventory to customers in Fort-de-France. For reasons that are not entirely clear, St. Lucia's Mabouya Valley has acquired a region-wide reputation as the base for those who control the drug trade between the neighboring islands. The ability of some valley residents to monopolize the trade despite its obvious economic attractions to outsiders rests on their continuous use or threat of violence against newcomers. Within the valley itself, what began as an attempt by younger men to offset their declining fortunes in the banana industry has had further disintegrating effects in a community already torn by conflicting loyalties over the Banana Salvation Committee, anti-government protests in the early 1990s, and the partisan distribution of government anti-poverty aid since then. Only with the passage of time, the incarceration of the smugglers with the most violent reputations, and the gradual ebbing of the crack cocaine epidemic they enabled have some of these wounds begun to heal. Yet a brisk trade in marijuana and cocaine continues between St. Vincent and Martinique to this day, most of it said to be in the hands of young men from the Mabouya Valley.

According to long-term residents, the use and sale of marijuana in the Mabouya Valley goes back at least to the 1960s, with most of the drug grown clandestinely in forest reserve lands remote from the main areas of banana cultivation. For decades, sales and use of the drug were limited to the local area and some of its younger men, many coming to identify themselves as Rastafarians during the 1970s and 1980s. By all accounts, the valley's involvement in the inter-island drug trade did not begin until 1992–93. At that time, as farm employment contracted for the first time in three decades, young men who had formerly worked in the banana industry began leaving for extended travel to the neighboring islands, most apparently to seek wage opportunities. Their absences at first elicited only speculation, but the illicit purposes of some migrants were soon betrayed by fancy clothes, jewelry, and then their acquisition of vehicles and houses far beyond the reach of any local banana worker. Although the more cautious among them attempted to conceal the source of their earnings, not a few boasted of the profits to be made selling drugs in Martinique or of narrow scrapes with police patrols at sea. Before long, when local men announced that they were leaving for St. Vincent, this was recognized throughout the valley as shorthand for an impending drug deal. As Patricia Mathurin, a teacher in the La Ressource elementary school recalled, "One young man, I hadn't seen him for quite some time, and then he showed up, wearing some nice clothes and lots of gold—what do they call it, bling bling? I asked him where he had been, and he said St. Vincent and Martinique. I didn't have to ask him anything else" (pers. comm. 2004).

By the mid 1990s, approximately forty men from the Mabouya Valley were known to be vying with one another to supply the Martinican market with marijuana they purchased or grew themselves on the north coast of St. Vincent. Competition with one another and with traffickers from other islands was already beginning to drive down prices and to cause conflict among dealers. The potential profits and dangers of trafficking increased dramatically as cocaine entered the trade during the first major marijuana eradication program in St. Vincent. Men were soon returning from their travels with not only expensive clothing and jewelry, but also handguns to intimidate rivals or to protect themselves while at sea. As the value of the trade increased, the extended passage from St. Vincent to Martinique became an especially hazardous part of the circuit between islands. "Pirates" in fast boats occasionally lay in wait along St. Lucia's leeward coast to overtake other traffickers and rob them of their drugs or earnings, after which they were usually killed. Seeking an alternative to the increasingly crowded and dangerous Martinican drug trade, in 1995 some traffickers introduced crack cocaine into the valley, where people had little prior experience with cocaine or any other drugs with physically addictive properties. As in US neighborhoods ravaged by the drug, crack fueled a local epidemic of burglary, hold-ups, and prostitution as addicts sought all available means to supply their habits. Even more ominously, by 1997 two rival gangs had organized to fight for control of the Mabouya Valley's drug trade and for access to the Martinican market. Recalling that time, valley residents say that they regularly heard gunfire in the evening, while morning's light revealed the victims of gang-related shootings strewn along roadsides or dumped in banana fields.

"Water House" and "Forty Foot," Mabouya Valley gangs named for a local rum shop and foot bridge that marked the centers of their territories, were comprised mostly of what are locally referred to as "school leavers," teens who had dropped out of school before the legal minimum of Standard Six (eighth grade). Valley residents report that most gang members grew up in "barrel households" with no parental supervision. In the absence of family role models, they say, younger gang members emulated the now very wealthy men in their twenties who had pioneered the drug trade several years before. Armed by the gang leaders, a group of twelve men largely responsible for the local crack trade, young men vied for a share of drug profits by threatening, assaulting, and occasionally killing their counterparts in rival gangs. For these actions, leaders rewarded their followers with cash or, more commonly, drugs to sell on their own. The gangs' territories met in an area between the settlements of Belmont and Deniere Riviere, a zone that became known as "the Gulf" where gun-fire was frequently exchanged between gang partisans.[9] While the largest number of shootings occurred among gang members, Patricia Mathurin notes that over the years several bystanders were also wounded and killed in their crossfire. When members of rival gangs unexpectedly encountered each other at local social events, they invariably clashed and frequently exchanged shots. As recently as 2002, a barbecue organized for teens in one of the valley settlements ended in the shooting death of an innocent bystander. In 2004, Mathurin recounted her daughter's harrowing escape from that event:

> Just two years ago, Jasmine, my 17-year-old daughter at the time, she was at a dance sponsored by one of the social clubs. Well, a young man there saw somebody from the other gang, and just like that, without any words or any warning, the guns come out and they start shooting. My daughter was terrified. As soon as she run from there she see some of the Water House controlling that road from the Community Centre. When she turn, she see some of the Forty Foot come from the other direction. She and her friends, well, they finally escape into a banana farm and make their way to another road and come on home that way. Mind you it was dark that night, and her friend fall in a ditch and twist her ankle bad. Even so, we don't dare take her to the doctor until morning. That was the last time my Jasmine gone out to any event here at night. Two years ago. Now I ask you, what kind of a way is that to live, like a prisoner in your own house? (Pers. comm. 2004)

The demise of the crack epidemic, killing of gang leaders at the hands of their rivals, and incarceration of others have caused much gang activity and organized violence in the valley to ebb since 2003. Most of the leaders responsible for the local crack trade in the 1990s are now dead or behind bars (to the readily admitted relief of many valley residents), while several others are known to have migrated to New York. The large majority of incarcerated drug dealers are serving their prison terms in Martinique or France. Fr. Laurent, whose sister serves as St. Lucia's consul to Martinique, asserts that that island's prison is filled with valley men arrested on the island, the majority of them for drug trafficking. "Whenever the police arrest a man from St. Lucia, she is the first to find out," Fr. Laurent stated. "She tells me about our young men in prison over there because I know a lot of them. You know, regardless of where they end up, most of them were babies that I baptized in this church." Beyond this anecdotal evidence, it is difficult to identify the specific places of origin of St. Lucians incarcerated on French territory. However, a former diplomatic source claims that more than half of Martinique's prison population is of St. Lucian origin, and that "90 percent of the St. Lucian prisoners jailed in the French colony are ones who have been displaced by the banana industry" (Weekes 2004: 5).

If open gang warfare in the valley has largely subsided, residents still encounter unsettling evidence of the everyday violence used to maintain control over the drug trade. Every few months, a dead body appears in the valley showing signs of mutilation or point-blank execution. Even the island's usually sensationalist press appears to have grown numb to this drumbeat of casual violence, relegating most drug-related murders (especially those in rural areas) to the back pages. The victims of most killings today are reportedly men who cheated or in some way defied the traffickers for whom they once worked, many killed for seemingly petty transgressions. In an especially gruesome case that made it to the newspapers' front pages in 2004, a mentally disabled man from the valley was hideously tortured and left to die along an isolated roadside in Belmont. "They hit him over and over again with a two by four that had nails driven through it," Fr. Laurent shook his head sadly. "By the time they finished with him, the poor man looked like hamburger." Discovered the next day by valley residents who transported him to Castries, the man expired after eight agonizing days in the hospital. His offense was reportedly the theft of less than an ounce of marijuana from a dealer. Like the prison terms now experienced by the high-flying traffickers of a decade ago, such killings advertise the dangers of the drug trade to potential newcomers. These hazards, valley residents are quick to point out, do not discourage many among the valley's large number of young men without jobs or other prospects from seeking their own share in it.

Notes

1. "Employment" is meant in the broadest sense, as many Mabouya Valley residents are engaging in smuggling rather than wage-based livelihoods.
2. The facile explanation occasionally offered for terrorist attacks directed against the United States, i.e., that "they hate us for our freedom," precludes a critical examination into the US actions abroad that generate such furious responses. Islamic scholar Ebrahim Moosa identified the dilemmas facing US citizens who think critically about US policies and the responses they generate elsewhere in the world: "The irony is that most Americans think they are moral yet remain unconcerned about the immoral way their government exercises power. That's what I find hardest to understand: the level of self-delusion that Americans allow themselves. Then again, I suppose that if Americans really thought about what their government is doing, they might go crazy" (quoted in Bremer 2006: 12).
3. Many islanders distinguish between adherents of Rastafarianism and those who simply adopt the symbols associated with it as a matter of style (i.e., dreadlocks, clothing in Rastafarian colors, reggae music, and marijuana use). Many will also offer some guarded praise for "legitimate" Rastafarians, who are "people of peace," while dis-

tinguishing them from a much larger group of "Rastaphonians" who are "rascals and criminals," in the words of an older informant.

4. One exception to this is Barbados, where a relatively high standard of living and large expatriate British population create a drug market almost as lucrative as that of Martinique.

5. The term *ganja*, by which all sectors of Caribbean society refer to marijuana, is of Hindi origin.

6. Some farmers on St. Lucia and St. Vincent admit to cultivating both bananas and marijuana, but never in the same field. Marijuana is always grown in remote, inaccessible places to diminish the possibility of detection by authorities and crop theft by other islanders. Moreover, growing marijuana on banana farms runs the risk of easy detection (given their comparatively accessible location) and loss of both legal and illicit crops through eradication.

7. In a belated effort to stave off defeat at the polls in 2001, even the NDP government, which favored eradication, stopped enforcing laws against possession and use of marijuana.

8. Such exemptions would prevent the prosecution of US nationals, including members of the armed forces, who are indicted for human rights abuses committed in other countries. At a White House luncheon for leaders from the Eastern Caribbean prior to a critical UN vote on the matter, Prime Minister Gonsalves was conspicuously absent from the guest list (*The Voice* 2003e: 9).

9. This name alluded to the Persian Gulf, site of the 1991 Iraq war, because of the warlike conditions that prevailed there.

— *Chapter Nine* —

FAIR TRADE IN DISCOURSE
AND PRACTICE

[L]abor and land are no other than the human beings themselves of which every society consists and the natural surroundings in which it exists. To include them in the market mechanism means to subordinate the substance of society itself to the laws of the market.
— Karl Polanyi, *The Great Transformation* (1944)

The Fair Trade Paradox

If the growth in the drug trade and related violence represent the grim underside of neoliberal globalization in the Caribbean, other local responses to the banana industry's decline may offset its corrosive effects for farmers and the communities in which they live. Since 2000, when it was widely believed that the WTO ruling would prove the death knell for farmers already battered by the Single European Market and rising production costs, Caribbean banana growers and European consumers have embraced an new market initiative not guided by the principle of global price competition. As defined by a coalition of European organizations involved in what has become known as "alternative trade,"

> Fair Trade is a trading partnership, based on dialogue, transparency, and respect, that seeks greater equity in international trade. It contributes to sustainable development by offering better trading conditions to, and securing the rights of, marginalized producers and workers – especially in the South. Fair Trade organizations (backed by consumers) are engaged actively in supporting producers, awareness raising, and in campaigning for changes in the rules and practice of conventional trade. (Quoted in Moore 2004: 73)

By selling bananas grown and labeled as certified Fair Trade produce, Windward Islands farmers receive a higher price than they would for conventional fruit. In addition to higher returns to the grower, a portion of the box price of all Fair Trade bananas is returned to farming communities to support local development projects designed by farmers themselves. Consumers pay appreciably more for certified Fair Trade fruit than for the cheaper bananas grown on Latin American plantations. Yet they do so with the stated assurance that their purchase helps to sustain small-scale farmers, their communities, and the environment through certified agricultural practices that limit chemical use and maintain watersheds. Discursively, Fair Trade redefines the relationship between producer and consumer as one that is personal and reciprocal, in which both parties benefit by making ethical decisions about production and consumption. Its advocates in the developed world view Fair Trade as one of the most significant contemporary alternatives to a global trading system in which multinational corporations regularly engage in socially and environmentally destructive practices.

Many advocates of free markets and unfettered global trade felt vindicated by history after the collapse of Soviet communism in 1990 and the demise of centrally planned economies in all but a few remaining enclaves. But their heady optimism must have been tempered by the ensuing years, which have witnessed a worldwide proliferation of grassroots movements opposing the spread of free market capitalism. By and large, anti-globalization movements have not sought to resurrect bureaucratic socialism. Rather, they assert the causes of social justice and local traditions in the face of neoliberal trade policies that have resulted in growing unemployment, declining wages, landlessness, and the dismantling of social safety nets throughout the global economy. Because anti-globalization movements are so strongly rooted in local concerns, these efforts have been highly diverse in their composition and strategies. Institutions heavily associated with neoliberal trade doctrines, specifically the IMF, WTO, and Group of Eight (G-8) developed nations, have drawn the most vigorous forms of public opposition, prompting tumultuous demonstrations involving tens of thousands of participants in locales as disparate as Seattle, Genoa, and Buenos Aires.

In the less developed countries, the role of these institutions in shaping national economies has prompted a wide range of political responses, many of which have either forced national governments from power or compelled them to modify their debt repayment and trade policies. Public protests against IMF-sponsored structural adjustment programs, which entail steep increases in both the cost of living and unemployment, became commonplace in heavily indebted countries during the 1980s and 1990s.

Many of the initial public demonstrations against structural adjustment were uncoordinated, spontaneous, and often destructive of private property, giving rise to the term "IMF riots" (Edelman 1999). When channeled into electoral politics, however, widespread indignation at structural adjustment and free market policies later helped anti-debt activists assume power in Brazil, Argentina, Bolivia, and elsewhere, and has added to the allure of leaders who, like Venezuela's Hugo Chavez, advocate a more equitable international economic order. In southern Mexico, opposition to neoliberal policies embodied in the North American Free Trade Agreement (NAFTA) has fueled the ongoing Zapatista uprising, which draws heavily on the grievances of indigenous farmers displaced by cheap agricultural imports from the US. Clearly, then, the waning of Marxism-Leninism as an official political and economic doctrine in most of the world has not been accompanied, as some political conservatives had triumphantly predicted (e.g., Fukuyama 1992), by an unquestioned acceptance of the free market as the most desirable mechanism for the satisfaction of human needs.

In all their manifestations, the movements and constituencies opposed to the effects of globalization have framed local concerns in broader moral, political, and economic terms. Hence, European environmentalists, farmers, food safety advocates, and even chefs and restaurateurs have combined forces to challenge the importation of genetically modified crops and food additives promoted by global agribusiness. In 1996, Pope John Paul II called on wealthy countries to forgive the developing world's foreign debt, invoking biblical injunctions against taking advantage of the destitute and oppressed. In response, people of faith belonging to many denominations worldwide organized the Jubilee Campaign[1] to pressure Western governments and the IMF to cancel the debt burdens of the world's poorest countries, a movement that has resulted in significant cancellation in some cases. While not rejecting public protest as a means of expressing grievances, food safety and anti-debt coalitions have relied much more heavily on political lobbying, editorial and letter writing campaigns, and internet-based organizing to effect change. With its reliance on private consumer choice in retail purchasing, Fair Trade remains relatively diffuse compared to these more formally orchestrated strategies, let alone to large-scale demonstrations and pleas for social justice by world religious leaders. Nonetheless, as measured by the number of commodities that it now embraces and its annual double-digit percentage increases in worldwide sales, Fair Trade has become arguably the fastest-growing segment of the anti-globalization movement.

Yet for all its recent growth, in several respects Fair Trade occupies an anomalous place among contemporary social movements. It is distinct from all other anti-globalization efforts in its reliance on individual consumer choice rather than collective experience or concerted political action. In the absence of ongoing relationships between its participants, other than market relations mediated by Fair Trade organizations, some have questioned whether Fair Trade could even be considered a social movement in the first place (Creed 2006; Fisher 2007; see also Edelman 2001). Apart from such semantic issues, a greater paradox arises from its underlying assumptions about effecting social change through consumer behavior. Unlike all other anti-globalization movements, which to a greater or lesser degree challenge the underlying assumptions of market economics, Fair Trade attempts to marshal market forces against the market's own logic of global price competition. As one recent analysis points out, Fair Trade's "voluntarist, non-statist program has been viewed by public institutions and corporations as being fundamentally compatible with neoliberal reforms" (Fridell 2007: 21); indeed, market-based Fair Trade has been encouraged by the World Bank as an alternative to government-based commodity control schemes and labor standards (Fridell 2007: 4). How, then, is political action based on consumer choice in the market to be understood relative to other forms of anti-globalization politics? Most importantly, does Fair Trade pose a genuine challenge to a longstanding global trading system that has historically benefited Western consumers and corporations at the expense of producers in the developing world?

Given Fair Trade's meteoric rise in the marketplace over the short span of a decade, it may be too early to answer the latter question. As will be seen in the next chapter, the experiences of Mabouya Valley farmers thus far suggest that Fair Trade's capacity for fundamentally changing the global commodity trading system may be overstated. For all the tangible benefits provided by Fair Trade, a substantial rift exists between the movement's promises to consumers in the developed countries and its reality for producers on the ground. Further, just as other social movements have been gradually co-opted by the very forces that they initially opposed, the threat of co-optation by global corporations is especially pronounced for a movement relying exclusively on consumer choice as a mechanism for social change.

A Postmodern Social Movement?

Relatively inconspicuous beside mass political protests and electoral victories by anti-globalization forces, the Fair Trade movement seeks to quietly challenge global agribusiness on the market's own terms. Despite its recent dramatic growth, the movement is less novel than its proponents might suggest, for consumer buying power has long been used as a mechanism to force changes in business practices and government policies.² Throughout the twentieth century, boycotts and "Buy Union" campaigns were widely adopted by organized labor to either punish firms that suppressed unions or patronize those that recognized them. In a sense, Fair Trade applies similar strategies to international commerce in artisanal goods and tropical agricultural commodities, which have often been subject to discriminatory pricing by a few "middleman" corporations that controlled their sale in the developed nations. The contemporary Fair Trade movement grew out of several initiatives in Europe and North America as early as the 1940s that sought to redefine the terms on which small-scale producers in the developing countries sold their goods to consumers in the developed North.³ In contrast to the priorities of profit maximization that motivate agribusiness corporations, Fair Trade organizations approach the marketing of such commodities as a means of sustainable development. They do so by promoting goods produced by family farmers, cooperatives, and ethically run businesses as certified Fair Trade products, while refusing to certify items produced by firms that engage in unfair pricing, labor repression, child labor, ethnic or gender discrimination, or environmental destruction.

In their early years, Fair Trade efforts in Europe operated through international aid NGOs such as OXFAM in the United Kingdom and SOS-Kinderhof in the Netherlands, while in North America the Ten Thousand Villages initiative was closely affiliated with Mennonite churches. These initial Fair Trade efforts involved the direct marketing of handicrafts and textiles from artisans in developing countries to consumers in the developed North. By averting the middlemen and traditional retailers who had previously appropriated much of the market price for handicrafts, alternative trade organizations provided artisans with higher returns for their products. In the US, the marketing of food and beverages along Fair Trade lines accelerated in close conjunction with the Central American solidarity and non-intervention movements of the 1980s. The most prominent of these initiatives, Equal Exchange, developed direct marketing relationships with Nicaraguan coffee cooperatives to offset the Reagan administration's trade embargo against the Sandinista revolutionary government.

Since their inception, these and other US Fair Trade groups have focused on mail-order and online systems of distribution, although recently they have expanded their sales to coffeehouses and other retail businesses in larger US cities. In contrast, three European alternative trade organizations, TransFair, Max Havelaar, and Fairtrade Mark, were already promoting Fair Trade products in conventional supermarkets by the late 1980s. Over the following decade, Fair Trade labeling initiatives proliferated in seventeen nations of Europe, North America and Japan, each geared to their respective national markets. In 1997, all of these organizations sought to coordinate their efforts with the creation of an umbrella group, the Fairtrade Labeling Organizations International (FLO), which is based in Bonn, Germany. FLO is responsible for formulating consistent certification standards for Fair Trade products among its member organizations and creating a unified retail market through labeling and promotional efforts (Raynolds 2000). To promote a recognizable presence in the retail market, in 2002 FLO introduced a standardized green and black Fair Trade logo for display on the packaging of all products that it certifies.

Embedded in FLO's Fair Trade logo on products in English-speaking countries are the words "Fair Trade guarantees a better deal for producers." Growers of FLO-certified Fair Trade goods receive prices above world market averages for their crops, which at a minimum are supposed to cover farmers' costs of production. In addition, Fair Trade producers generate a "social premium," or a monetary rebate corresponding to the amount of goods that they sell under the FLO label. These earnings are returned to the producers' association to which the farmer belongs and are invested in community projects devised by the association itself. In exchange for FLO certification, producers must satisfy standards for social and environmental sustainability. By 2006, FLO had established certification standards for producers of coffee, tea, cacao, bananas, a wide array of other fresh fruit and vegetables, sugar, honey, orange juice, wine, spun cotton, and cut flowers, as well as manufactured goods such as sports balls.

To receive Fair Trade certification small-scale farmers must belong to democratically run producers' associations or formal cooperatives. Alternately, if Fair Trade products are grown or manufactured on commercial farms and businesses, workers employed by them must be represented by independent unions or other workers' organizations. Fair Trade producers are required to abide by the United Nations' International Labor Organization (ILO) standards, which uphold rights to free association, freedom from discrimination, prohibition of child or involuntary labor, and workplace safety. They must also adhere to agronomic practices that minimize the impact of farming on watersheds, top soils, and the overall environment (Murray and Raynolds 2000). In general, Fair Trade farmers must refrain from using most chemical herbicides and nematicides, minimize the application of a narrow range of approved farm chemicals, and maintain uncultivated buffer zones adjacent to waterways. Compliance with these criteria is assessed by independent monitors engaged by FLO's certification branch (FLO CERT) to conduct periodic "social audits" onsite among producers' groups.

In the United States, Fair Trade sales are still largely limited to coffee, tea, chocolate, and handicrafts (rather than fresh produce), most of which remain available only through coffeehouses, co-ops, and online retailers. Some large regional supermarket chains in the US, such as Whole Foods, have recently increased their inventory of Fair Trade products. In contrast, Fair Trade items have been a staple in European supermarket chains for more than a decade, largely thanks to FLO's promotional efforts. Recent years have witnessed an explosive growth in the range and quantity of Fair Trade products consumed in the developed countries, with North America now the fastest-growing overall market, despite Fair Trade's limited penetration into US supermarket sales. By 2005, Fair Trade certification had been extended to 508 producers' groups or firms in fifty-eight countries, an increase of 127 percent in four years (FLO 2006: 11). The same time period saw a 132 percent increase in the number of importers registered with Fair Trade organizations, to 1,483 firms worldwide in 2005 (FLO 2006: 11). By 2005, the volume of Fair Trade sales in the developed world reached US $1.45 billion, a nearly fivefold increase in just three years (FLO 2006: 12; FLO 2004). Global Fair Trade sales increased another 42 percent in the following year (FLO 2007: 11). On a per capita basis, Switzerland and the United Kingdom represent the largest Fair Trade markets; these two countries combined account for 34 percent of Fair Trade retail sales worldwide (FLO 2007: 12). In 2006, annual per capita Fair Trade sales in the UK reached US $9.19, well behind Switzerland's $25.67 but more than four times their level in the United States (FLO 2007: 11).[4]

In the United Kingdom and most European countries, Fair Trade enjoys a retail and advertising profile far exceeding its public prominence among US consumers. By 2003, Fair Trade products comprised about 15 percent of all imported bananas, tea, coffee, and cocoa entering the UK in that year, with importers aiming ultimately at 30 percent of the retail market for such items (Hoggarth, pers. comm. 2003).[5] More than a thousand items bearing Fair Trade certification, ranging from mangos and chocolate bars to cotton socks, may now be purchased in the UK, most of them in conventional retail supermarkets. In addition to prominently featuring Fair Trade items on their shelves, most British supermarket chains heavily promote their commitment to Fair Trade principles on company websites as a measure of their social responsibility (e.g., Tesco 2006; Sainsbury's 2006; Marks and Spencer 2006). When the UK and US governments found themselves on opposite sides of the banana trade war, British retailers exhorted consumers to express solidarity with the former British West Indies by purchasing Fair Trade Windward Islands bananas. In addition to its prominent place in stores and on company websites, Fair Trade has been the subject of ongoing national promotional campaigns in the British mass media. In association with the Fair Trade Foundation, the UK affiliate of FLO, UK retailers have held annual "Fair Trade Fortnights" since 1994. Each two week–long advertising blitz is held in conjunction with community- and nationwide events to promote awareness of Fair Trade principles and encourage British consumers to sample a range of Fair Trade products. These events, which include essay and recipe contests and educational campaigns, are intended, according to one retail representative, to "create a Fair Trade community organized around the principle of ethical buying" (Hoggarth, pers. comm. 2003).

Born of the same anger at deepening global poverty that has motivated protests against the IMF and WTO, the Fair Trade movement has turned not to the streets but to the private realm of consumer choice as the arena of political action. In its early guises Fair Trade retained explicitly oppositional qualities, especially by its association with revolutionary movements in Central America and southern Africa. Given its initially low levels of sales, Fair Trade remained largely a symbolic political gesture until the movement's entry into the retail supermarket trade within the last decade. Since then Fair Trade products, in Europe at least, have quickly matured into a distinct niche market within a dizzying array of retail choices.

The supermarket prices of Fair Trade items compared to their conventional counterparts, ranging from 65 percent higher in the case of coffee to at least 100 percent higher for fresh produce in the UK, ensure that the most consistent Fair Trade consumers are also likely to be comparatively affluent. Produce managers for several British supermarkets interviewed in 2003 confirmed that Fair Trade sales are much more robust in upper middle-class neighborhoods and among educated professionals than in chain stores in working-class areas. They attributed this increased effective demand to the greater disposable income among affluent consumers as well as their putatively greater "health-consciousness" in food-buying decisions. In its reliance upon consumer preference in upscale suburban supermarkets, Fair Trade might be characterized as the quintessential postmodern social movement—one that is private, consumption-based, and overwhelmingly market-driven. Efforts to create a Fair Trade "community" through promotional campaigns such as Fair Trade Fortnights and municipal declarations of support do not alter the fact that participation in these events is secondary to their main purpose: encouraging greater purchases of Fair Trade–branded items. All that Fair Trade ultimately demands of its supporters in the way of political engagement is conscientious retail choice, a relatively risk-free gesture for consumers with higher than average levels of disposable income.

In this sense, the embrace of Fair Trade products by mainstream supermarkets could be seen as one facet of the "flexible accumulation" that has emerged in the developed countries in recent decades, a process that Harvey (1989: 141ff.) identifies as an economic hallmark of the condition of postmodernity. Between the immediate postwar period and the mid 1970s, Western economies were organized on the basis of "Fordist" mass consumption of standardized products geared to working- and middle-class consumers. The process of flexible accumulation that has arisen since then has been marked by a proliferation of higher-priced product lines and specialized niche markets. These new consumer choices cater to the upwardly mobile minority in the developed countries that has benefited from economic restructuring involving the decline of manufacturing industries and rise of financial and information sectors. For manufacturers, niche marketing to the comparatively affluent under flexible accumulation helps to offset the declining effective demand of much of the North American and European working class, which finds its employment and economic status increasingly precarious (Harvey 1989: 179). In a similar vein, the marketing of relatively expensive "specialty coffees" in the 1990s (once known as "yuppie coffees") sought to reverse a long-term drop in per capita coffee consumption and the resulting loss of earnings for coffee roasters (Roseberry 1996). Coffee was the first agricultural commodity to be widely marketed as a Fair Trade product, and it remains the most readily available Fair Trade item in North America. From its formerly marginal position in mail-order and internet sales, Fair Trade coffee now occupies a significant retail niche within the array of other "high-end" coffees available for purchase by comparatively privileged consumers.

Much of the appeal of Fair Trade, and no doubt a major reason for its phenomenal growth, is its capacity to engage a newfound sense of consumer agency. In an influential essay on the global cultural economy, Appadurai writes that a critical facet of postmodern marketing is the "fetishism of the consumer ... [who] is consistently helped to believe that he or she is an actor, where in fact he or she is at best a chooser" (1990: 307). Niche marketing draws upon this illusion of choice by creating a multiplicity of brands and retail commodities, each superficially differentiated by packaging and minor product details. Each, in turn, is targeted at selected demographic groups whose personal identities (including their political beliefs) increasingly center on the goods they consume (Klein 2000). Lyon identifies the appeal of certified shade grown coffee to environmentally-minded shoppers in precisely such terms, for "the dominant *modus operandi* of identity construction has become our 'lifestyle,' which we shape through our choices as sovereign consumers" (2006: 380). The "branding" of personal identities and beliefs through an ever-proliferating array of products and transitory fashions belies a continuing tendency toward the consolidation of wholesale and retail markets in the hands of fewer and fewer corporations. From the belief, however illusory, that individuals can transform their social identities through branded consumption, it is but a short logical step to the conclusion that as consumers they can also transform the condition of society. Or, as the advertisement for an English Fair Trade chocolate bar succinctly encourages buyers, "shopping can change the world!" (Dubble 2006).

Yet against the claims of Appadurai and other theorists who have examined the relationship between postmodern culture and economy since the 1970s, the very premises of the Fair Trade movement also herald a break with the postmodern condition, at least as they initially characterized it. As Harvey (1989) outlined in his far-reaching if humbly subtitled "enquiry into the origins of cultural change," the production, transportation and marketing innovations of recent decades have massively transformed the nature of consumption in the developed countries. The post-Fordist consumer comes into contact with an unprecedented array of commodities whose points of origin differ radically in space and time. Supermarkets once stocked with a limited array of slightly differentiated products now permit a vicarious sampling of many exotic cultures and geographies. Yet these products are marketed to the consumer "in such a way as to conceal almost perfectly any trace … of the labor processes that produced them, or of the social relations implicated in their production" (Harvey 1989: 300). Mediated by market and advertising, then, the consumer's relationship to those who actually produce the commodities filling retail shelves is viewed as one of emotional detachment. Where producers are featured in product advertising, they are typically represented in highly idealized ways that further obscure the actual conditions of production. Hence the romanticized figure of Juan Valdez used to market Colombian coffee effaced the desperately low earnings and endemic political violence experienced by small-scale coffee growers in that country.[6]

Harvey described the end result of this process as a sort of alienation on a global scale, as if the postmodern celebration of consumer choice drowned out the pleas of poor farmers and child workers whose labor made such choices possible in the first place. Appadurai concurred that the unprecedented spatial dispersion of production and consumption "generates alienation (in Marx's sense) twice intensified, for its social sense is now compounded by a complicated spatial dynamic which is increasingly global" (1990: 307). Other analyses, identifying postmodern sentiments and aesthetics as the "cultural logic" of late capitalism, reached a similar conclusion from the endpoint of the commodity chain. The mass consumption of items grown and manufactured under repressive and inhumane conditions requires, as Jameson put it, a "mass effacement of the traces of production" (1991: 314). How else, he asked, could the individual enjoy the self-indulgent experiences upon which capitalism depended if continually reminded of the injustices implicated in the very act of consumption? In like fashion, the mass media's celebration of the upwardly mobile during the 1980s and 1990s required the "disappearance" of the unemployed, homeless, and other victims of economic restructuring from the public eye. From such processes emerged the signature emotional stance of postmodernity, an ironic and self-absorbed detachment that made this disappearance possible.

In retrospect, it can be seen that these early assessments of postmodernity could not have anticipated how recent information technologies would overcome some of the efforts of corporations and retailers to conceal the origins of globally traded commodities from their consumers. The internet has emerged as arguably the most effective tool employed by anti-globalization activists to disseminate information about global inequities and abusive working conditions and to organize mass protests against them. Long before the end of the 1990s, a global capitalist economy widely considered triumphant a mere decade before was drawing renewed public opposition, much of it from younger, internet-based activists. As the anti-globalization movement marshaled evidence of sweatshops, child and forced labor, and environmental degradation before corporate shareholders and middle-class consumers alike, millions in the developed North sought to reconcile consumption with conscience. For many consumers, the answer to this paradox was also readily available on the internet, and increasingly in retail stores, in the form of certified Fair Trade products. Yet just as consumers began turning to Fair Trade as an alternative to conventionally marketed products, the very corporations whose workplace and environmental practices had been criticized by anti-globalization activists began to recognize the commercial potential of the Fair Trade market as well. Fair Trade, which originated as a threat to the prerogatives of global corporations, also offered them a mechanism for redeeming their often tarnished reputations.

Co-opting Justice

During the final two years of his life, as he stepped up his criticism of the US war on Vietnam and neglect of social justice at home, Dr. Martin Luther King, Jr., was vilified in the mainstream media as a dangerous demagogue. For several years after his assassination, conservatives such as then California Governor Ronald Reagan described him as a "near-communist" (Rockwell 1995). Ironically, the federal holiday that bears his name was later signed into law by President Reagan and in recent years has been annually (if carefully) commemorated by another Republican White House. Meanwhile, King's image is used to sell Apple computers, Bell South internet connections, and a host of other products not remotely connected with the man or his ideas. The civil rights movement that he helped to lead, vigorously opposed during his lifetime by the US Chamber of Commerce, has recently inspired advertisements for everything from clothing ("The United Colors of Benetton") to General Motors pickup trucks and corporate charitable campaigns. These posthumous evocations of King's image and words may suggest to some that his message has finally been embraced by corporations and political conservatives. Those who actually worked with King, however, see in such commercial appropriations a highly sanitized portrait of the activist who once inspired discomfort and loathing among US politicians and big business. Indeed, it is likely that the pacifist who advocated massive nonviolent resistance to authority and proclaimed the "spiritual death" of a country that spends more on weaponry than on programs that help people to live, would be declared a terrorist sympathizer in today's climate, and possibly be prosecuted as such under federal statutes enacted since September 11, 2001.

This co-opting of the image of King and the civil rights movement for commercial purposes is a fate shared by other social movements that have acquired a mass following and modicum of success in attaining some of their goals. Earth Day, conceived in 1970 as a nationwide mobilization to change America's environmentally destructive habits, is often regarded as the dawn of modern environmental activism. The movement's demands for greater regulation of industrial and automotive emissions brought it into direct conflict with US manufacturers and oil companies, who in turn characterized early environmentalists as alarmist and utopian, even un-American. In ensuing years, environmentalists overcame industry opposition to advocate successfully for federal environmental protection laws. To avert additional legal oversight, manufacturers changed their tactics to appropriate the rhetoric of environmentalism in their advertisements and public relations activities (see especially Bruno and Karliner 2002). To blunt the demands of environmental activists, they contributed conspicuously to some national organizations and formed pro-industry "grassroots environmental" organizations of their own (Moberg 2002). Annual celebrations of Earth Day were increasingly underwritten by the very companies that had earlier been criticized by environmentalists, among them waste management and oil companies with the nation's worst pollution records (Dowie 1995).

The 1990s saw a proliferation of advertising campaigns by oil companies that heralded their ostensible commitment to environmental protection, notwithstanding continued accidents in the years after Exxon Valdez.[7] Similar "green merchandising" was launched by companies directing their products at environmentally conscious consumers. In 1999, the Oxford English Dictionary extended formal recognition to these strategies through its inclusion of the verb "greenwash" in the English lexicon: "To mislead or deflect (the public, public concern, etc.) by stressing the environmental credentials of a person, company, product, etc., esp. when these are unfounded or irrelevant" (*OED* 2007).

The Fair Trade movement may be of much more recent origin than those for civil rights and environmental causes, but already there is evidence that the global corporations originally opposed by it are seeking to co-opt its principles in similar fashion. The US $2.2 billion spent on Fair Trade commodities in 2006 (Downie 2007) represents a loss, albeit still a relatively minor one, in potential earnings for Chiquita, Cadbury's, Nestlé, Procter and Gamble, and other global middlemen. Yet with its sustained 30 to 40 percent annual growth in demand over the past decade, Fair Trade has attracted the attention of these and other companies eager to break into new markets and rehabilitate damaged corporate images. By 2000, with Fair Trade scarcely present in the US market apart from mail-order and internet sales, Murray and Raynolds already recognized that "transnational corporations [are] seeking to capture these initiatives and redefine them in ways that advance not progressive agendas, but their own private profits" (2000: 73).

Apart from the history of the civil rights and environmental movements mentioned above, there is ample recent precedent for reaching such a conclusion. In response to anti-sweatshop initiatives mounted internationally during the 1990s, major clothing retailers, such as Gap, adopted high-profile "codes of conduct" to be observed by their suppliers in the developing world. Yet because the codes lacked effective third-party certification or enforcement, there is little evidence that they greatly altered conditions for most apparel workers; indeed, most workers ostensibly covered by them were entirely unaware of the existence of the codes, much less their provisions (Breslin 2001, Mohanty 2003). Similar codes adopted to regulate the marketing of infant formula in developing nations are routinely violated by the largest formula manufacturer, Nestlé, despite the company's claim that it supports them (Bruno and Karliner 2002: 24). Because Fair Trade, unlike the civil rights and environmental movements, does not wield a political or constituent community apart from the retail market, the risks associated with corporate co-optation are even greater than in these instances. Neither grassroots civil rights nor environmental activists are likely to be deterred in their work by the appropriation of their movements' symbols by corporations (although other types of organizations might be). Should global agribusiness companies come to dominate the Fair Trade market, however, those who originally viewed Fair Trade as a mechanism to reform the world market are likely to see its goals changed beyond recognition.

Since 2000, corporate responses to Fair Trade have recapitulated, if in greatly accelerated fashion, the transformation of business attitudes toward once adversarial social movements. In the case of both the civil rights and environmental movements, corporations revised their public stances from open hostility to adoption of much of the movements' rhetoric. In 1999, Starbucks, the largest specialty coffee retailer in the US, became the target of a boycott by the US human rights campaign Global Exchange because of its coffee buying policies. The boycott drew attention to the huge disparities between Starbucks's retail prices (between US $10 and $12 per pound of whole coffee) and rising profit margins, on the one hand, and the declining price its roasters paid Central American growers for their coffee beans (then about US $0.30 to $0.50 per pound) (Global Exchange 2000). Boycott organizers drew attention to the ruinously low coffee prices then prevailing in many producing communities, associated with unprecedented economic hardship for farmers and their families. Following a year of damaging public relations and boycott efforts that had widened to Starbucks operations in the UK and Canada, the company announced that it would purchase and stock certified Fair Trade coffee in all of its stores.

The "resolution" of the Global Exchange boycott left many Fair Trade advocates dissatisfied. Claiming that it lacks access to adequate supplies of Fair Trade coffee to make it available in the brewed form that constitutes most of its stores' sales, Starbucks relegates Fair Trade to sales of whole beans.[8] The company's professed inability to locate sufficient volumes of Fair Trade coffee struck many alternative trade advocates as implausible (Jaffee 2007: 200). As is the case for most Fair Trade commodities, there is a substantially larger supply of coffee grown by Fair Trade producers than there is market demand: indeed, about 80 percent of all coffee that could potentially be labeled as Fair Trade is instead sold through conventional channels at lower prices (Ten Thousand Villages 2007). While Starbucks boasts that it now imports 10 percent of the Fair Trade coffee entering the United States (Starbucks 2006), critics contend that this commitment appears less than wholehearted when compared with the 20 percent of the US specialty coffee market that the company commands (Global Exchange 2007). Notwithstanding persisting concerns about company policies among some members of the Fair Trade movement, Starbucks has publicly recrafted its image from that of a hostile opponent of Fair Trade to a supporter of it. Company websites extol its decision to stock Fair Trade coffee "as part of a larger effort by Starbucks to be socially responsible in our relationships with coffee farmers and communities" (Starbucks 2006). Yet despite such claims, Fair Trade makes up only 3.7 percent of Starbucks's coffee sales, which is less than Fair Trade's overall percentage share of the US specialty market (Grant 2007).

Starbucks's strategy of deriving maximum public relations benefits by incorporating a single Fair Trade item into a much wider line of products has been seized upon by other global corporations. In 2004, Procter and Gamble, the largest single coffee retailer in the US, announced that its specialty Millstone brand would now offer a certified Fair Trade selection in supermarkets. Comprising minute levels of sales compared to its mainstream Folgers label, Millstone Fair Trade allowed Procter and Gamble to adopt the mantle of social responsibility without altering the way it purchases the vast majority of its coffee. After the experience of Starbucks and Procter and Gamble, Fair Trade advocates were little surprised when McDonald's later announced plans to serve Fair Trade coffee in its stores on the US East Coast. By 2007, even Sam's Club, the warehouse chain subsidiary of Wal-Mart, had introduced its own brand of Fair Trade coffee (Downie 2007). Other companies that earlier vowed not to bow to pressure from Fair Trade advocates have also adopted Fair Trade labels. Responding to criticisms that it relied upon repressive human rights climates in West Africa to source cacao below growers' costs of production, Cadbury's, one of the world's largest chocolate manufacturers, angrily asserted that "Yorkie and all our other chocolate products are produced fairly" (Tiffin 2002: 390). As criticism continued, however, the company announced a plan to introduce a certified Fair Trade chocolate bar produced with Belizean cacao. While conferring Fair Trade respectability on a small segment of the company's sales, the decision did not entail any change in Cadbury's supply policies elsewhere.

Few corporations have so audaciously redefined themselves with respect to Fair Trade as the Swiss multinational Nestlé, which controls significant shares of both the world's coffee and cacao markets. The target of a consumer boycott for nearly three decades because of its infant formula marketing practices in the developing world, the company amassed a record of labor repression in its Latin American and African divisions. Nestlé steadfastly refused to reform its marketing, labor, and pricing policies, and testily answered complaints about its sourcing policies by claiming that "all Nestlé cocoa is fairly traded" (Tiffin 2002: 390). From the company's perspective, Fair Trade was not only unnecessary but a violation of "free-trade policies" (O'Nions 2006). But in 2005, the company abruptly ceased its rhetorical battle with the Fair Trade movement and introduced into the UK market its Partners' Blend freeze-dried coffee, identified on its label as "coffee that helps farmers, their communities, and the environment." Out of more than 8,500 products manufactured by Nestlé, Partners' Blend is the only one to carry FLO's Fair Trade logo.

FLO's certification of Partners' Blend prompted angry exchanges within the European Fair Trade movement. Harriet Lamb of the Fairtrade Foundation praised FLO's decision as "a turning point ... Here is a major multinational listening to people and giving them what they want – a Fair Trade product" (O'Nions 2006). Others perceive more than a trace of irony in the Fair Trade certification of Nestlé's newest coffee line. Because Nestlé's control of much of the global coffee industry has enabled it to force down producers' prices, the company is widely regarded as responsible for the conditions that made Fair Trade necessary in the first place. The UK-based World Development Movement responded to Partners' Blend with a challenge: "If Nestlé really believes in Fair Trade coffee, it will alter its business practices and lobbying strategies and radically overhaul its business to ensure that all coffee farmers get a fair return for their efforts. Until then, Nestlé will remain part of the problem, not the solution" (O'Nions 2006). Short of such measures, many feel that to certify a single product without reference to a company's wider behavior is to allow corporations with abysmal labor, human rights, and environmental records to cheaply redeem themselves in the eyes of consumers while leaving most of their business practices unchanged. Indeed, while surveys indicate that FLO's Fair Trade logo and Fair Trade principles are recognized and understood by about half of all English consumers, many mistakenly believe that FLO certification extends not to individual products but to the company that markets them (O'Nions 2006). Such buyers may indeed assume that Nestlé as a whole has been certified by FLO, despite the fact that just an infinitesimal one-tenth of one percent of the coffee sold by the company worldwide will be purchased through Fair Trade channels.

FLO's decision to certify Partners' Blend points to a growing rift within the Fair Trade movement. Some segments of the movement, including representatives of TransFair, a FLO affiliate and the largest US-based Fair Trade organization, claim that the desire of multinational corporations to acquire a socially responsible image creates new marketing opportunities for Fair Trade producers. Many activists consider this view of Fair Trade as a niche market remaining under corporate control to be a betrayal of the movement's original intention to reform the whole global trading system. Following intense debate over these positions at the 2005 Fair Trade Futures Conference in Chicago, several groups broke away from TransFair (and thereby FLO) to establish certifying Fair Trade organizations of their own. Dean Cycon, founder of the Dean's Beans coffee company, argued against a Fair Trade system dominated by multinational corporations in these terms: "Is the goal of Fair Trade to have every roaster use five percent Fair Trade coffee, thereby dooming the other 95 percent of farmers to deepening debt? Or, is the goal to transform the world coffee market into a more just system of trade?" (Caldwell and Bacon 2006). Indeed, the former approach, which appears to be gaining ground, points to a central paradox in the Fair Trade movement as a whole. By stimulating the production of traditional exports, such as coffee and bananas, Fair Trade may well contribute to global overproduction of such commodities, which accounts in large part for their declining producer prices worldwide. The effect, ironically, may be lower prices for the large majority of growers lacking access to Fair Trade certification and markets (*The Economist* 2006).

Following the recent decision of TransFair USA to extend Fair Trade certification to bananas grown on some of Chiquita's Central American plantations, other organizations have broken away from FLO and a certification process that they no longer believe to be an alternative to traditional trade. Yet the absence of a single certifying body applying a consistent set of criteria also poses new hazards to Fair Trade principles. A number of companies already "self-certify" the conditions under which their products are grown, further raising the possibility of meaningless and self-serving claims. As divisions arise within the alternative trade movement concerning the certification of goods marketed by multinational corporations, consumers and industry observers alike have begun to ask who benefits from the retail prices charged for many Fair Trade products.

Many consumers assume that all or most of the difference that they pay for Fair Trade as opposed to conventional products is returned to the producer in the form of higher prices. This assumption is far from the reality. While retail price markups are often in excess of 100 percent, especially for goods sold in supermarkets, the lion's share of this price difference accrues to retailers and wholesalers. According to FLO, a grower of Fair Trade coffee in 2006 was guaranteed a price of US $1.26 per pound, or $0.44 per pound more than the current world market price. But Fair Trade coffee sold in that year at Tesco, Britain's largest supermarket chain, cost the consumer the equivalent of US $3.46 more per pound than conventional coffee. Similar or even greater discrepancies between producer and retail prices exist for other commodities. At Sainsbury's supermarkets, the biggest retailer of Windward Islands bananas in the UK, Fair Trade fruit in 2003 retailed for the equivalent of US $1.29 per pound, compared to about $0.59 per pound for conventional bananas from Central America and the Caribbean. Yet while its retail price is about 120 percent higher than that of generic fruit, the price per pound paid to Caribbean growers for Fair Trade fruit is only about US $0.07 (41 percent) greater than that paid for generic fruit (Moberg 2005: 10).[9]

Asked about the disparities in retail and producer prices for Fair Trade versus conventional bananas, a spokesperson for Sainsbury's pointed out, correctly, that some of the retail price difference is returned to growers' communities as a social premium (Stecklow and White 2004). However, the social premium generated by each 42-pound box of Fair Trade fruit is

US $1.75. Given that the contents of each box will retail for about $53, it can be seen that the social premium is a very small share of the total value of each box. Clearly, then, much of the retail price differential between Fair Trade and conventional products is not returned to producers or the communities to which they belong.

For both Fair Trade coffee and bananas, Tesco and Sainsbury's maintain that their profit margins are lower than those for their much cheaper conventional counterparts. Despite such assurances, retailers are reluctant to disclose their actual margins, and FLO is similarly less than forthcoming about the share of the Fair Trade price appropriated for its administrative and certification costs. In this respect, the wholesale and retail end of the Fair Trade commodity chain falls considerably short of the "transparency" identified as one of the movement's guiding principles. This again points to a significant long-term challenge to Fair Trade's viability in the retail market. If the movement is premised upon consumers' willingness to pay a premium to ensure a higher price for producers, their commitment is sure to be lessened if they learn that supermarkets and other middlemen benefit more from the Fair Trade retail price than do the producers themselves.

Chiquita Fair Trade Bananas?

In 1998, two reporters for the *Cincinnati Enquirer*, the daily newspaper in the hometown of Chiquita Brands International, ran a series of reports based on secret company documents detailing Chiquita's labor and environmental practices in Latin America. For the first time, a major daily newspaper brought meticulous evidence to the broad public documenting the company's persecution of union activists, defiance of local labor laws, and agricultural practices that poisoned both workers and the environment. As the authors of the series emphasized, these abuses were not isolated incidents in the company's remote past but continued until the late 1990s as an integral part of its operating policies. Chiquita moved swiftly to contain the public relations damage from the reports: after threatening lawsuits against the newspaper, the company extracted an apology from the *Enquirer* and compensation of $10 million in damages. The newspaper was forced to retract the series not because of any alleged factual lapses but because its reporters relied on documents and voice mails obtained without Chiquita's permission.

Notwithstanding the publisher's renunciation, the *Chiquita Secrets Revealed* series was widely disseminated internationally among Chiquita's critics and can be readily accessed to this day on numerous internet sites. Based on highly detailed internal memos and communications, the articles were particularly damaging because they flatly contradicted years of heavily publicized efforts by the company to reform its image in the face of international criticism. In the early 1990s Chiquita developed the Better Banana Project, an initiative with the Rainforest Alliance to certify the elimination from its farms of chemicals not approved by the US and European governments. The *Enquirer's* reporters revealed that by 1998 at least one banned chemical continued to be widely used and that other environmental reforms remained largely rhetorical gestures on the company's part (Gallagher and McWhirter 1998a). Another article detailed how the company paid for an ostensibly "independent" onsite visit by Conservation International to document its compliance with the Rainforest Alliance agreement (Gallagher and McWhirter 1998c).

In addition, the UK-based Fair Trade organization Banana Link and the European Banana Action Network (EUROBAN) revealed that wages and union representation on Chiquita plantations had deteriorated throughout the 1990s as the company sought to cut costs to improve its financial position. EUROBAN crafted a continent-wide consumer awareness campaign in conjunction with COLSIBA (*Coordinadora Latinoamericana de Sindicatos Bananeros*), a coalition of unions representing 42,000 banana workers in seven Latin American countries. COLSIBA had been organized to challenge the multinationals' increased reliance on bananas grown on non-union farms and efforts to replace independent unions with pro-management *solidarismo* ("solidarity") organizations (Riisgaard 2004: 10).[10] Negative publicity from the *Chiquita Secrets Revealed* series and a growing European campaign against Chiquita led the UK supermarket giants Asda and Tesco to demand that the company address its environmental and labor relations problems. In the US, the Interfaith Center on Corporate Responsibility (ICCR) also urged its member organizations, mostly church-affiliated groups, to acquire some Chiquita stock in order to introduce shareholder resolutions demanding that the company change its practices. At one annual general meeting following the *Enquirer* series, the Chiquita directors found themselves lectured by a nun from the Sisters of Charity who reproached them at length for their ill treatment of workers. In the face of shareholder challenges, a de facto European boycott, pressure from Latin American unions, and sharply declining share prices, the company opted to acknowledge its critics and adopt a code of corporate social responsibility (Riisgaard 2004: 10).

After three years of meetings, in 2001 Chiquita and COLSIBA signed an agreement affirming the rights of Chiquita's workers to join an independent union of their choosing and bargain collectively for wages and working conditions, and requiring the company to uphold International Labor Organization conventions banning discrimination and forced and child labor. Moreover, these standards were to apply as well to the independent farms, contractors, and venture partners from which Chiquita sourced much of its branded fruit. Since the early 1980s, the company had increasingly divested itself of production and transferred lands and sourcing to independent contractors in order to reduce its operating expenses and risks. Contractors who acquired former Chiquita holdings and continued to sell to the multinational typically dissolved unions and lowered wages when they took control of farms. Hence, the extension of union rights to Chiquita's suppliers could be viewed as a significant potential victory for banana worker unions that had seen memberships, earnings, and working conditions plummet as a result of the company's subcontracting policies.

Chiquita's agreement with COLSIBA, its publication of annual reports on its social responsibility, and its acceptance of independent auditors of company operations to certify compliance with ILO conventions have won the company some newfound respectability in the market. Its collaboration with social and environmental activists to reform on-farm practices has "transformed a tarnished brand," according to a recent, if controversial, account upholding the company as a model of proactive corporate social responsibility (Taylor and Scharlin 2004). The company's willingness to meet its critics and sign an agreement with banana workers' unions has quickly paid off via its redemption in the marketplace. A pariah in social and environmental terms less than a decade ago, Chiquita is now poised to enter the Fair Trade banana market in the United States, which remains rudimentary compared to that of Europe. In June 2005, COLSIBA and TransFair USA signed an agreement under which Chiquita bananas grown on unionized plantations could be labeled and sold as Fair Trade produce in North American supermarkets, with distribution aimed at the Safeway, Stop and Shop, Whole Foods, and Wild Oats chains.

Yet in the wake of the COLSIBA agreement with the banana multinational, there is little evidence that working conditions on most of the Central American plantations that supply Chiquita-branded fruit have improved. Recent on-site assessments in four Central American countries by an ILO representative found that "Chiquita showed a bad record [in publicizing the agreement] since none of the workers interviewed had been informed about it by Chiquita management" (Riisgaard 2004: 13). More seriously, although the agreement guaranteed workers the right to organize on farms belonging both to Chiquita and its independent suppliers, union representatives were in every case turned away by managers when they attempted to set foot on independent farms. Only one farm in all of Central America had gained union representation as a result of the agreement, and that was because union organizers circumvented farm managers to meet with workers after hours.

Ultimately, the refusal of managers to permit farm visits by union representatives is traceable back to Chiquita's failure to inform subcontractors of their responsibilities as specified in its agreement with the union. Hence, it is not surprising that the ILO's compliance assessment found that rights of association and general working conditions on the farms of most of Chiquita's suppliers had either remained the same or deteriorated since the agreement was signed (Riisgaard 2004: 14). While bananas produced on farms that violate workers' rights will presumably not carry the COLSIBA-endorsed Fair Trade emblem, they will, like the fruit marketed as Fair Trade, bear Chiquita's familiar blue oval label. In this way, Chiquita anticipates that the Fair Trade certification of some of its bananas will increase sales of all Chiquita-branded fruit, whether or not it is produced under socially and environmentally sustainable practices. Because TransFair adopted FLO's Fair Trade banana certification criteria as its own, there is at this point no impediment to Chiquita's marketing of Fair Trade fruit in Europe as well.

For many residents of the Caribbean and EU who support the Windward Islands banana industry, the possibility that Chiquita could enter the European market as a Fair Trade producer evokes the same painful ironies that trade activists experienced with the certification of Nestlé's Partners' Blend coffee. In the UK, the marketing of Fair Trade bananas arose specifically as a means of protecting farming communities of the Windward Islands against the ravages of "free trade" as championed by Chiquita. The Fair Trade market was to be a refuge for banana farmers unable to compete on the global market's terms of price and quantity, which were driving a worldwide "race to the bottom" in earnings and environmental conditions. After Caribbean growers were targeted by Chiquita in its efforts to eliminate EU market regulations, Fair Trade was also seen as a gesture of support for family farmers in their struggle with global agribusiness corporations. Hence, as in the earlier case of Nestlé, the very conditions in the global banana market that necessitated Fair Trade were largely created by Chiquita's policies in the first place. The company's possible entry into the European Fair Trade market, whereupon it could compete with Caribbean growers on *their* terms, indicates how drastically the Fair Trade movement has changed in a few short years. It also highlights what is likely to be an intense battle within its ranks over the movement's goals and principles in the years to come.

Notes

1. Although not affiliated with any particular Christian denomination, the movement followed the Pope's declaration of 2000 as a jubilee year, a claim rooted in the Old Testa-

ment practice in which the wealthy were called upon to forgive the debts of the poor every fifty years.

2. It is likely that consumer boycotts are as old as capitalism itself. Breen (2004) illustrates how colonists' refusals to purchase British goods played a critical role in the years prior to and following the American Declaration of Independence. The term for withholding patronage as a form of protest owes its origin about a century later to mass protests by Irish tenants against a Captain Boycott, the exceptionally brutal manager for an absentee English landlord. Unable to harvest his crops because of Irish tenants' refusal to work for him, Boycott was socially ostracized and forced to return to England.

3. The term Fair Trade actually arose during the 1950s and 1960s to encompass an agenda among U.N. member states favoring more equitable exchange between the developed and developing worlds (Fridell 2007: 24). Arguing that the global South's reliance on primary product exports placed it at a disadvantage relative to the industrialized North, developing nations in the United Nations Economic Commission on Latin America (ECLA) and UN Commission on Trade and Development (UNCTAD) lobbied for "fairer" prices for primary product exporters of the developing world. Hence, the notion of Fair Trade originally involved a multilateral agenda opposed in principle to the deregulation embraced by later neoliberal policies, and did not entail the consumer-based initiatives with which Fair Trade is now associated.

4. These per capita figures were derived from FLO's most recent annual sales data by country, divided by each nation's 2007 estimated population. These data indicate that demand for Fair Trade items in the most established markets may be leveling off: while the US experienced a greater than 40 percent increase in Fair Trade sales between 2005 and 2006, sales in Switzerland increased just 1 percent (FLO 2007: 15).

5. Figures for each of these commodities vary considerably, ranging from 18 percent of the UK retail market for coffee to about 8 percent for bananas. Switzerland, which leads the world in per capita Fair Trade product sales, achieved a watershed in 2007 when Fair Trade bananas claimed a majority (55 percent) of that country's retail market for the fruit (Ten Thousand Villages 2007).

6. In a similar vein, FLO and UK supermarkets feature Windwards Fair Trade banana growers in their product advertisements, but the testimonials delivered by these individuals never mention the hierarchical and locally resented aspects of Fair Trade marketing detailed in Chapter Ten.

7. It might be noted that industry contributions, welcomed as windfalls by otherwise poorly funded environmental organizations, undoubtedly represented less of a cost to industry than stricter emissions controls or, in the case of Exxon, double-hulled tankers.

8. The company says that upon request its stores will brew individual cups of Fair Trade coffee for customers who request them. But several groups involved in the original boycott claim that in practice such requests are met infrequently, as many Starbucks stores have not been made aware of the policy or do not even stock Fair Trade coffee.

9. These figures are based on a supermarket survey in March 2003, a period of historically low banana prices in the UK. Retail prices from 2005 published elsewhere indicate that as much as a fourfold price differential separated Fair Trade from conventional bananas at Sainsbury's.

10. Since the early 1990s, *solidarismo* organizations have been widely promoted by the owners and managers of independent banana farms in Central America as alternatives to unions. Although they claim to represent workers and offer them credit and some social and recreational services, they do not engage in collective bargaining or grievance procedures.

— Chapter Ten —

FAIR TRADE AND CONVENTIONAL FARMING IN THE MABOUYA VALLEY

Our organization put enough furniture in the school so that school could be going on a full day. Before then, you constantly have kids on the street, because they could only get a half day of school … And this is why I give Fair Trade a lot of respect, because the social premium it has made a real difference in the community. We were not using it on behalf of the farmers to build a pretty house or buy a vehicle, it was circulating in the community, where kids can go to school, where youth can play sports, and all these things

— Amos Wiltshire, National Fair Trade Federation of Dominica (2004)

Here you have a farmer who maybe cannot read and write and these Fair Trade requirements become mind boggling to him. Because now we have even more record keeping, where he must put down the type of chemical he used, the quantity, and who applied them on what dates. So you find that the farmer has had real problems keeping up. They always seem to be raising the bar.

— Ministry of Agriculture Extension Agent, Mabouya Valley (2004)

New Masters?

Apart from the frenetic activity of harvest days, banana farms in the Mabouya Valley are serenely quiet places that belie the political and economic turmoil experienced by the region since 1992. Employing neither the cableways nor the spray irrigation systems found in Central America, the only sounds heard on most valley farms, apart from the conversations of those who work on them, are the rustle of the breeze and the sporadic drumming of raindrops on banana leaves. Since the 1980s, when farmers replaced a good deal of hand weeding with herbicides, even the steady chopping rhythm of cutlasses clearing undergrowth has gradually disappeared from most area farms. But in June 2000, the valley's relative silence was broken by sputtering two-cycle motors and whirring monofilament grass cutters, a noise more often associated with well-manicured suburban lawns than banana farms in the tropics.

The sound of gasoline-powered weed eaters, infrequent and incongruous at first, is now widely heard on local farms, testifying to an ongoing transformation in the way that many farmers grow and market their bananas. Under the environmental criteria mandated by FLO, most of the chemical herbicides formerly used in the area are now banned from farms that produce Fair Trade bananas. At FLO's urging, the weed eater has emerged as the most widely used tool for performing the job formerly done with chemicals dispensed from backpack sprayers. The Mabouya Valley's Fair Trade group collectively owns eight of the machines, which rotate among the membership according to a waiting list maintained by the association's secretary. The sound of the weed eater is the most obvious indicator that a particular farm is Fair Trade certified.

If the weed eater is emblematic of the changes that farmers have had to adopt in becoming Fair Trade certified, it also symbolizes much of their ambivalence to the Fair Trade movement. Overwhelmingly, farmers state that they are grateful for the higher prices and other benefits they receive for their bananas as Fair Trade produce. In the same breath, most will express their frustration with the weed eater as an impractical and often ineffective tool for local farms, one that they view as an imposition by outsiders possessing little knowledge of the realities of farming or the labor constraints under which they operate.[1] With few exceptions, farmers outside the Fair Trade group continue to utilize herbicides, ostensibly within the limits established by EUREP-GAP, and all have spurned weed eaters as alternatives to chemicals.

With 119 members, the Mabouya Valley Fair Trade Group is the largest of five Fair Trade farmers' associations active on St. Lucia. Its membership comprises about 40 percent of all active banana growers in the valley. Six years after the introduction of FLO's no-herbicide policy, the Fair Trade environmental criteria continue to dominate discussion during monthly meetings of the Mabouya Valley group. The primary complaint aired about them concerns the effects of low-chemical farming on labor inputs and operating costs. Older farmers in particular protest that they lack the strength required to wield and operate the 35-pound weed eaters effectively, at least for a period long enough to clear several acres of undergrowth from their farms.[2] The average age of the Mabouya Valley's

Fair Trade farmers is 50.9 years, significantly greater than the average age of conventional banana farmers (40.1 years).[3] More than 46 percent of the Fair Trade group's members are 51 years of age or older. Three members are in their seventies, and the oldest is 83. Many older farmers working under Fair Trade's herbicide ban now must hire younger men to clear their farms of weeds, a task they had previously been able to easily perform themselves with backpack sprayers. One FLO-approved alternative to the weed eater would be to return to hand weeding by cutlass, a practice abandoned by most farmers in the 1980s.[4] This also involves increased labor expenditures and inevitably requires farmers (both young and old) to hire more workers. In addition, weeding with cutlasses is difficult if not impossible on the approximately 20 percent of valley farms employing drip irrigation, for the blades would sever rubber drip lines, a danger not posed by weed eaters' monofilament grass cutters.

A majority (55 percent) of Fair Trade farmers report that their wage expenses have increased as a result of the no-herbicide policy, with each farmer expending on average an additional EC $116 in wages per fortnight. Because of limited demand for Fair Trade bananas in the UK market, considerably less than half the fruit produced on Mabouya Valley Fair Trade farms is actually labeled and sold as such. Like other Fair Trade groups on St. Lucia, the Mabouya Valley group maintains a roster in which members are assigned to pack labeled Fair Trade bananas in about one out of every three shipments that they make. In the shipments in which farmers are assigned to pack Fair Trade fruit, they will usually also pack fruit for two or even three other price and label categories. For any given shipment, then, some fruit may earn Fair Trade prices while other bananas harvested from the same farm, or even the same plant, will be sold at lower prices. As originally formulated, FLO's environmental criteria are to apply permanently to all farms with Fair Trade certification, regardless of how much Fair Trade fruit they sell or the how often they sell it. Hence, Fair Trade criteria have required St. Lucian farmers to accept continuously higher production costs, despite the fact that those higher costs are only occasionally offset by higher fruit prices.

Given farmers' perception that labor costs and labor availability are their most significant problems after the costs of inputs and price of bananas, it is little surprise that many believe that FLO's environmental policies have aggravated their economic circumstances. To their further dismay, farmers learned of an unanticipated agronomic problem resulting from the ban on herbicides: a recently introduced weed easily eradicated by chemical means (*Commelina sp.* or watergrass) is actually propagated when its stems are cut by weed eaters and machetes. When *Commelina* is chopped rather than killed chemically, the broken stems send out new roots of their own. This has led in turn to additional pest problems on Windwards farms. Watergrass is a host species for nematodes, which destroy banana plants by burrowing into their roots and corm. Because FLO's environmental criteria prohibit the use of all currently existing nematicides, many farmers argue that Fair Trade policies have amplified pest problems without providing effective alternatives to chemical use. Farmers who were able to demonstrate the presence of nematodes after the loss of infected banana plants were, after appeal of the policy to WINFA and a dispensation granted by FLO officials in Europe, allowed to apply limited amounts of several less toxic nematicides to affected areas of their farms. For most, the added bureaucracy required in gaining authorization for a decision that they would ordinarily have made on their own led to nearly a month's delay in treating their farms, during which they were unable to halt the widening infestations. As a result, affected farmers experienced substantial losses in production and earnings that otherwise could easily have been averted.

The ban on herbicides is one component of a set of environmental criteria that have dramatically changed the way Fair Trade farmers grow bananas. Some of these changes are poorly understood by farmers, and even the Windwards-based certification officer who is responsible for enforcing them on behalf of FLO openly acknowledges that several of the environmental criteria are inappropriate for local conditions. Among these is the requirement that Fair Trade farmers maintain a 20 meter–wide buffer zone on farms adjacent to streams and main roads in order to minimize soil erosion and protect watersheds. While such requirements may be feasible in Europe, on a three- to four-acre Caribbean farm the 20-meter buffer requirement requires farmers to remove a large percentage of their land from production. The certification officer himself describes the requirement as "an unreasonable economic demand on farmers." After vociferous complaints from farmers, WINFA requested and obtained from FLO a modification of the policy intended to offset the economic losses incurred by affected farmers. The revision permits the buffer zone to consist of tree crops having commercial value, such as citrus, mangos, and coconuts. Because these trees require at least five years to reach bearing maturity, during which the farmer recoups no earnings from the buffer zone of his or her farm, the modified requirement still poses a considerable economic sacrifice for farmers (un)fortunate enough to be located near roads and streams. Several such Mabouya Valley farmers volunteered that because of the buffer zone requirement, they chose to remain conventional producers after being invited to join the Fair Trade group.

Concerns about the new environmental criteria are fervently discussed at most monthly meetings of Fair Trade farmers' associations. As required by FLO, each Fair Trade group convenes general membership meetings at least once per month, with attendance required of all members other than those with prior excused absences.[5] In practice, about 70 percent of the membership attends any given meeting of the Mabouya Valley group, and most of those present appear to be avidly engaged in the animated debates that take place during the sessions. Meetings of the Mabouya Valley Fair Trade group are presided over by President Cornelius Lynch and First Secretary Daniel Sandiford, both of whom are younger and possess much more formal education than most of the group's membership. Lynch, who grew up in the Mabouya Valley in a farming household, earned a bachelor's degree in agronomy from the University of the West Indies in Trinidad. He is articulate, well-traveled, and especially well-versed in the principles of the Fair Trade movement. As a former extension agent for the SLBC, Lynch was employed for a time to educate the island's farmers about Fair Trade principles, and he played a key role in organizing the Mabouya Valley Fair Trade Group during its initial stages in 2000. Such informal gatherings in the early days of the island's Fair Trade movement have been replaced by regular monthly meetings that last between two and four hours. Monthly meetings serve as opportunities for officers to disseminate technical information and marketing news to members. The members also share information, propose and debate uses for social premiums in local development projects, and formulate requests to be directed to umbrella organizations such as the National Fair Trade Committee on each island and WINFA. Each local farmer's group elects a delegate to the National Fair Trade Committee, which also meets monthly, either in the Mabouya Valley at La Caye or the Cul de Sac Valley at Odsan.

As the president of the Mabouya Valley Fair Trade group, Lynch finds that his work has shifted from educating farmers about Fair Trade criteria to defending the criteria against the opposition of much of the membership. During the group's August 2003 meeting, he announced a change in the rotation schedule for the group's weed eaters because two of the machines had broken down in the previous several weeks. This announcement, the third of its kind that year, provoked a chorus of complaints. Fitz Roy Alexander, also one of the group's younger members and one of the few to have completed secondary school, took the opportunity to challenge the Fair Trade no-herbicide policy altogether. Alexander claimed that his labor expenses regularly ran EC $75 more per week than those of his conventional farming neighbor, the difference being the increased labor requirements of clearing his farm without chemicals. "I weed eater [sic] my whole farm, but I only get to ship Fair Trade a third of the time. So what's fair about Fair Trade when the farmer who weed eaters has to pay more to grow his bananas but doesn't get the benefits?" Lynch was immediately besieged with angry affirmations of this point from other members unhappy with the herbicide ban. After managing to quiet the assembly, he appealed to environmental and social considerations to justify the weed eater policy, attempting to draw a contrast between local farmers and their agribusiness adversaries in Latin America:

> We, as Fair Trade farmers, we use the weed eater because we are more concerned about the environment, and we want to leave a decent world for our children. Do you think Chiquita cares about this? Do you? You should be proud that we are not like those big companies poisoning the environment with their chemicals and their pollution. We are getting a social premium because we are Fair Trade farmers. The minute we stop taking care of the environment we are no longer Fair Trade farmers and we will no longer receive the social premium.

Lynch's explanation was greeted with a restive silence punctuated by murmurs of disagreement, although even this was short-lived. Undaunted, Alexander responded: "But our grandmothers and grandfathers grew bananas and they cared about the environment. Who are these people from outside to tell us they know better than we how to take care of the environment and grow bananas?" This comment was greeted by calls of "That's right, that's right!" from many quarters, leading Lynch to look nervously about the room as if in search of potential allies. "That's where I would disagree with you," the president called out over the chorus of discontent. "Our grandparents and parents did *not* take good care of the environment. They cut down forests, they planted on slopes and next to streams. As Fair Trade farmers we can't do those things. Now you can grow fruit the way your grandparents did, and you can use herbicide *and still* export to England, but you can't be a Fair Trade farmer if you choose to do that."

The meeting immediately dissolved into a half-dozen animated arguments between members and the group's president. As was usually the case when members departed from meeting agendas, the discussion gravitated from the formal meeting's English to Kwéyòl, from which the English word "weed eater" occasionally surfaced, uttered almost as an epithet. Gradually regaining the attention of the group, Lynch offered a compromise. "Here's an idea that has been discussed with the National Committee,[6] and I know that WINFA has approved it. Maybe the solution is to divide your farm and use conventional practices on one side, while you use the weed eater on the other one. Then, when you harvest Fair Trade fruit, it would come just from that part of the farm. But if you are to do this, it is absolutely crucial that you never take fruit from the conventional side of your farm and box it as Fair Trade bananas." Were pesticide residues detected on even a single box of Fair Trade bananas in Britain, he explained, the reputation of all Fair Trade growers would be damaged.

Lynch cautioned growers that their unique identification numbers meant that every box of fruit could be traced back to the farm that produced it. "But that's not all," he warned.

> I'm old enough to remember when growers used to put anything they could in boxes to achieve their box weight. I'm not just talking about bad fruit, but even sticks and stones. That was an embarrassment and shame to every serious farmer. We all knew growers like that, and we all know that they're out of the industry because they didn't have the quality that the supermarkets expect. Now the supermarkets are just asking us to keep our word when we call ourselves Fair Trade. Let me warn you: if anyone here puts fruit that has Gramoxone on it in a Fair Trade box and I find out about it, I will *personally* ensure that that member is delisted as a Fair Trade grower.

When interviewed privately after the meeting, Lynch admitted that he had long known of the compromise of dividing individual farms between Fair Trade and conventional parcels. He had hesitated to announce it at all until late in the meeting, when the vociferous opinions of some made him fear that they would defy the ban in its entirety. Privately he worried about the effect of the compromise on farmers eager to both reduce their soaring production costs and garner the benefits of Fair Trade prices. "What if you have two acres grown conventionally and one acre that uses no herbicide?" he asked rhetorically. "Maybe your Fair Trade quota is forty boxes but you only have twenty boxes available from the Fair Trade part of your farm. You see how tempting it would be to divert fruit from the other part of your farm and label it as Fair Trade? The alternative is to lose twenty boxes at the Fair Trade price. We only have to get a single box of bananas misrepresented in that way to destroy the Fair Trade market." Lynch noted that the herbicide ban had generated more opposition from farmers than any other aspect of the Fair Trade criteria, causing two to abandon Fair Trade on their own and leading two others to be decertified for defiance of the ban.

While forced at the group's meetings to defend the new environmental requirements in order to maintain the integrity of the Fair Trade market, he also sympathized with farmers' discontent about those policies. The new requirements meant only one thing to most members: that they were, once again, finding their actions dictated by powerful "outsiders" making what many farmers consider to be unreasonable demands on their labor and resources:

> Look, you can talk all you want about Fair Trade as a partnership between the customer in England and the grower in the Caribbean. I've seen the websites, I know what they say. But from the farmer's perspective, it looks like more of the same old thing. First WIBDECO tells them how to grow the fruit. Then the

supermarkets tell them how to pack it, and they have to pay for the privilege of using the supermarket's boxes and materials. Then EUREP-GAP comes along and tells them to put toilets and first aid kits in their farms. Now it's FLO telling them to use weed eaters and keep buffer zones. Can you blame farmers for viewing the Fair Trade people as a new set of masters? For them, anything that reduces their independence, anything that comes from "outside," causes resentment. Because in their experience the effect is always the same: more work, higher costs, less control over their time, lower earnings. (Lynch, pers. comm. 2004)

Perhaps the strongest evidence of farmers' attitudes toward the new requirements was suggested by their response to the president's suggestion that they divide their farms into "conventional" and "Fair Trade" sections. This compromise measure received cautious approval by FLO only after its administrators were warned by WINFA and local Fair Trade associations of possible widespread defiance of the herbicide ban. By May 2004, the practice of dividing lands into "herbicide" and "non-herbicide" zones was already in place on a third of the surveyed valley Fair Trade farms. Less than a year had passed since Cornelius Lynch had reluctantly offered the compromise to the valley's Fair Trade farmers.

Building Community

If FLO's environmental criteria require a significant change in local agricultural practices, its social criteria have promoted a form of cooperative development that is in many places also without recent precedent. Growers may sell Fair Trade fruit only if they belong to a producer's association that is democratically organized, self-governing, and nondiscriminatory with regard to gender, age, religion, or political identity. With few exceptions, formal cooperatives in rural communities of the Windwards either did not exist or were nonfunctioning immediately prior to the creation of Fair Trade farmers' groups. Moreover, the fate of the region's cooperatives may not seem to augur well for Fair Trade associations patterned on cooperative models.

Beginning during the depression of the 1930s, missionaries and other church-based organizations promoted cooperatives and credit unions throughout the Caribbean to offset the deep economic crisis experienced by the region, whose effects were felt most acutely by the rural poor. Following World War II, agricultural cooperative development was also embraced by British authorities as a mechanism of both enhancing rural economic viability and preparing island societies for some degree of self-governance in the final years of colonial control. This official commitment

survived past the era of decolonization, and most of the region's governments maintained field offices and entire departments devoted to cooperative promotion and development well into the 1990s. Yet with few
exceptions, formal cooperatives in the Caribbean have evidenced a poor
record of economic viability. Most failed to survive for more than a few
years. Some observers have inferred from the dissolution of church- and
government-sponsored farming cooperatives that the ostensibly individ-
ualistic nature of Afro-Caribbean culture is inconsistent with cooperative
forms of economic activity (e.g., Feuer 1984).

   Much more likely, however, such efforts were doomed instead by the
limited prospects of agricultural production for domestic markets, to
which most cooperatives were oriented. Where domestic demand for food
crops is limited and easily satisfied, there are few advantages to be gained
by cooperative marketing efforts. Indeed, a farmer's best chance for dis-
posing of produce when markets are glutted is to fall back upon his or
her individual contacts and wiles. In contrast, bulking produce with other
farmers for sale—a customary strategy of farmers' cooperatives—simply
contributes to glutted markets in town and leads to lower prices for all.
Defying the claim that the history of failed co-ops demonstrates that the
poor in the Caribbean are unable to work together, the region presents
some notable instances of commercially successful and democratically run
cooperative ventures. Among them are the lobster fishing cooperatives of
Belize (King 2004), the Jamaica Banana Producers Association prior to its
disruption by Chiquita (Holt 1992), and all of the Windward Islands' Banana Growers' Associations before they came under government control
in the 1960s (Romalis 1975). Nonetheless, it remains the case that most of
the Fair Trade farmers' groups introduced into rural communities after
2000 arrived there without any local precedent of cooperative community
development, successful or otherwise, in recent memory.

   Compared to the formal cooperatives that preceded them a generation
ago, Fair Trade groups have the opportunity to make a much more tangible material contribution to their local communities. They do this by
allocating "social premiums," a share of the retail price of each box of fruit
produced by Fair Trade members, for development projects of their own
devising. Any member of a group may propose projects to be funded with
Fair Trade premiums, and such proposals are voted on by the membership at large. Among the first expenditures of social premiums by Fair
Trade groups was the purchase of weed eaters needed to comply with Fair
Trade environmental regulations, an expenditure that one grower likened
to "robbing Peter to pay Paul."[7] The Mabouya Valley Fair Trade Group
also uses a portion of its social premiums to underwrite some of the costs
of production experienced by its members. The use of social premiums

for such purposes enables Fair Trade farmers to spend approximately 20 percent less on boxes and other packaging material than do conventional growers. Although some social premiums have been expended in this manner on Fair Trade compliance and production-related expenditures, the majority of the projects underwritten by social premiums are not agricultural in nature.

The only restriction imposed by the National Fair Trade Committee on the use of social premiums is that projects must benefit the farmers' group or community as a whole. The committee has vetoed a number of proposed uses that were deemed to be too narrowly directed toward particular individuals. In addition to agricultural projects, social premiums have been used to purchase equipment for local schools, improve roads, create and maintain sports fields, provide night-time lighting in crime-prone areas, and offer vocational training programs for rural youth. On St. Lucia, a novel health insurance fund has been established through a joint effort involving all Fair Trade groups on the island. This initiative reimburses farmers and their families for medical expenses up to EC $1,000 (US $375) that are not covered by government health clinics and hospitals. Another project initiated by the Mabouya Valley Fair Trade Group attempts to in-

Figure 10.1 | President and vice president of the Mabouya Valley Fair Trade Group distributing packaging supplies to members. The social premium earned from Fair Trade sales helps offset the cost of such materials.

crease the level of secondary school attendance for rural students. Rural youth have always been far less likely than their counterparts in town to attend high school because of the costs of daily transportation to and from school. A scholarship fund for farmers' families offsets transportation and school expenses for students who make satisfactory progress toward graduation.

Apart from such lasting infrastructural and educational investments, social premiums are used to support activities that "help to build community," in the words of a National Fair Trade Committee member. These include community-wide events such as sports competitions, talent shows, commemorations of national holidays, and "Seniors' Days," which honor the valley's senior citizens for their community contributions. Fair Trade farming groups underwrite such events by providing food and drink, entertainment, educational materials, t-shirts, trophies, and other services that help to generate a sizeable local turn-out. Herbert Rosarie, an SLBC representative who formerly helped organize Fair Trade groups around the island, noted that by reinvesting their social premiums, Fair Trade groups are providing social services no longer offered by the neoliberal state. "It used to be that people looked to government to do these things," Rosarie explained.

> But since the nineties, when the bottom fell out of bananas, government tells us it doesn't have the funds. It can't even provide essential services, like schools and roads. Government tells us that we have to get used to living in a new age, a time of self-reliance. So where does that leave us? Sometimes political parties do these things, but only in a partisan way, a way that poisons relationships. Churches do some of these things, too, but it's not like the old days when everyone was a Catholic. You're not going to find a whole community coming together for church-sponsored events, not anymore. As for most people, especially the ones in rural areas, they are hurting even more than government. How can you be self-reliant if you've have your livelihood kicked out from under you? So Fair Trade groups are stepping into this vacuum. They're providing services and development that don't come from anywhere else. What we're seeing is the creation of civil society; this is people themselves building up community. We've never experienced anything like this before. This, to me, this is the most exciting part of Fair Trade. (Rosarie, pers. comm. 2003)

Those involved in Fair Trade groups often state that their common participation in planning community events and development projects creates bonds of trust that extend into a broader sense of mutual support. Quoting a member of the Grace Fair Trade Group at the southern end of the island, an SLBC official commented similarly on the changed outlook: "She said that ... since we became part of the Fair Trade Group, when a family member dies, the group comes and provides monetary support through a collection. But she said to me, when we sold before to this company, you never encouraged us to do that. And I told her, well … this is the good thing about Fair Trade, that it builds up community" (Faisal, pers. comm. 2003).

The magnitude of Fair Trade financial contributions to community development is both considerable and rapidly growing, even as the overall prospects for the region's banana industry remain uncertain or largely negative. Every box of Fair Trade fruit exported from St. Lucia generates a US $1.75 social premium, of which US $0.20 is allocated to WINFA and $0.55 to the St. Lucia National Fair Trade Association (SLNFTA), an umbrella group representing all Fair Trade farmers island-wide.[8] The remaining net social premium of US $1.00 per box is deposited into the accounts of local Fair Trade Farmers' groups according to their share of the island's Fair Trade output. The SLNFTA incurs some administrative costs, notably salaries for its three staff members and rent for a very modest office in Vieux Fort. Most of its share of the social premium is ultimately returned to farming communities in the form of development aid, however. Most of the expenses required of EUREP-GAP compliance, for example, were offset by direct grants from the SLNFTA to each Fair Trade group on St. Lucia, as were some of the costs of establishing buffer zones required by FLO. Reflecting the rapid expansion of the Fair Trade market in Britain, between 2000 and 2005 annual imports of certified Fair Trade bananas to the UK increased from 43,000 to over 1.33 million boxes. In the latter year, Fair Trade bananas accounted for nearly half of all the fruit exported by growers in the Windwards and generated US $2.33 million in social premiums. Of this, US $1.33 million was directly returned to the local groups that produced Fair Trade bananas for use as growers saw fit to benefit agricultural or community development.

Since 2000, there has been a corresponding increase in the number of Fair Trade groups and certified Fair Trade farmers throughout the region, although this increase has not been evenly distributed among the islands. The first Fair Trade banana shipments in 2000 were filled by twelve farmers' groups containing 466 members. By mid 2003, thirty-two groups had been registered with a membership of 1,368 farmers, and thirteen more were awaiting certification (WINFA 2003). In part because of supermarket preferences, the growth and distribution of Fair Trade production has not occurred evenly among the islands. When the UK-based Tesco supermarket chain began marketing Fair Trade bananas from the Caribbean in 2002, it insisted that all its fruit be sourced from Dominica, a decision that overrode WINFA's ostensible role in allocating island Fair Trade quotas. Some in the region attribute Tesco's insistence on Dominican fruit to self-interested promotional strategies by the supermarket rather than principles of social equity. Often identified in travel literature as the "Nature Isle" because of its rugged volcanic topography and lack of large-scale tourism development, Dominica has received considerable recognition from international environmental organizations for its conservation policies. By purchasing all its fruit from Dominica, some on St. Lucia argued, Tesco was attempting to simultaneously enhance its reputation for both social and environmental responsibility, a claim that at least one company representative denied.[9] Regardless of its motives, Tesco's desire to appear socially responsible by marketing Fair Trade bananas led it—paradoxically—to disregard the policy-making role of Fair Trade producers themselves, who are ostensibly represented through WINFA.

One result of Tesco's sourcing strategy has been a rapid expansion of Fair Trade producers' groups on Dominica, but a much slower growth of such groups elsewhere. Over 85 percent of Dominica's approximately 1,000 remaining banana farmers were certified Fair Trade producers in 2004, compared with just 22 percent of the approximately 1,500 farmers remaining in production on St. Lucia. Despite the fact that St. Lucia by itself produces approximately one-half of all bananas exported from the Windward Islands, its share of Fair Trade production is less than 25 percent of the total. Some Fair Trade representatives on St. Lucia also suspect that WINFA, which is supported by voluntary assessments made by producers' groups from each island's total social premium, discriminates against St. Lucia in the allocation of Fair Trade quotas. The reason for this, they contend, is that the Vincentian and Dominican National Fair Trade Associations choose to allocate a larger share of their social premium to WINFA than does the SLNFTA. Indeed, unstructured interviews with Fair Trade participants on all three islands reveal a much more skeptical attitude toward WINFA among St. Lucians, who often describe the umbrella organization as more of a self-interested bureaucracy than an advocate for farmers' interests.[10] Whether or not such suspicions are warranted, the proportionately larger Fair Trade quotas awarded to St. Vincent and Dominica are regularly cited by St. Lucians as evidence of WINFA's alleged favoritism. Most St. Lucian farmers are unaware, however, of how heavily British supermarket sourcing preferences influence the current distribution of Fair Trade quotas.

Fair Trade farmers in St. Lucia are quick to point out what they see as the inequitable aspects of their relationship to WINFA and FLO. Yet they also acknowledge that Fair Trade has encouraged among them a greater degree of community involvement than in the past. For most farmers, participation in a Fair Trade group is the first opportunity they have had to contribute to a democratically run community organization not affiliated

Figure 10.2 | Bus stop in rural Dominica bearing FLO's Fair Trade logo. The structure was built with social premiums generated by area banana farmers.

with party politics. Levels of participation in monthly meetings vary between groups, but judging from their avid participation most members in the Mabouya Valley attend out of a sense of commitment rather than obligation. Meetings provide farmers with a novel opportunity to plan local development using funds they themselves have generated, rather than passively accept whatever largesse and priorities the state, political parties, and NGOs intend for them. From this process has emerged both a discernible identity and a sense of community that extend beyond the allocation of the material benefits of Fair Trade. Throughout the Eastern Caribbean, Fair Trade banana farmers are often recognizable by their proudly worn lapel pins, which bear the same logo that FLO displays on all the products it certifies. Just as Fair Trade farmers distinguish themselves outwardly from their conventional counterparts, the distinction between Fair Trade and conventional growers is evident in their economic circumstances and outlook as well. These factors may well determine who among the region's banana growers is able to survive in a newly configured European market as the last remnants of quota protection are dismantled in the wake of the WTO ruling.

"Our Last Chance"

After the conclusion of a meeting of the Mabouya Valley Fair Trade Group in July 2004, two members who looked to be well into their seventies waited patiently to ask the group's president whether they were on the roster of those packing Fair Trade fruit that week. Standing not ten feet away from them, the vice president, one of a few persons under the age of forty in a room of gray-haired men and women, reviewed minutes from the Kwéyòl portion of the preceding meeting with me. Suddenly gesturing at the nearby farmers, he interrupted our discussion to make a point about the future of the banana industry:

> This is one of the problems we are facing here now. You see these old men? They won't pass the farm on to their children because they can't afford to. They need the farm because they don't have a pension. Meanwhile, they don't have the education you need to make their farms modernized, and they don't have the energy to make them produce even as much as they used to. As long as men like this have no other support, we're not going to see young people coming into the industry. (Edwin, pers. comm. 2004)

Even as the vice president pointed them out as an illustration of "the problems" faced by the banana industry, the older men betrayed no irritation or discomfort at his assertion. It was apparent from their lack of response that they were either ignoring his comments or lacked sufficient English fluency to understand them. When asked about this point later on, the officer claimed that the latter was the case. This only proved his point, he said, about the farmers' lack of education as well as age. His assertion about the relative lack of education among older farmers is borne out by responses offered by the 133 Mabouya Valley growers surveyed in 2004. Farmers older than the mean age of 44.5 years had completed an average of 6.2 years of schooling, compared to 8.6 years of formal education for those below that age.[11] This figure drops off dramatically for the oldest cohort of farmers: those age 70 and above reported an average of just 2.3 years of schooling, with 29 percent having received no formal education at all. This is reflected as well in levels of English-Kwéyòl bilingualism, for while virtually all valley farmers under 45 are fluent in English, only about 40 percent of those above 70 have a working command of it.

Among governments and NGOs in the Eastern Caribbean and among Fair Trade advocates in Europe, there is ardent agreement about securing the future of the Windward Islands banana industry. Almost all policy recommendations about how to achieve the industry's survival have centered on economic questions, notably costs of production, yields per acre, and returns to growers, as well as macroeconomic factors such the permissible level of tariff protection in the wake of the WTO ruling. In the midst of this often heated policy discussion, one fundamental issue affecting the industry's future—its aging demographic structure—is almost never mentioned. Yet to attend any gathering of banana growers on St. Lucia is to be in the presence of many people who are obviously beyond their prime working years, leading even the most casual observer to note how few young men and women on the island now select farming as a way of life. If a Caribbean banana industry of any size is to survive beyond the immediate future, it must be able to recruit farmers of a younger generation. This it will do only when it can also demonstrate its economic viability relative to other choices of livelihood, whether or not they are based on legal alternatives or require foreign migration. To determine whether Fair Trade can secure a place for growers in the transition to a more open European banana market, it is first necessary to ask how Fair Trade affects those farmers that it purports to help. In turn, this question may be assessed by comparing the circumstances of Fair Trade and conventional farmers living and working side by side in the Mabouya Valley.

In the course of this research, 133 commercial banana farmers residing in the Mabouya Valley were surveyed during a seven-week period between May and July 2004. To ensure the inclusion of a cross-section of active growers, farmers were interviewed as they waited to deliver their fruit for sale to the buying depot at La Caye, which services all Mabouya Valley farms. Four St. Lucians, all having some experience with banana farming, were recruited and trained as ethnographic interviewers. They also collaborated in the preparation of a Kwéyòl version of the survey instrument, which was administered in that language in about 80 percent of the farmers' interviews. Of those farmers surveyed, 58 were members of the Mabouya Valley Fair Trade Group; the remaining 75 were conventional farmers. In total, the sample represented about a third of all active growers in the valley, according to data maintained by BERU. In terms of its demographic and landholding characteristics and proportion of Fair Trade and conventional farmers, the overall sample (whose parameters are suggested in Table 3.1 in Chapter 3) closely approximates the broad parameters of the local farming population as indicated in BERU's database of all the valley's growers.

The differences between Fair Trade and conventional farmers in the Mabouya Valley are so striking in many instances that the two groups might be taken for entirely separate populations or communities. Tables 10.1, 10.2, and 10.3 summarize some of the key differences between the groups with respect to their demographic, landholding, and economic characteristics.

The survey results indicate that on average, Fair Trade farmers are significantly older (by 10.8 years) than their conventional counterparts and

Table 10.1 | Demographic Characteristics of Fair Trade and Conventional Farmers

		N	Mean	Std. Deviation
Age of Farmer	Fair Trade	58	50.9*	9.0
	Conventional	75	40.1	11.6
Household Size	Fair Trade	58	5.3	2.3
	Conventional	75	4.9	1.8
Years of school	Fair Trade	58	6.9	3.1
	Conventional	75	7.9	2.9
Years farming in valley	Fair Trade	58	25.1*	12.1
	Conventional	75	17.5	8.1

Cross-tabulation of Gender and Fair Trade Status

		Fair Trade Status		
		No	Yes	Total
Gender of farmer	Female	21	19	40
	Male	54	39	93
Total		75	58	133

Chi-Square = .352, not significant at p < .05

Table 10.2 | Landholdings: Fair Trade and Conventional Farmers

		N	Mean	Std. Deviation
Number of parcels farmed	Fair Trade	58	1.2	0.4
	Conventional	75	1.3	0.5
Acreage in bananas	Fair Trade	58	4.3	1.5
	Conventional	75	4.2	2.2
Acreage of owned land	Fair Trade	58	2.4*	2.6
	Conventional	75	1.2	1.9
Acreage of rented land	Fair Trade	58	2.0	2.9
	Conventional	75	1.9	2.4
Acreage of family land	Fair Trade	58	0.4	1.1
	Conventional	75	1.8*	2.6

*t-statistic significant at p < .05

Source: Author's survey data

Table 10.3 | Economic Characteristics: Fair Trade and
Conventional Farmers

		N	Mean	Std. Deviation
Annual income:	Fair Trade	58	4,229	8,583.9
other crops (EC $)	Conventional	75	4,406	7,642.5
Annual income:	Fair Trade	58	2,141	7,553.7
other sources (EC $)	Conventional	75	3,095	8,587.5
Paid nonharvest	Fair Trade	58	2.8*	1.0
workers on farm	Conventional	75	2.4	0.9
Paid workers on	Fair Trade	58	6.9*	1.9
harvest days	Conventional	75	5.8	1.7
Wages paid	Fair Trade	58	$410*	324.5
fortnightly	Conventional	75	$285	195.5
Gross sales from	Fair Trade	57	$1,458*	1074.8
most recent harvest	Conventional	74	$968	703.3
Net earnings from	Fair Trade	57	$776*	544.3
most recent harvest	Conventional	74	$538	400.1
Most recent shipment	Fair Trade	58	82.7*	51.4
(boxes)	Conventional	75	70.1	63.6

*t-statistic significant at p < .05

Source: Author's survey data

have been farming in the valley for a significantly longer period of time
(by 7.6 years). Reflecting the general negative association between age and
completed education, Fair Trade farmers report 1.1 fewer years of schooling than conventional growers. This difference between the groups is not,
however, statistically significant. Interestingly, in a farming population
characterized by a relatively high level of female participation, women
are even more highly represented among Fair Trade farmers (48 percent of
whom are female) than among conventional farmers (28 percent). Despite
their heavy representation among the general membership, it is notable
that only one out of the five officers of the Mabouya Fair Trade group is a
woman.

There is virtually no difference in the amount of land cultivated in bananas by either conventional or Fair Trade farmers or in the number of
parcels that each farms. Yet such outward similarities conceal huge underlying differences in land tenure. Fair Trade farmers, on average, privately
own more than twice the acreage owned by conventional farmers, while
the latter on average utilize more than five times the amount of family

land farmed by their Fair Trade counterparts. Nearly 16 percent of Fair Trade farmers (9 out of 58) have access to irrigation, an infrastructural improvement claimed by just one of the 75 conventional farmers (1.3 percent). These differences, all of which are statistically significant, suggest that conventional farmers enjoy much less security of land tenure than Fair Trade growers, and are less able to make permanent investments in banana production as a result. Many of these investments represent the very commitments expected of farmers under the Fair Trade regime.

A host of reasons could explain why Fair Trade farmers represent the older and most heavily invested segment of the valley's farming population. Chief among these is the manner in which farmers were initially recruited into the Fair Trade group when it was formed in 2000. For more than two decades, the region had been the site of the Mabouya Valley Development Project (MVDP), an ambitious integrated rural development initiative begun by the St. Lucian government during the Compton administration and funded in part by the Organization of American States. Broadly speaking, the project's goal was to promote agricultural "modernization" (in the form of individualized land tenure and technological change) and community formation. Participating farmers were afforded the opportunity to purchase five-acre parcels of land from the government-owned Dennery Farmco estate with low-interest loans, to receive government-subsidized irrigation services,[12] and to participate in a "grassroots" community association linked to the MVDP. Although not operating officially as a cooperative, the MVDP promoted some degree of common interest and community participation through monthly meetings of valley farmers with representatives of the government, Ministry of Agriculture extension agents, and BGA staff. The formal project was winding down at about the same time that the SLBC began promoting Fair Trade farming in 2000, during which time the banana company disseminated information about Fair Trade through the MVDP project headquarters at Riche Fond. That office became a meeting place for the first organizational gatherings of what was to become the Mabouya Valley Fair Trade Group, which continues to meet in a building at the same site. Hence, the first local farmers to be invited to participate in Fair Trade were those who had previously participated in the MVDP; as such, they were also among the most established local farmers in terms of their individualized land tenure, farming experience, and length of local residence.

When asked how they had first learned about Fair Trade, 37 of 58 (66 percent) said they had been told about it directly by the MVDP office or by another farmer associated with the project. While networking of this sort appeared to play a critical role in initial recruitment to the Fair Trade group, the association has thus far managed to stay clear of the political and religious divisions that have ensnared cooperatives elsewhere. In Belize, for example, even successful cooperatives often draw their members from a single political party or religious affiliation, resulting in an inequitable distribution of benefits that heightens both village factionalism and class divisions (Moberg 1991). Similarly, farmers' cooperatives in Jamaica have been notoriously prone to partisan infighting among supporters of the two major national political parties. In the Mabouya Valley, political and religious differences are acknowledged openly by Fair Trade members, but significantly, the group itself draws members from both political parties as well as most of the various churches active in the region. In contrast to cooperatives elsewhere, the leadership of the Fair Trade group has discouraged and even penalized efforts of some members to steer the association in a partisan direction. In two instances, where members persisted in engaging in politically partisan and divisive arguments during monthly meetings, those individuals were decertified after failing to heed warnings about their behavior. Also interesting is that many growers were unable to identify the party affiliation of the group's president when asked to do so, or responded, in effect, that his beliefs did not affect the way he conducted association business.

The absence of a distinctly partisan identity to the Fair Trade group does not imply that all local farmers have enjoyed equal opportunities to participate in it. Indeed, it is likely that some of the requirements of Fair Trade farming have unintentionally precluded participation by the many local farmers who lack individual titles to land. Slightly over 60 percent of all Fair Trade farmers own all or some of their land outright, while 72 percent of conventional farmers lack formal titles over any land. As noted above, while Fair Trade farmers control significantly more land under individual ownership than do conventional farmers, the latter group occupies significantly more family land. Farmers without individual land titles would find it difficult to comply with some of the Fair Trade environmental criteria. Chief among these is the creation of buffer zones along streams and roads, a requirement affecting about one in five Fair Trade farms. To establish a buffer zone, a farmer occupying family land would have to secure the permission of all other family members claiming rights to his or her parcel to leave a portion of it uncultivated or planted in tree crops. Such arrangements are likely to be strongly opposed by kin who rely on the land for subsistence. Indeed, the most commonly encountered complaint by those who cultivate family land regards the pressure placed upon a given parcel by many competing demands from kinsmen. Similarly, few farmers would be willing to invest in the planting of tree crops on land that they rented on a year-to-year basis but did not themselves own. Because the buffer zone requirement presupposes that farmers have complete discretion over the use of their land and would solely benefit from improvements such as tree crops, it has in effect limited participation in the Fair Trade group in many instances to those who exercise independent ownership of their land.

Because Fair Trade and conventional farmers are so distinct in terms of demography and land tenure, it might be anticipated that identifying the effect of Fair Trade participation on banana farmers is complicated by other confounding variables. However, in one critical respect—the extent of acreage cultivated under bananas—Fair Trade and conventional farmers are virtually identical (an average of 4.34 vs. 4.26 acres under bananas, respectively). It can be plausibly argued, then, that whatever other differences characterize the two groups, their distinct experiences with regard to growing and selling bananas could be largely attributed to whether or not they participate in Fair Trade. Table 10.4 summarizes some of these differences.

As mentioned earlier, Fair Trade farmers report that their labor requirements have increased as a result of FLO's no-herbicide policy, a perception borne out by their reported heavier reliance on hired workers and greater overall wage expenditures than conventional farmers. These differences in labor inputs and wage expenses are statistically significant.

Fair Trade growers on average sell 17 percent more fruit over a given fortnight (82 versus 70 boxes). While not quite statistically significant at the .05 level of probability, this disparity may point to a critical difference between the groups with regard to incentives for production. The box price paid to growers for premium conventional bananas during 2004 lagged between 12 percent and 16 percent below that of Fair Trade fruit, while unbagged fruit destined for the wholesale market sold for approximately 40 percent less than the Fair Trade bananas did. It is probable that for many conventional farmers these lower prices constitute major disincentives to increased banana production.

Compared to Fair Trade farmers, conventional growers experience a lower opportunity cost for their labor, which often brings a higher return when deployed off the farm than on it, especially during the first months of the year when fruit prices are lowest. This fact, which is reflected in their higher average nonfarm incomes, means that conventional farmers are prone at times to reduce their overall labor contributions to their farms. This, in turn, reduces their average overall farm output. An additional factor that may contribute to aggregate productivity differences between Fair Trade and conventional farmers is the higher incidence of irrigation on Fair Trade farms, although this pertains to a relatively small minority of parcels. Regardless of its causes, the difference in farm productivity, combined with the higher prices of Fair Trade fruit, corresponds to statisti-

Table 10.4 | Attitudinal Measures: Fair Trade and Conventional Farmers

		N	Mean	Std. Deviation
Are conditions better or	Fair Trade	58	3.5*	1.2
worse than 5 years ago?	Conventional	75	2.6	1.4
(1 = much worse, 5 = much better)				
Estimated % of assets	Fair Trade	58	66.6*	19.4
from banana farming	Conventional	75	58.9	24.6

*t-statistic significant at p < .05

Cross-tabulation: Amount of Bananas You Grow Today
Compared to Five Years Ago by Fair Trade Status

		Fair Trade Status		
		No	Yes	Total
Growing more or less	Less	33	22	55
bananas than 5 years ago?	Same	12	17	29
	More	30	19	49
Total		75	58	133

Chi-Square = 3.4, not significant at p < .05

Cross-tabulation: Will You be Growing Bananas in 5 Years?
by Fair Trade Status

		Fair Trade Status		
		No	Yes	Total
Will you be growing	No	16	2	18
bananas in 5 years?	Yes	49	53	102
	Don't know	10	3	13
Total		75	58	133

Chi-Square = 12.8, significant at p < .05

Source: Author's survey data

cally significantly higher earnings from banana production for Fair Trade growers. On average, the gross sales receipts of Fair Trade farmers every fortnight are 53 percent higher than those of their conventional counterparts (EC $1,458 vs. $968). Even after deductions for inputs, supplies, and labor, Fair Trade growers report net returns 36 percent higher than those of conventional farmers (EC $776 vs. $538).[13]

While these are the measurable material benefits associated with Fair Trade, the higher incomes received by farmers translate directly into what industry and local Fair Trade representatives openly call "a changed outlook" in banana-producing communities. This might be characterized as a perceptible degree of optimism and confidence absent from most sectors of the Eastern Caribbean banana industry since 1993. Conventional farmers have attempted, within the limited means available to them, to diversify their sources of household income, with an attendant decline in their attention to farming and on-farm investments. In comparison, Fair Trade farmers remain heavily committed to banana farming as a livelihood, notwithstanding the costly sacrifices expected of them by the new environmental protocols. Somewhat over 62 percent of Fair Trade farmers reported that they were growing the same or a greater amount of bananas than five years earlier, compared to 56 percent of conventional farmers. The difference between groups is not statistically significant, but given the demographic composition of the Fair Trade group it is notable that a sizable majority of the Fair Trade farmers have maintained or increased their commitment to banana production in recent years. As noted earlier, Fair Trade farmers in the Mabouya Valley disproportionately comprise older growers and women, segments of the rural population that have otherwise reduced their reliance on banana farming more than younger male growers have. When asked to estimate the percentage of their personal and household assets derived from bananas, Fair Trade farmers report a figure of 66.6 percent, statistically significantly higher than the 58.9 percent estimated by conventional farmers. The improved outlook that industry observers have attributed to Fair Trade growers is borne out by these farmers' perceptions of recent change in the industry, which reveal significantly more optimism about current circumstances than among their conventional counterparts. Not surprisingly, such attitudes translate to a greater degree of future commitment to the industry among Fair Trade farmers. Asked to predict whether they expected to remain in banana production in five years' time, Fair Trade growers were significantly more likely than conventional farmers to answer in the affirmative.

Perhaps the most telling indicator that Fair Trade has benefited Windward Islands banana farmers is the very low rate of attrition among Fair Trade farmers' groups. All the groups have experienced some losses in membership when participants found the new requirements too burdensome or costly, or insisted on injecting partisan issues into group discussions. But even though they grumble about the new requirements they are subject to, the large majority of Fair Trade farmers would not trade places with their conventional counterparts. Tellingly, just seven farmers either resigned from the Mabouya Valley group or were decertified by it in the first four years of operation, a figure amounting to less than 6 percent of its 2004 membership. On the other hand, just one of the 75 surveyed conventional farmers said that he would not join the Fair Trade group if offered the opportunity (although several other farmers did express this sentiment in unstructured interviews).

In contrast to the history of previous agricultural cooperatives in the Eastern Caribbean, which is littered with far more failures than successes, just one of the six Fair Trade groups organized on the island in 2000 has since been dismantled. This fact was widely attributed to the fact that its members were geographically dispersed and had had little prior familiarity with one another. Many of its members have since joined other Fair Trade groups on the island. Like the other remaining Fair Trade groups on St. Lucia, the Mabouya Valley group maintains a waiting list of local farmers wishing to join in the event of resignations or increased production quotas, which would enable the group to expand beyond its current membership of 119. In 2001, the group admitted fifty "provisional" members in anticipation of an increase in Fair Trade quotas with the news that the Tesco chain was increasing its commitment to Fair Trade retailing. As seen earlier, the quota increase, when it came, was allocated entirely to Dominica's growers, and the provisional members in the Mabouya Valley were dropped from the group's roster as a result.

The contributions that Fair Trade groups have made to island economies, in terms of both somewhat higher export revenues and community development through social premiums, have gained the attention of government agencies formerly uninterested in, and even distrustful of, social movements organized outside the political party system. Until 2004, the official position of the St. Lucian government toward banana industry revitalization was evidenced by BERU's insistence on technological change, which made little accommodation for low–chemical usage farming. Indeed, the shift to meristem tissue culture bananas, with their higher preparation, labor, and input costs, threatened (like other Green Revolution innovations) to achieve higher average productivity at a steep social cost in terms of stratification. Having witnessed Fair Trade's tangible contribution in terms of rural incomes and community development, the St. Lucian government now welcomes the expansion of Fair Trade farming as a key to the banana industry's salvation. The government's changed attitude signals an implicit endorsement of community and environmental sustainability in place of its earlier promotion of a technologically modernized farming sector based on a smaller number of more "efficient" farms. Over the long term it remains to be seen whether the promises of Fair Trade will entice a new generation to enter banana farming after the present, aging generation has retired.

On January 1, 2006 the last vestiges of the tariff-quota system were eliminated, a moment once predicted to be the death knell of the banana industry in the Windwards. Ironically, by that point there were signs that the surviving banana farmers had weathered the worst of globalization. Soon two of the largest supermarket chains in the UK, Sainsbury's and Waitrose, announced that they would begin to carry exclusively Fair Trade bananas in their retail stores, with the fruit to be sourced from the Windward Islands, the Dominican Republic, and Colombia. The announcement anticipated the eventual conversion of all of the remaining growers in the Windwards to Fair Trade certification. It also prompted a modest but measurable increase in cultivation among farmers who had dropped out of production over previous years. By the following year, according to WINFA, the number of commercially active banana farmers on St. Lucia, St. Vincent, and Dominica had reached 3,347 (Fairtrade 2007), representing the first time since 1990 that the industry's productive base had actually grown instead of declined. No one in the islands expects that the industry will ever comprise more than a tiny fraction of its size during the heyday of Green Gold. Farmers also realize that Fair Trade has fallen far short of the promises made to them when they were recruited into the initiative. Notwithstanding its all too evident limitations, however, Fair Trade has become, in the words of one Mabouya Valley resident, "our last chance to survive here."

Notes

1. Similar attitudes have been reported among growers of other Fair Trade and "eco-friendly" products, such as shade-grown coffee (see especially Lyon 2006).
2. The machines are far more heavy-duty (and much heavier) than the electric weed eaters typically employed on suburban lawns. Nonetheless, they remain ill suited for agricultural use: farmers are advised not to run them for more than four consecutive hours, lest their motors overheat and seize up.
3. Two-tailed t-test significant at $p < .05$ with 131 df.
4. The cutlass does continue to be widely used on those portions of banana farms intercropped with staple foods, where farmers are usually reluctant to apply chemicals.
5. St. Lucia's National Fair Trade Association, which establishes general membership requirements for all local Fair Trade groups, requires the decertification of farmers who fail to attend three consecutive meetings. Although four members were expelled from the Mabouya Valley group during its first four years of existence, failure to attend meetings was not indicated as a reason for the expulsions.
6. He is referring to the National Fair Trade Committee, which is comprised of representatives of each of the Fair Trade farmers' groups on the island.
7. The expenditure of some of the first social premiums on weed eaters prompted some growers to compare Fair Trade assistance policies to those of Geest and the BGA in the

past. "They talk about giving you aid, but it's only to ensure that you do things on your farm the way they want them done."

8. The proportion of this allocation varies from island to island. The share of their social premiums that farmers on St. Vincent and Dominica contribute to WINFA is nearly twice that contributed on St. Lucia, with correspondingly less being made available to their island-wide Fair Trade associations.

9. A representative of Tesco visiting St. Lucia confirmed that the supermarket had chosen to source its Fair Trade bananas from Dominica, but denied that environmental considerations had entered into the decision. He stated that the sourcing decision was reached because of Dominica's especially severe economic contraction in the years after 1993. The company felt that Fair Trade's higher prices and social premiums would have greater potential to alleviate economic hardship on that island than on the more economically diversified islands of St. Lucia and St. Vincent.

10. St. Lucia's Fair Trade representatives were incensed when they learned, belatedly, that WINFA had organized a regional conference on the future of the Caribbean banana industry in June 2004 but had failed to invite them to the meeting or even inform them about it. The St. Lucians who were invited to participate included the island's prime minister and several other political leaders, the heads of the island's banana companies, and representatives of BERU, but no farmers or Fair Trade representatives.

11. The negative correlation between age and years of completed schooling is strongly statistically significant (Pearson's r of -.44, significant at $p < .05$).

12. These initial efforts at irrigation eventually failed because of engineering and construction errors made by the original contractor. All of the irrigation lines presently operating in the valley resulted from a much more recent initiative funded by the European Union in the late 1990s.

13. For gross earnings, two-tailed t-test is significant at $p < .05$ with 130 df. For net earnings, two-tailed t-test is significant at $p < .05$ with 130 df.

— Chapter Eleven —

CONCLUSION
A New World or a New Kind of Dependence?

More than 2,000 feet above sea level, in the cool, mist-enshrouded hills ten miles east of Roseau, Dominica, two Rastafarians cultivate potatoes, broccoli, tomatoes, and a variety of herbs for sale in the town's markets. Their farm clings to the edge of a steep slope. Its fields are painstakingly terraced and layered with green manure to prevent erosion. Conrad "Bull" Barrow and his friend Leonel "Lion" Williams grew bananas for export on land at lower elevations until declining prices led them to abandon the crop in 1994. The partners describe themselves as among the handful of former banana growers still residing in their hamlet of Giraudel, many others having left for the US and UK over the previous fifteen years.

Dominica, whose banana farms are even smaller than those on the other Windward Islands and almost always found on precipitous hillsides, has the highest costs of production per yield on any of the four islands. It has also experienced an even higher level of attrition than St. Lucia or St. Vincent, with the number of active banana farmers dropping to just 800 at one point in 2002. Here the combined effect of a declining industry and few legal economic alternatives has been especially heavily felt in rural areas. Export earnings from banana production declined by two-thirds between 1990 and 2000, during which time the island lost more than 10 percent of its population to emigration. Meanwhile, the country's trade imbalance was further aggravated by increasing oil prices and a recession in the US economy that caused Dominicans abroad to send fewer remittances back home. On the island itself, government expenditures climbed as officeholders, who are never far removed from popular discontent in such close-knit places, attempted to lessen the impact on consumers by subsidizing gasoline and other imports. With its foreign debt service payments approaching 100 percent of gross domestic product, the Dominican government was forced to negotiate a standby agreement with the International Monetary Fund in 2001. In addition to cutbacks in jobs, wages, and benefits in the public sector (now the island's largest employer), the IMF's structural adjustment program for Dominica has imposed strict austerity measures that affect all islanders' standards of living. Under structural adjustment, the Dominican government has imposed a new 7.5 percent sales tax on all purchases, followed by an additional 5 percent value-added tax (VAT) in 2004 (Edwards, pers. comm. 2004). In that year, more than 25 percent of all government revenues were used to repay the country's foreign debt, forcing sharp curtailments of public spending on domestic needs such as education and health care.

Like much of the island's sizable rural Rastafarian population, Barrow and Williams cultivate some marijuana and regularly use it themselves, in addition to a host of other plants traditionally used for medicinal purposes. Barrow admits that "there's money to be made" growing marijuana in larger quantities, but states that he is reluctant to plant more than what he himself uses given the dangers involved in trafficking. His brother, he volunteers, is serving a three-year prison term in Guadeloupe for doing so. Occasionally US Drug Enforcement Agency helicopters can be seen flying inland over the adjacent valley, almost at eye level with their farm, in search of the much larger drug-producing operations that are now the country's largest source of export earnings. While Barrow has not followed in his brother's path, his farm is very much the product of the same global economic forces that have seen an increase in drug production and trafficking. For four years, the men have employed no manufactured chemical inputs of any kind on their farm. Barrow learned organic farming from his father, saying that it was not until they began growing bananas for export in the 1970s that local farmers began using farm chemicals. Having abandoned bananas and the attendant array of chemical inputs in the last decade, he says, they've since "gone back to the old ways." Clearing secondary growth is performed by cutlass, not herbicide. The men prepare a compost of mulch and cow manure to sow into the soil around their potato plants. Insects and other pests are repelled by spraying their crops with an emulsion containing ground cinnamon and marigold blossoms.

Across the island, hundreds of other farmers are similarly experimenting with organic methods and striving to recover agricultural techniques largely abandoned over the last generation. Many of these techniques are being tested at a government agricultural station, as are field tests with organic bananas. Farmers such as Barrow and Williams are the first to acknowledge that their interest in organic farming did not grow out of their ecological consciousness; rather, it was fueled, at least initially, by the soaring cost of chemical inputs. Rising import duties, sales taxes, and VAT, all resulting from the IMF's structural adjustment program, have priced fertilizer and herbicide beyond the reach of many farmers, compelling them to replace chemicals with human labor and organic substitutes. Ironically, one Dominican agronomist, recently returned from training in Cuba, brought with him many of the same organic methods being employed in that country's agriculture, which has also embarked on a low-chemical regimen since the loss of subsidized Soviet oil and agricultural inputs.

The decision of many rural Dominicans to become organic farmers might be seen as one response to the forces of globalization. Amidst the declining living standards of much of the population, there has also been a forced attempt at autarky, or economic self-sufficiency, accompanied by some degree of withdrawal from the world market. Unable to afford heavily taxed manufactured goods, Dominica's farmers and town dwellers alike have rediscovered some local, low-cost substitutes for the things the world market had formerly made available to them. These trends are not experienced in similar fashion by all island residents, however. For those like Barrow and Williams who make their living from the land, the rediscovery of older farming techniques and the resulting reduction in their dependence on imported inputs have resulted in a newfound pride in island traditions and a sense of economic independence. They also contribute marginally to the government's effort to market the island to socially and environmentally conscious tourists as an ecological haven distinct from the Caribbean's better known beach and resort destinations. In this sense, peaceful Rastafarians engaged in organic farming have become symbols to be employed in promotional advertising for the "Nature Isle."

Autarky may be a source of pride for some rural Dominicans, but for many other island residents it poses a difficult and even hazardous contraction in the standard of living to which they have become accustomed. Local alternatives to imported goods do not always exist, and those that do are not necessarily viewed as equally effective substitutes. With the decline of government subsidies for imported pharmaceuticals, poorer residents in town and country alike have returned to an extensive repertoire of "bush medicine" to treat their ailments. Whether local plants such as bay leaf and estaphagil treat high blood pressure as well as commercial beta-blockers or other anti-hypertensive drugs remains a point of contention in the local medical community. Many of its members remain concerned because the traditional medicines, unlike more expensive commercial drugs, have never been tested for their pharmaceutical properties, so their dosage and effectiveness remain largely unknown. Entirely apart from such questions, most town dwellers, whose aesthetics and sensibilities as consumers continue to be informed by the ubiquitous global media

Figure 11.1 | Former banana growers, now organic farmers, on the island of Dominica.

culture, experience autarky simply as greater material poverty and relative deprivation.

Fair Trade represents a different response to globalization, one that simultaneously embraces, yet seeks to transform, the world market. Because Fair Trade grew to maturity in conjunction with the anti-globalization protests that swept the world in the late 1990s, it was, and is still, viewed by many critics of the global economy as a blueprint for a new world. Here was a practical measure that all individuals could undertake to alter the way the international economy operates. In the process, the incomes, local decision-making, and cultural traditions of farmers whose products found their way into global markets would be enhanced. The exponential growth in consumer interest in Fair Trade items in recent years attests to a widespread distrust of the promises of unfettered globalization and growing desire for an alternative route.

If, however, the central objectives of Fair Trade are seen in ameliorative rather than transformative terms, as organizations such as Transfair and FLO have increasingly defined them, then some argue that there is no reason *in principle* to exclude large corporations from Fair Trade certification. No longer seen as a means of subverting global capitalism, Fair Trade in this sense is decidedly remote from its origins as a gesture of solidarity with revolutionary movements in Central America and southern Africa. It is not surprising that this "soft" definition of Fair Trade has been seized upon as a marketing opportunity by powerful corporations and retail supermarkets. Given the fate of other social movements whose objectives to transform the political and economic systems were eventually co-opted by them, this de-radicalization of Fair Trade may disillusion many of its advocates, but it should not surprise them. Much as corporations once ignored or disparaged the advocates of civil rights and environmentalism only to eventually adopt their rhetoric, companies have discovered that Fair Trade on a carefully circumscribed basis offers a cost-effective way to redeem tarnished reputations in the eyes of politically aware consumers.

What, then, is to be made of the Fair Trade movement as it encompasses growing numbers of Caribbean farming communities? There is general agreement among farmers, other industry segments, and national governments that Fair Trade has materially benefited farmers and rural communities in the Windward Islands. Recent trends suggesting a stabilization and even slight increase in the region's grower base provide further, if tentative, proof of this. Evidence from this study also strongly suggests that on balance, the economic circumstances of farmers have demonstrably improved from the higher price paid for Fair Trade bananas. Yet questions remain about how that price is determined and whether it meets Fair Trade's stated pricing criteria. According to FLO's promotional literature and website, the higher producer prices received by Fair Trade farmers are designed to cover their costs of production and afford them a sustainable standard of living. Some Fair Trade farmers dispute this, arguing that higher fruit prices do little more than offset the higher production costs of low-chemical farming. Still, as seen in the previous chapter, even after the higher costs of production are deducted from the gross receipts of Fair Trade farmers, most receive higher net earnings than their conventional counterparts. Nonetheless, little information is available either to growers or to the public about how the producer price of Fair Trade bananas is actually established and who is involved in setting that price. What is apparent is the final price that WIBDECO pays for bananas of various categories from each island, as this information is readily made available to producers through the local banana companies (St. Lucia and Dominica) or the BGA (St. Vincent). How WIBDECO's box price is set is a question that no one at the importing and retail end of the commodity chain appears inclined to answer. No one interviewed in the course of this project recalls WIBDECO, FLO, or WINFA personnel conducting production cost studies for each of the islands and the various topographical conditions existing on them, which would have been a precondition to establishing a genuine Fair Trade price.

At a broader level, while Fair Trade represents the relationship between producers and consumers as a reciprocal one, farmers see themselves as continuously subject to seemingly arbitrary or inappropriate production decisions made elsewhere. FLO's insistence on mechanical methods of weed control and its ban on nematicides—practices that often worsen problems of weed and pest infestation—and buffer zone requirements ill suited to the small size of Caribbean farms aptly illustrate the hierarchical, nonlocal, and nondemocratic nature of these decisions. FLO has not been unresponsive to farmers' appeals of these decisions through their National Fair Trade Committees and WINFA, but the time-consuming and cumbersome nature of the appeal process highlights the asymmetric nature of the relationship between producers and those who certify their Fair Trade status. In terms of the "transparency" of decision making, an attribute upheld by FLO as a distinctive feature of the Fair Trade producer-consumer relationship, then, it can be seen that the reality of Fair Trade in the Windward Islands has fallen far short of its rhetorical promises.

Within the dimensions of pricing and production, Fair Trade farmers remain subject to criteria determined by WIBDECO and FLO, but with little or no input from farmers themselves. Hence, Fair Trade has done little to transform the market in which growers participate; indeed, in some respects it has heightened the vagaries to which they are exposed. As previous observers have pointed out (Slocum 1996, 2006; Grossman 1998, 2003), despite their nominal independence as producers, Windwards farmers have experienced a profound erosion in their autonomy in recent decades within the realms of production and post-harvest handling. As responsibility for packaging shifted in the last three decades from retailer to importer, then to the local BGAs, and finally to the growers themselves, fruit specifications and production techniques became increasingly standardized and demanding. The recent shift in the UK retail banana market from undifferentiated loose bananas to products geared for segmented niche markets, in which Fair Trade plays a significant role, has not reversed this trend. Rather, the proliferation of pack types designed for specific market segments and retail outlets, each with their own specifications for hand size and box weight, has greatly compounded the complexity of the production and packaging routines to which farmers are subjected.

Confronted with a retail market differentiated into loose, organic, "kids' sized," and finally Fair Trade bananas, the English consumer likely does not realize that fruit from the very same farm may be packaged differently and sold in highly distinct price categories. While retailers reap most of the benefit of this segmented market, farmers perform all of the additional labor that makes it possible. In this sense, Fair Trade has not reversed the trend toward nonlocal control over the production process. As retail niches have broadened, the demands for farmers to comply with market expectations have increased, as have the costs for doing so. Further, the most recent changes associated with niche marketing have come in a breathtakingly short period of time, forcing farmers to modify their production routines with little notice and heightening their uncertainty about impending future changes in marketing and packaging. It is little surprise, then, that the Fair Trade movement's rhetoric of reciprocity and partnership rarely finds expression among growers themselves. While remaining optimistic about Fair Trade's potential, a WINFA official accurately summed up the ambivalence and even foreboding expressed by many Windwards residents about the movement:

> Fair Trade has done a lot of good things for farmers and their communities, and we're grateful to still sell our bananas. But there have been so many changes in this industry in the last ten years that many of us wonder whether *this* will last. A lot of farmers now know that Fair Trade doesn't give him any more control over what he produces, how he produces it, or how he packages it. It's a new kind of dependence. (Bobb, pers. comm. 2004).

Notwithstanding their diminished control over production and the dictates of the market, in one especially critical dimension Fair Trade has offered banana farmers a kind of independence they had not before experienced, at least not in recent decades. Much of this book has attempted to demonstrate the forms of political and economic control to which rural St. Lucians are subject. Over the last generation, unlike the colonial era that preceded it, rural residents have been critical actors in their island's history. Farmers and rural workers in St. Lucia have proven most of the time to be *the* key constituency for those seeking political and economic power. Yet like peasantry everywhere, as Wolf (1969) once famously observed, they have played a societal role that is in some ways a tragic one. Having supplied the massed crowds, the indignation, and the votes needed to fulfill others' political ambitions, the rural poor have rarely set the agenda of those who ride their grievances to power. Once safely in their electoral and bureaucratic positions, both government and corporate officeholders view rural residents as an afterthought, a force to reckon with—or more likely, manipulate—only during crises or the approach of elections. At such times, farming communities are "rediscovered" by their ostensible champions, who deliver, in unsolicited form, road maintenance, some infrastructural improvements, higher banana prices in the form of "cross-subsidization," and a good measure of temporary public works employment. All of these benefits tend to fade away conspicuously in the weeks and months following elections. Opposition candidates or rival business leaders inevitably draw upon the ensuing disillusionment, promising better than their opponents but delivering little differently upon their own rise to power.

It is no surprise then that St. Lucian politics, for all its partisan intensity, has long been accompanied by a "client" rather than a class consciousness (Johnson and Earle 2000: 341–342), a belief that only influential patrons spouting populist rhetoric can deliver farmers and rural workers from their plight. Banana farmers may have made recent St. Lucian history by their power at the ballot box. But despite the tumultuous events in which they participated, such as the 1993 growers' strike, in too many instances they have cast their votes as the passive objects of others' ambitions rather than active subjects of their own.

The achievements of Fair Trade thus far are replete with ironies. The movement has fallen short of its primary stated goal of substantively transforming the world market, for the structures that govern banana growers' incomes, decision making, and overall well-being remain largely unchanged by it. Further, given the increasing number of global corporations seeking the redemption of Fair Trade certification, this goal appears ever more elusive even as the movement captures a greater share of the world market for coffee, cacao, tea, and bananas. Yet in what might be considered a footnote to its central motivation—namely, Fair Trade's social criteria for producers' groups—the movement has brought about a revolution in the arena of community governance and local development.

Until now, none but the most elderly of the island's small farmers had had any direct participatory experience in democratically self-governing community organizations. Since 1967, when the island BGA was restructured as a statutory board from which the large majority of growers were excluded in terms of voting privileges and representation, most farmers have had little or no voice in the operations of their industry. Much as the BGA came under the control of the government, so too did labor unions and other community organizations eventually lose their former independence. By the 1970s, all of these segments of civil society were more or less absorbed by the island's political parties as appendages to the parties' electoral strategies. The experience of the dissident movement SLAM (the St. Lucia Action Movement) in the same decade, which originated as a trenchant critic of the island's party-based political system but evolved into an arm of the St. Lucia Labour Party, highlights the extent to which independent organizations and activists in the past inevitably succumbed to the juggernaut of the two dominant parties.

A generation later, Fair Trade farmers are learning direct democracy all over again. This time they are doing so independently of politicians and the parties they represent, in part by supplying services that an atrophied neoliberal state has abandoned. In addition to their democratic operating principles, Fair Trade groups provide their members with access to community development resources that are not tied to the demands of one or the other segments of the island's political elite. The ability of farmers to generate funds for local development and plan how those resources are utilized has proven to be an extraordinarily empowering tool. No longer mere recipients of government and party largesse during times of political crisis, farmers are learning to identify their communities' chief concerns and to address them with the products of their own labor. As a Mabouya Valley farmer observed after one marathon group meeting, "We debate and debate, but this is not a debating society. This is political *and* economic democracy. None of us have experienced this before. I honestly think sometimes we go on and on and even argue just because, like all good new things, you don't want it to end."

The survival of Fair Trade farmers' groups, and the novel forms of grassroots democracy that they embody, hinge closely on a number of issues that remain very contentious at this writing. First of these is a world market whose terms and contours continue to be defined by both the architects of globalization and the countervailing pressure of their opponents. Caribbean residents have much to say about these issues, and their voices, with others in the global South, are increasingly heard by thousands of community-based, national, and religious organizations working for a more socially just distribution of the world's resources. The outcome of this story also turns on the evolving definition of the Fair Trade movement and whether corporate entities such as Chiquita may gain entry into it. The ending of that particular story remains in the hands of the broad coalition of consumers, anti-globalization activists, and producers who constitute the Fair Trade movement worldwide. Ultimately, though, the movement's achievements will be measured by its accomplishments at the local level, perhaps most notably the freeing of community development and decision making from the aspirations of outside power seekers. Should Fair Trade associations like those in the Mabouya Valley survive the coming years of uncertainty to take root and become the model for other community-based organizations throughout the Windward Islands, banana politics may yet become the route to a new, better world.

References

Interviews

Blanchard, Earl, Docks Manager for St. Lucia Ports Authority. Personal communication, Castries, St. Lucia, 1 July 2004.

Bobb, Arthur, WINFA Fair Trade Coordinator. Personal communication, Kingstown, St. Vincent, 14 July 2004.

Boxill, Mecia, CARITAS Programs Administrator. Personal communication, Vigie, St. Lucia, 28 June 2004.

Celestine, Edme, retired farmer. Personal communication, Dennery, St. Lucia, 22 June 2004.

Charles, Lucien, WIBDECO fruit buyer. Personal communication, Riche Fond, St. Lucia, 18 June 2004.

Compton, Sir John, then former Prime Minister. Personal communication, Castries, St. Lucia, 8 June 2004.

Cottle, Junior "Spirit," Community Development and Sustainability Officer, Ministry of Agriculture. Personal communication, Kingstown, St. Vincent, 19 July 2004.

Edwards, Rosamund, Chief Economist in the Ministry of Finance, Government of Dominica. Personal communication, Roseau, Dominica. 7 July 2004.

Edwin, Victor, First Vice President of the Mabouya Valley Fair Trade Farmers Group. Personal communication, Riche Fond, St. Lucia, 18 June 2004.

Faisal, Nicholas, Financial Director, St. Lucia Banana Corporation. Personal communication, Castries, St. Lucia, 8 August 2003.

Francois, Matthew, Royal St. Lucia Police. Personal communication, Castries, St. Lucia, 8 June 2004.

Henry, Jacinta, Principal of St. Michael's Primary School. Personal communication, La Ressource, St. Lucia, 28 June 2004.

Hoggarth, Marcus, Head Produce Buyer for Sainsbury's Supermarkets. Personal communication, London, UK, 13 March 2003.

James, Perpetua, Community Development Officer for Dennery South. Personal communication, Dennery, St. Lucia, 18 June 2004.

Jn Pierre, Tony, Communications Director, St. Lucia Banana Corporation. Personal communication, Castries, St. Lucia, 16 May 2000.

Joseph, Patrick, former Secretary of the Banana Salvation Committee. Personal communication, Mon Repos, St. Lucia, 1 July 2004.

LaForce, Hillary, Programme Manager for Banana Emergency Recovery Unit. Personal communication, Cul de Sac, St. Lucia, 13 August 2003

Laurent, Fr. Raymond, parish priest of St. Michael's Catholic Church. Personal communication, La Ressource, St. Lucia, 24 and 28 June 2004.

Lynch, Cornelius, President of the Mabouya Valley Fair Trade Farmers Group. Personal communication, Osdan, St. Lucia, 12 August 2003 and Riche Fond, St. Lucia, 18 June 2004.

Mathurin, Patricia, teacher at St. Michael's Primary School. Personal communication, La Ressource, St. Lucia, 28 June 2004.

Rosarie, Herbert, Field Officer, St. Lucia Banana Corporation. Personal communication, Castries, St. Lucia, 8 August 2003.

Sandiford, Daniel, Secretary of the Mabouya Valley Fair Trade Farmers Group. Personal communication, Riche Fond, St. Lucia. 18 June 2004.

Serieux, Peter, Executive Director, Total Quality Fruit Company. Personal communication, Castries, St. Lucia, 23 May 2000.

Wiltshire, Amos, National Fair Trade Coordinator. Personal communication, Roseau, Dominica, 5 July 2004.

Archival Sources

CO 1031/2809a.
Report of D.D. McGoun, Chief of Police, regarding a public meeting held at La Ressource, 26 April 1957, to Administrator of St. Lucia. Public Records Office, Kew, Great Britain.

CO 1031/2809b
Dispatch from Administrator of St. Lucia to Acting Governor Lindo of Windward Islands, dated 15 May 1957, marked Secret. Public Records Office, Kew, Great Britain.

CO 1031/2808
Telegram from Governor of Windward Islands to Secretary of State for the Colonies, dated 31 March 1957, marked Secret. Public Records Office, Kew, Great Britain.

DO 200/19a
Confidential memo in West Indies Department, April 1963, entitled Pressure to Remove Quantitative Restrictions in the British Market, in "West Indies Bananas." Brief no. 43, Public Records Office, Kew, Great Britain

DO 200/19b
"The Secretary of State's Visit to the West Indies – January 1962," marked Secret, in "West Indies Bananas." Brief no. 43, Public Records Office, Kew, Great Britain.

Secondary Sources

Abu-Lughod, Janet. 1989. *Before European Hegemony: The World System A.D. 1250–1350*. New York: Oxford University Press.

Acheson, James M. 1989. "Management of Common Property Resources." In *Economic Anthropology*, ed. Stuart Plattner. Stanford, CA: Stanford University Press.

Acosta, Yvonne, and Jean Casimir. 1985. "Social Origins of the Counter-Plantation System in St. Lucia." In *Rural Development in the Caribbean*, ed. P. I. Gomes. New York: St. Martin's.

Adrien, Peter. 1996. *Metayage, Capitalism, and Peasant Development in St. Lucia, 1840–1957*. Mona, Jamaica: Consortium Graduate School of the Social Sciences.

Ames, Barry. 1987. *Political Survival: Politicians and Public Policy in Latin America*. Berkeley: University of California Press.

Anderson, Rachel, Timothy Taylor, and Timothy Josling. 2003. "The Caribbean and the Banana Trade." In *Banana Wars: The Anatomy of a Trade Dispute*, ed. Timothy E. Josling and Timothy G. Taylor. Cambridge, MA: CABI Publishing.

AP (Associated Press). 2007. "Dow Pesticide Focus of Trial." *Saginaw News* (Saginaw, Michigan). 22 July. URL http://www.mlive.com/business/sanews/index.ssf?/base/business-2/1185099761180270.xml&coll=9 (14 August 2007).

Appadurai, Arjun. 1990. "Disjuncture and Difference in the Global Cultural Economy." *Theory, Culture and Society* 7 (2): 295–310.

Bailey, F. G. 1969. *Strategems and Spoils: A Social Anthropology of Politics*. Oxford: Blackwell.

———. 1988. *Humbuggery and Manipulation: The Art of Leadership*. New York: Cornell University Press.

Barber, Benjamin. 1995. *Jihad vs. McWorld: How Globalism and Tribalism are Reshaping the World*. New York: Ballantine Books.

Barlett, Donald L. and James B. Steele. 2000. "How to Become a Top Banana." *Time*, 7 February, 155 (5): 42–47.

Barlett, Peggy F. 1987. "The Crisis in Family Farming: Who Will Survive?" In *Farm Work and Fieldwork: Anthropological Studies of North American Agriculture*, ed. Michael Chibnik. Ithaca: Cornell University Press.

Barrow, Christine. 1992. *Family Land and Development in St. Lucia*. Cave Hill, Barbados: Institute for Social and Economic Research, University of the West Indies.

Barth, Frederik. 1959. *Political Leadership among Swat Pathans*. London: Athlone.

———. 1966. *Models of Social Organisation*. London: Royal Anthropological Institute.

Basch, Linda, Nina Glick Schiller, and Cristina Szanton-Blanc. 1994. *Nations Unbound: Transnational Projects, Postcolonial Predicaments, and Deterritorialized Nation-States*. Amsterdam: Gordon and Breach.

Bauman, Zygmunt. 1998. *Globalization: The Human Consequences*. New York: Columbia University Press.

Beckles, Hilary. 1996. "Where Will All the Garbage Go? Tourism, Politics, and the Environment in Barbados." In *Green Guerrillas: Environmental Conflicts and Initiatives in Latin America and the Caribbean*, ed. Helen Collinson. London: Latin American Bureau.

Bernstein, Henry, and Terence J. Byres. 2001. "From Peasant Studies to Agrarian Change." *Journal of Agrarian Change* 1 (1): 1–56.

Bérubé, Nicolas and Benoit Aquin. 2005. "Chiquita's Children." *In These Times*, 10 May. URL: http://www.inthesetimes.com/article/2096/ (17 August 2007).

BGA (St. Lucia Banana Growers' Association). 1963. *Tenth Annual Ordinary General Meeting*. Castries: The Voice Publishing Company.

BGH Bulletin. 2000. "News of Lawsuit Exposing Media Cover-up of Suspected Dangers in Milk." *BGH Bulletin*. URL: http://www.foxbghsuit.com/ (28 August 2005).

Boissevain, Jeremy. 1968. "The Place of Non-Groups in the Social Sciences." *Man: Journal of the Royal Anthropological Institute* 3 (4): 542–556.

———. 1974. *Friends of Friends: Networks, Manipulators and Coalitions*. Oxford: Blackwell.

———. 1977. "Of Men and Marbles: Notes toward a Reconsideration of Factionalism." In *A House Divided? Anthropological Studies of Factionalism*, ed. Marilyn Silverman and R. F. Salisbury. St. John's, Newfoundland: Memorial University of Newfoundland.

Bolland, O. Nigel. 1981. "Systems of Domination after Slavery: The Control of Land and Labor in the British West Indies after 1838." *Comparative Studies in Society and History* 23 (4): 591–619.

———. 1995. *On the March: Labour Rebellions in the British Caribbean, 1934–1939*. Kingston, Jamaica: Ian Randle.

Bourgois, Philippe. 1989. *Ethnicity at Work: Divided Labor on a Central American Banana Plantation*. Baltimore: Johns Hopkins University Press.

———. 1995. *In Search of Respect: Selling Crack in El Barrio*. New York: Cambridge University Press.

———. 2003. "One Hundred Years of United Fruit Company Letters." In *Banana Wars: Power, Production, and History in the Americas*, ed. Steve Striffler and Mark Moberg. Durham: Duke University Press.

Breen, Henry H. 1844. *St. Lucia: Historical, Statistical, and Descriptive*. London: Longman, Brown, Green and Longmans.

Breen, T.H. 2004. *The Marketplace of Revolution: How Consumer Politics Shaped American Independence*. Oxford: Oxford University Press.

Bremer, Krista. 2006. "In God's Name: Muslim Scholar Ebrahim Moosa on Freedom, Fundamentalism, and the Spirit of Islam." *The Sun* 364 (April): 4–12.

Brennan, Teresa. 2003. *Globalization and Its Terrors: Daily Life in the West*. London: Routledge.

Breslin, Jimmy. 2001. "In Sweatshops, Plundered Lives." *Newsday*, 11 April, A2.

Browne, Katherine. 2005. *Creole Economics: Caribbean Cunning under the French Flag*. Austin: University of Texas Press.

Bruce, John W. 1983. *Family Land Tenure and Agricultural Development in St. Lucia*. Research paper no. 79. Madison, WI: Land Tenure Center.

Bruno, Kenny, and Joshua Karliner. 2002. *Earthsummit.biz: The Corporate Takeover of Sustainable Development*. Oakland: Food First Books.

Caldwell, Zarrin T., and Christopher Bacon. 2006. "Fair Trade's Future: Scaling Up without Selling Out?" URL: http://us.oneworld.net/article/view/123087/ (1 September, 2006).

Campbell, Dunstan, Gavin Olney, and Millan L.B. Mulraine. 2001. *Windward Islands' Banana Farmers Livelihood Study*. St. Michael, Barbados: DFID Caribbean.

Cancian, Frank. 1992. *The Decline of Community in Zinacantan: Economy, Public Life, and Social Stratification*. Stanford, CA: Stanford University Press.

Cargill. 1995. *Action Plan for the Restructuring of the Windward Islands Banana Industry: Draft Report*. Surrey, UK: Cargill Technical Services Ltd.

————. 1998. *Socio-Economic Impact of Banana Restructuring in St. Lucia (Draft Report)*. Surrey, UK: Cargill Technical Services Ltd.

Charles, George F. 1994. *The History of the Labour Movement in St. Lucia, 1945–1974: A Personal Memoir*. Castries, St. Lucia: Folk Research Centre.

Chayanov, A.V. 1966. *Theory of Peasant Economy*, ed. D. Thorner, B. Kerblay, and R. E. F. Smith. Chicago: American Economics Association.

Clapp, Roger. 1994. "The Moral Economy of the Contract." In *Living Under Contract: Contract Farming and Agrarian Transformation in Sub-Saharan Africa*, ed. Peter D. Little and Michael J.Watts. Madison: University of Wisconsin Press.

Clarke, Edith. 1966. *My Mother Who Fathered Me: A Study of the Family in Three Selected Communities in Jamaica*. London: Allen and Unwin.

Clegg, Peter. 2002. *The Caribbean Banana Trade: From Colonialism to Globalization*. Basingstoke, UK: Palgrave Macmillan.

Cole, Joyce. 1994. "Socio-Political Problems of the Tenurial System in St. Lucia." In *Land Tenure and Development in the Eastern Caribbean: A Symposium*, ed. Frank W. Alleyne. Bridgetown, Barbados: Caribbean Research and Publications, Inc.

Collier, George. 1994. *Basta! Land and the Zapatista Rebellion in Chiapas*. Oakland: Food First Books.

Collins, Jane L. 2003. *Threads: Gender, Labor, and Power in the Global Apparel Industry*. Chicago: University of Chicago Press.

Compton, Jacques. 2004. "On the Question of Visas for Martinique." *The Crusader* (Castries, St. Lucia), 24 January, 41 (55): 7.

Compton, Sir John. 2003. "A Short History of the Banana Industry (Part I)." *The Voice*. (Castries, St. Lucia), 18 December, 115 (8990): 10.

Conway, D. 2002. "Tourism, Agriculture, and the Sustainability of Terrestrial Ecosystems in Small Islands." In *Island Tourism and Sustainable Development*, ed. Y. Apostopolous and D. Gayle. Westport, CT: Praeger.

Cook, Scott. 2004. *Understanding Commodity Cultures: Explorations in Economic Anthropology with Case Studies from Mexico*. Lanham, MD: Rowman and Littlefield.

Cornibert, Bernard. 1980. "Trends in Windward Islands Bananas." Unpublished ms. in Government Documentation Centre, Castries, St. Lucia.

Cowater International Inc. 2000. *Poverty Reduction Fund Social Assessment Study Final Report.* Castries, St. Lucia.

Creed, Gerald W. 2006. "Community as Modern Pastoral." In *The Seductions of Community: Emancipations, Oppressions, Quandaries,* ed. G. W. Creed. Santa Fe: School of American Research Press.

Crichlow, Michaeline. 1994. *Land Use and Land Tenure Patterns in the Windward Islands.* Port of Spain, Trinidad: Caribbean Network for Integrated Rural Development.

Da Breo, D. Sinclair. 1981. *Of Men and Politics: The Agony of St. Lucia.* Castries, St. Lucia: Commonwealth Publishers International.

Davies, Peter N. 1989. *Fyffes and the Banana: A Centenary History, 1888–1988.* London: Athlone.

Deere, Carmen Diana, and Alain De Janvry. 1981. "Demographic and Social Differentiation among Peruvian Peasants." *Journal of Peasant Studies* 8 (3): 335–367.

De Janvry, Alain. 1981. *The Agrarian Question and Reformism in Latin America.* Baltimore: Johns Hopkins University.

De Janvry, Alain and Ann Vandeman. 1987. "Patterns of Proletarianization in Agriculture: An International Comparison." In *Household Economies and Their Transformation,* ed. Morgan Maclachlan. Lanham, MD: University Press of America.

Dole (Dole Food Company). 2006. "Dole Food Company Inc. Announces Settlement of 16 Lawsuits of Banana Workers Claiming Injuries as a Result of Exposure to DBCP." Press Release. 8 December. URL: http://www.dole.com/CompanyInfo/PressRelease/PressReleaseDetail.jsp?ID=1059 (14 August 2007).

Domhoff, G. William. 1983. *Who Rules America Now?* New York: Simon and Schuster.

Dowie, Mark. 1995. *Losing Ground: American Environmentalism at the Close of the 20th Century.* Cambridge: MIT Press.

Downie, Andrew. 2007. "Fair Trade in Bloom." *New York Times,* 2 October, C1–5.

Dubble. 2006. URL: http://www.dubble.co.uk/fairtrade/ (24 October 2006).

Dubois, Laurent. 2004. *A Colony of Citizens: Revolution and Slave Emancipation in the French Caribbean, 1787–1804.* Chapel Hill: University of North Carolina Press.

Durrenberger, E. Paul, ed. 1984. *Chayanov, Peasants, and Economic Anthropology.* New York: Academic.

The Economist. 2006. "Good food?" 381 (8507): 12.

Edelman, Marc. 1999. *Peasants against Globalization: Rural Social Movements in Costa Rica.* Stanford, CA: Stanford University Press.

———. 2001. "Social Movements: Changing Paradigms and Forms of Politics." *Annual Review of Anthropology* 30: 285–317.

Edmunds, Joseph F., and Clayton Shillingford. 2005. "A Program for the Resuscitation of the Windward Islands Banana Industry and Recommendations to Contribute to Its Sustainability in World Trade." URL: http://www.da-academy.org/banana_project.html (21 January 2007).

Escobar, Arturo. 1995. *Encountering Development: The Making and Unmaking of the Third World.* Princeton: Princeton University Press.

Evans, Peter, Dietrich Rueschemeyer, and Theda Skocpol. 1985. "On the Road toward a More Adequate Understanding of the State." In *Bringing the State Back In,* ed. Peter B. Evans, Dietrich Rueschemeyer, and Theda Skocpol. Cambridge: Cambridge University Press.

Fairtrade (Fairtrade Foundation, UK). 2007. *Press Statement.* 24 August. URL: http://www.fairtrade.org.uk/pr240907.htm (8 October 2007).

FAO (Food and Agriculture Organization). 2005. *FAO Banana Statistics 2005.* URL: http://www.fao.org/es/esc/common/ecg/109399_en_BAN_STAT_.06.pdf/ (15 August 2007).

Farmer, Paul. 1996. "On Suffering and Structural Violence: A View from Below." *Daedalus, Journal of American Academy of Arts and Sciences* 125 (1): 261–283.

———. 2003. *Pathologies of Power: Health, Human Rights and the New War on the Poor.* Berkeley: University of California Press.

Feuer, Carl. 1984. *Jamaica and the Sugar Worker Cooperatives: The Politics of Reform.* Boulder, CO: Westview.

Fischer, Edward F., and Peter Benson. 2006. *Broccoli and Desire: Global Connections and Maya Struggles in Postwar Guatemala.* Stanford, CA: Stanford University Press.

Fisher, Carolyn. 2007. "Selling Coffee, or Selling Out?: Evaluating the Consequences of Different Ways to Analyze the Fair Trade System." *Culture and Agriculture* 29 (2): 78–88.

FLO (Fairtrade Labeling Organizations International). 2004. *Impact.* URL: http://www.fairtrade.net/sites/impact/impact.html (8 March 2004).

———. 2006. *News Bulletin.* July. URL: http://www.fairtrade.net/news_bulletin.html (17 September 2006).

———. 2007. *2006/7 Annual Report.* URL: http://www.fairtrade.net/uploads/media/Final_FLO_AR_2007_01.pdf (3 September 2007).

Foley, Michael, and Karl Yambert. 1989. "Anthropology and Theories of the State." In *State, Capital and Rural Society,* ed. Benjamin Orlove, Michael Foley, and Thomas Love. Boulder, CO: Westview.

Fontaine, Thomson. 2007. "Tracing the Diaspora's Involvement in the Development of a Nation: The Case of Dominica." URL: http://www.thedominican.net/articles/diasporaPaper.pdf (27 August 2007).

Foucault, Michel. 1994. "Two Lectures." In *Culture/Power/History: A Reader in Contemporary Social Theory,* ed. Nicholas B. Dirks, Geoff Eley, and Sherry B. Ortner. Princeton: Princeton University Press.

France, L. 1998. "Sustainability and Development in Tourism on the Islands of Barbados, St. Lucia and Dominica." In *Resource Sustainability and Caribbean Development,* ed. Duncan F. M. McGregor, D. Barker, and S. Evans. Kingston, Jamaica: University Press of the West Indies.

Francois, Martinus. 2004. "Before 361 There Was 651." *The Star* (Castries), 11 June, 12–13.

Frank, Thomas. 2004. *What's the Matter with Kansas?: How Conservatives Won the Heart of America.* New York: Metropolitan.

Frederick, Rhonda. 2005. *Colon Man a Come: Mythographies of Panama Canal Migration.* Lanham, MD: Lexington Books.

Freeman, Carla. 2000. *High Tech and High Heels in the Global Economy: Women, Work and Pink-Collar Identities in the Caribbean.* Durham: Duke University Press.

French, Hilary. 2000. *Vanishing Borders: Protecting the Planet in the Age of Globalization.* New York: W.W. Norton.

Fridell, Gavin. 2007. *Fair Trade Coffee: The Prospects and Pitfalls of Market-Driven Social Justice.* Toronto: University of Toronto Press.

Fried, Morton. 1967. *The Evolution of Political Society.* New York: Random House.

Friedemann-Sánchez, Greta. 2006. *Assembling Flowers and Cultivating Homes: Labor and Gender in Colombia.* Lanham, MD: Lexington Books.

Fukuyama, Francis. 1992. *The End of History and the Last Man.* New York: Free Press.

Gallagher, Mike, and Cameron McWhirter. 1998a. "Chiquita Secrets Revealed: Better Banana Program under Attack." *Cincinnati Enquirer.* 3 May. URL: http://www.mindfully.org/Pesticide/chiquita/chiquita06.htm (2 September 2007).

———. 1998b. "Chiquita Secrets Revealed: Island Economies on the Line." *Cincinnati Enquirer,* 3 May. URL: http://www.globalexchange.org/campaigns/bananas/chiquitaSecretsRevealed.html.pf (22 August 2007).

———. 1998c. "Chiquita Secrets Revealed: Unregistered Toxins Used Despite Claims." *Cincinnati Enquirer,* 3 May. URL: http://www.mindfully.org/Pesticide/chiquita/chiquita09.htm (2 September 2007).

Gettman, Jon. 2006. "Marijuana Production in the United States." URL: http://www.drugscience.org/Archive/bcr2/domstprod.html (31 August 2007).

Global Exchange. 2000. "An Open Letter to Starbucks." URL: http://www.globalexchange.org/campaigns/fairtrade/coffee/OpenLetterToStarbucks.html (3 September 2007).

———. 2007. "Starbucks Campaign." URL: http://www.globalexchange.org/campaigns/fairtrade/coffee/starbucks.html (3 September 2007).

Grant, Julie. 2007. "Does Fair Trade Coffee Work?" *The Environment Report*, 2 April. URL: http://environmentreport.org/transcript.php3?story_id=3374 (3 September 2007).

Gray, John. 2003. *Al Qaeda and What It Means to Be Modern*. New York: New Press.

Greider, William. 1997. *One World, Ready or Not: The Manic Logic of Global Capitalism*. New York: Simon and Schuster.

Grier, Jean Heilman. 2005. *Section 301 of the 1974 Trade Act*. Washington, D.C.: US Department of Commerce. URL: http://www.osec.doc.gov/ogc/occic/301.html (3 October 2007).

Grindle, Merilee. 1977. *Bureaucrats, Politicians and Peasants in Mexico*. Berkeley: University of California Press.

———. 1986. *State and Countryside: Development Policy and Agrarian Politics in Latin America*. Baltimore: Johns Hopkins University Press.

Grossman, Lawrence S. 1998. *The Political Ecology of Bananas: Contract Farming, Peasants, and Agrarian Change in the Eastern Caribbean*. Chapel Hill: University of North Carolina Press.

———. 2003. "The St. Vincent Banana Growers' Association, Contract Farming, and the Peasantry." In *Banana Wars: Power, Production and History in the Americas*, ed. Steve Striffler and Mark Moberg. Durham, NC: Duke University Press.

Haas, Jonathan. 1982. *The Evolution of the Prehistoric State*. New York: Columbia University Press.

Harvey, David. 1989. *The Condition of Postmodernity*. Oxford: Basil Blackwell.

Helleiner, Eric. 1994. "From Bretton Woods to Global Finance: A World Turned Upside Down." In *Political Economy and the Changing Global Order*, ed. Richard Stubbs and Geoffrey R. D. Underhill. New York: St. Martin's Press.

Heuman, Gad. 1994. *'The Killing Time:' The Morant Bay Rebellion in Jamaica*. Knoxville: University of Tennessee Press.

Hintzen, Percy. *The Costs of Regime Survival: Racial Mobilization, Elite Domination, and Control of the State in Guyana and Trinidad*. Cambridge University Press.

Holt, Thomas C. 1992. *The Problem of Freedom: Race, Labor and Politics in Jamaica and Britain*. Baltimore: Johns Hopkins University Press.

Hunting Technical Services, Ltd. 1998. *Protecting St. Lucia's Watersheds: Environmental Needs and Management Plans*. Hertfordshire, UK.

Ioannides, D. 2002. "Tourism Development in Mediterranean Islands: Opportunities and Constraints." In *Island Tourism and Sustainable Development*, ed. Yiorgos Apostopolous and Dennis Gayle. Westport, CT: Praeger.

Jaffee, Daniel. 2007. *Brewing Justice: Fair Trade Coffee, Sustainability, and Survival*. Berkeley: University of California Press.

Jameson, Frederic. 1991. *Postmodernism, or the Cultural Logic of Late Capitalism*. Durham: Duke University Press.

Jean, Ignatius. 2004. "New Deception Movement on the Banana Industry." *The Voice* (Castries, St. Lucia), 20 March, 116 (9025): 24–29.

Jessop, Bob. 1999. "Narrating the Future of the National Economy and the National State: Remarks on Remapping Regulation and Reinventing Governance." In *State/Culture: State Formation After the Cultural Turn*, ed. George Steinmetz. Ithaca: Cornell University Press.

Johnson, Allen W., and Timothy Earle. 2000. *The Evolution of Human Societies*. 2nd ed. Stanford, CA: Stanford University Press.

Josie, Peter. 2003. "Banana Blues." *The Crusader* (Castries, St. Lucia), 9 August, 40 (32): 4.

Josling, Tim. 2003. "Bananas and the WTO: Testing the New Dispute Settlement Process." In *Banana Wars: The Anatomy of a Trade Dispute*, ed. Timothy E. Josling and Timothy G. Taylor. Cambridge, MA: CABI Publishing.

Kairi Consultants. 1993. *Development of a Time-Phased Action Programme to Improve the International Competitiveness of the Banana Industry of the Windward Islands*. Report for the Caribbean Development Bank, Barbados.

————. 1996. *Poverty Assessment Report – St. Lucia.* Port of Spain, Trinidad: Kairi Consultants, Ltd.

————. 2000. *Study to Assess the Socio-Economic Impact of Restructuring in the St. Vincent Banana Industry. Draft Final Report.* London: Kairi Consultants Ltd.

Kay, Cristobal. 1974. "Comparative Development of the European Manorial System and the Latin American Hacienda System." *Journal of Peasant Studies* 2 (1): 69–98.

Kepner, Charles. 1936. *Social Aspects of the Banana Industry.* New York: Columbia University Press.

Kerblay, Basile. 1987. "Chayanov and the Theory of Peasant Economics." In *Peasants and Peasant Societies,* ed. Theodor Shanin. Oxford: Blackwell.

King, Thomas. 2004. *Success and Transformation: Collective Marketing and Common Pool Credit in a Belizean Fishing Cooperative: An Empirical Example of a Multi-Tiered Collective Action Problem.* PhD dissertation, Department of Anthropology. Pennsylvania State University.

Klein, Naomi. 2000. *No Logo: Taking Aim at the Brand Bullies.* New York: Picador.

Leahy, Stephen. 2006. "Central America: Workers Left Sterile by Pesticide Seek Justice." *Inter Press News Service,* 12 November. URL: http://www.ipsnews.net/africa/interna.asp?idnews=26266 (14 August 2007).

Lewis, Gordon K. 1968. *The Growth of the Modern West Indies.* New York: Monthly Review Press.

Little, Peter. 1994. "Contract Farming and the Development Question." In *Living Under Contract: Contract Farming and Agrarian Transformation in Sub-Saharan Africa,* ed. Peter D. Little and Michael J. Watts. Madison: University of Wisconsin Press.

Lowenthal, David. 1972. *West Indian Societies.* New York: Oxford University Press.

Lyon, Sarah. 2006. "Migratory Imaginations: The Commodification and Contradictions of Shade Grown Coffee." *Social Anthropology* 14 (3): 377–390.

Marks and Spencer. 2006. *How We Do Business.* URL: http://www2.marksandspencer.com/thecompany/trustyourmands/index.shtml (26 October 2006).

Marshall, Woodville K. 1985. "Emancipation and Labour Relations in Four Windward Islands." In *Abolition and Its Aftermath: The Historical Context, 1790–1916,* ed. D. Richardson. London: Frank Cass.

————. 1993. "Notes on Peasant Development in the West Indies since 1838." In *Caribbean Freedom: Society and Economy From Emancipation to the Present,* ed. Hilary Beckles and Verene Shepherd. Kingston, Jamaica: Ian Randle.

McCann, Thomas. 1976. *An American Company: The Tragedy of United Fruit.* New York: Crown.

Michels, Robert. 1958 [1915]. *Political Parties.* Glencoe: The Free Press.

Midgett, Douglas. 2003. "Spots on the Bananas." Unpublished ms.

————. 2004. "Cocky vs. Staffy: St. Lucian Electoral Politics since Independence." Unpublished ms.

Miliband, Ralph. 1983. "State Power and Class Interests." *New Left Review* 138 (1): 57–68.

Mintz, Sidney. 1974. *Caribbean Transformations.* Chicago: Aldine.

————. 1977. "The So-called World System: Local Initiative and Local Response." *Dialectical Anthropology* 2 (4): 253–270.

The Mirror. 2003. "CARICOM Defy U.S." *The Mirror* (Castries, St. Lucia), 4 July, 9 (42): 1.

Miyoshi, Masao. 1993. "A Borderless World? From Colonialism to Transnationalism and the Decline of the Nation-State." *Critical Inquiry* 19 (summer): 727–751.

Moberg, Mark. 1991. "Citrus and the State: Factions and Class Formation in Rural Belize." *American Ethnologist* 18 (2): 215–233.

————. 1994. "An Agency Model of the State: Contributions and Limitations of Institutional Economics." In *Anthropology and Institutional Economics,* ed. James Acheson. Lanham, MD: University Press of America.

————. 1997. *Myths of Ethnicity and Nation: Immigration, Work, and Identity in the Belize Banana Industry.* Knoxville: University of Tennessee Press.

————. 2002. "Erin Brockovich Doesn't Live Here: Environmental Politics and 'Responsible Care' in Mobile County, Alabama." *Human Organization* 61 (4): 377–389.

————. 2003. "Responsible Men and Sharp Yankees: The United Fruit Company, Resident Elites, and Colonial State in British Honduras." In *Banana Wars: Power, Production and History in the Americas,* ed. Steve Striffler and Mark Moberg. Durham, NC: Duke University Press.

————. 2005. "Fair Trade and Eastern Caribbean Banana Farmers: Rhetoric and Reality in the Anti-Globalization Movement." *Human Organization* 64 (1): 4–15

————. 2006. "Race, Class, and Environmental Justice: Eastern Caribbean Dimensions of a 'Southern' Problem." In *Caribbean and Southern: Transnational Perspectives on the U.S. South,* ed. Helen A. Regis. Athens: University of Georgia Press.

Moberg, Mark, and Tawnya Sesi Moberg. 2005. "The United Houma Nation in the U.S. Congress: Corporations, Communities and the Politics of Federal Acknowledgment." *Urban Anthropology* 34 (1): 85–124.

Moberg, Mark, and Steve Striffler. 2003. "Introduction." In *Banana Wars: Power, Production and History in the Americas,* ed. Steve Striffler and Mark Moberg. Durham, NC: Duke University Press.

Mohanty, Chandra. 2003. "'Under Western Eyes' Revisited: Feminist Solidarity through Anti-capitalist Struggles." *Signs* 28 (2): 499–537.

Moore, Geoff. 2004. "The Fair Trade Movement: Parameters, Issues, and Future Research." *Journal of Business Ethics* 53 (1): 73–86.

Murray, Douglas L., and Laura T. Raynolds. 2000. "Alternative Trade in Bananas: Obstacles and Opportunities for Progressive Social Change in the Global Economy." *Agriculture and Human Values* 17 (1): 65–75.

Myers, Gordon. 2004. *Banana Wars: The Price of Free Trade. A Caribbean Perspective.* London: Zed Books.

Nader, Laura. 1974. "Up the Anthropologist: Perspectives Gained from Studying Up." In *Reinventing Anthropology,* ed. Dell Hymes. New York: Vintage.

Nash, June. 1981. "Ethnographic Aspects of the World Capitalist System." *Annual Review of Anthropology* 10: 393–424.

————. 1994. "Global Integration and Subsistence Insecurity." *American Anthropologist* 96 (1): 7–30.

NDIC (National Drug Intelligence Center). 2005. *National Drug Threat Assessment 2005 Summary Report.* Washington, D.C.: US Department of Justice. URL: http://www.usdoj.gov/ndic/pubs11/13846/marijuana.htm (31 August 2007).

NERA. 2003. *Banana Exports from the Caribbean since 1992.* London: National Economic Research Associates.

The News. 1998a. "Ganja Farmers Against Eradication" *The News* (Kingstown, St. Vincent), 20 November, 487: 1.

————. 1998b. "Marijuana Farmers Send Protest Letter to Clinton." *The News* (Kingstown, St. Vincent), 4 December, 489: 1.

————. 1998c. "150,000 Marijuana Trees Destroyed." *The News* (Kingstown, St. Vincent), 11 December, 450: 1–2.

Noel, Jeana. 2004. EUREP-GAP: Challenges and Opportunities." *Focus* (Kingstown, St. Vincent), 2 (1): 5.

Nurse, Keith, and Wayne Sandiford. 1995. *Windwards Islands Bananas: Challenges and Options under the Single European Market.* Kingston, Jamaica: Friedrich Ebert Stiftung.

OAS (Organization of American States). 1991. *Integrated Land Development: The Case of the Mabouya Valley in St. Lucia.* Washington, D.C.: Executive Secretariat for Economic and Social Affairs.

————. 1995. *Background Information for Project Entitled: Technological Modernization of the Banana Industry in the Caribbean.* Castries: Inter-American Institute for Cooperation in Agriculture.

Ochoa, Enrique C. 2000. *Feeding Mexico: The Political Uses of Food since 1910.* Wilmington, Delaware: SR Books.

O'Nions, James. 2006. "Fairtrade and Global Justice." URL: http://www.grain.org/seedling/ ?id=430 (1 September 2006).

Oxford English Dictionary (OED). 2007. "Greenwash." URL: http://dictionary.oed.com.libproxy2 .usouthal.edu/ (1 October 2007).

Paggi, M., and T. Spreen. 2003. "Overview of the World Banana Market." In *Banana Wars: The Anatomy of a Trade Dispute,* ed. Timothy E. Josling and Timothy G. Taylor. Cambridge, MA: CABI Publishing.

Patullo, Polly. 1996a. *Last Resorts: The Cost of Tourism in the Caribbean.* London: Latin American Bureau.

———. 1996b. "Green Crime, Green Redemption: The Environment and Ecotourism in the Caribbean." In *Green Guerrillas: Environmental Conflicts and Initiatives in Latin America and the Caribbean,* ed. Helen Collinson. London: Latin American Bureau.

Polanyi, Karl. 1957 [orig. 1944]. *The Great Transformation.* Boston: Beacon Press.

Poulantzas, Nicos. 1978. *State, Power, Socialism.* London: New Left Books.

Purcell, Trevor. 1993. *Banana Fallout: Class, Color, and Culture among West Indians in Costa Rica.* Los Angeles: UCLA Center for Afro-American Studies.

Radio St. Lucia. 2003. *Evening News Report.* 19 August.

Raynolds, Laura T. 2000. "Re-embedding Global Agriculture: The International Organic and Fair Trade Movements." *Agriculture and Human Values* 17 (3): 297–309.

———. 2003. "The Global Banana Trade." In *Banana Wars: Power, Production and History in the Americas,* eds. Steve Striffler and Mark Moberg. Durham, NC: Duke University Press.

Reynolds, Anderson. 2004. *The Struggle for Survival: An Historical, Political, and Socioeconomic Perspective on St. Lucia.* Vieux Fort, St. Lucia: Jako Books.

Richardson, Bonham. 1997. *Economy and Environment in the Caribbean: Barbados and the Windwards in the Late 1800s.* Gainesville: University of Florida Press.

Riisgaard, Lone. 2004. *The IUF/COLSIBA – CHIQUITA Framework Agreement: A Case Study.* International Labor Organization Working Paper No. 94. URL: http://www.ilo.org/public/ english/employment/multi/download/wp94.pdf (10 September 2006).

Rockwell, Paul. 1995. "The Right Has a Dream: Martin Luther King as an Opponent of Affirmative Action." *FAIR: Fairness and Accuracy in Reporting* (May/June). URL: http://www.fair .org/index.php?page=1292 (1 September 2007).

Romalis, Rochelle. 1975. "Economic Change and Peasant Political Consciousness in the Commonwealth Caribbean." *Journal of Commonwealth and Comparative Politics* 13 (3): 225–241.

Roseberry, William. 1985. "Something About Peasants, History, and Capitalism." *Critique of Anthropology* 5 (3): 69–76.

———. 1996. "The Rise of Yuppie Coffees and the Re-imagination of Class in the United States." *American Anthropologist* 98 (4): 762–775.

Rosegrant, S. 1999. *Banana Wars: Challenges to the European Union's Banana Regime.* Kennedy School of Government Case Study. Cambridge: Harvard University.

Rowbotham, Michael. 1998. *The Grip of Death: A Study of Modern Money, Debt Slavery and Destructive Economics.* Charlbury, UK: Jon Carpenter.

Rubenstein, Hymie. 1999. "Ganja and Globalization: A Caribbean Case Study." *Global Development Studies* 1 (1–2): 233–250.

Sahlins, Marshall. 1972. *Stone Age Economics.* New York: Aldine.

Sainsbury's. 2006. URL: http://www.sainsburys.cok.uk/social/ (12 September 2006).

Sasidharan, V., and B. Thapa. 2002. "Sustainable Coastal and Marine Tourism Development: A Hobson's Choice?" In *Island Tourism and Sustainable Development,* ed. Yiorgos Apostopolous and Dennis Gayle. Westport, CT: Praeger.

Schumpeter, Joseph A. 1975 [orig. 1942]. *Capitalism, Socialism and Democracy.* New York: Harper.

Scott, James C. 1998. *Seeing Like a State: How Certain Schemes to Improve the Human Condition Have Failed*. New Haven, CT: Yale University Press.

Sealy, Theodore, and Herbert Hart. 1984. *Jamaica's Banana Industry: A History of the Banana Industry with Particular Reference to the Part Played by the Jamaica Banana Producers Association, Ltd.* Kingston: The Jamaica Banana Producers Association.

Service, Elman. 1975. *Origins of the State and Civilization*. New York: Norton.

Shanin, Teodor. 1972. *The Awkward Class: Political Sociology of Peasantry in a Developing Society; Russia 1910–1925*. Oxford University Press.

———. 1986. "Chayanov's Message: Illuminations, Miscomprehensions, and the Contemporary 'Development Theory.'" In *A.V. Chayanov on the Theory of Peasant Economy*, ed. Daniel Thorner, Basile Kerblay, and R. E. F. Smith. Madison: University of Wisconsin Press.

Sharma, Aradhana and Akhil Gupta. 2006. "Introduction: Rethinking Theories of the State in an Age of Globalization," In *The Anthropology of the State: A Reader*, ed. Aradhana Sharma and Akhil Gupta. Oxford: Blackwell.

Sklair, Leslie. 1998. "Social Movements and Global Capitalism." In *The Cultures of Globalization*, ed. Frederic Jameson and Masao Miyoshi. Durham, NC: Duke University Press.

Skocpol, Theda. 1979. *States and Social Revolutions*. Cambridge: Cambridge University Press.

Slocum, Karla. 1996. *Producing Under a Globalizing Economy: The Intersection of Flexible Production and Local Autonomy in the Work, Lives, and Actions of St. Lucian Banana Growers*. PhD dissertation, University of Florida.

———. 2006. *Free Trade and Freedom: Neoliberalism, Place and Nation in the Caribbean*. Ann Arbor: University of Michigan Press.

Smith, Carol. 1984. "Does a Commodity Economy Enrich the Few While Ruining the Masses? Differentiation Among Petty Commodity Producers in Guatemala." *Journal of Peasant Studies* 11 (1): 60–95.

Soluri, John. 2005. *Banana Cultures: Agriculture, Consumption, and Environmental Change in Honduras and the United States*. Austin: University of Texas Press.

Starbucks. 2006. URL: http://www.starbucks.com/aboutus/fairtrade.asp (7 September 2006).

Stecklow, Steve, and Erin White. 2004. "What Price Virtue? At Some Retailers, 'Fair Trade' Carries a Very High Cost." *Wall Street Journal*, 8 June, P A.

St. Lucia (Government of St. Lucia). 1973. *Report of the Commission of Inquiry into the Prolonged Stoppage of Work in the Cul-de-Sac and Roseau Group of Estates during the Months of April and May, 1973*. Printed in Guyana for the Government of St. Lucia.

———. 1980. *An Inquiry into the Banana Industry: Interim Report*. Castries: Government of St. Lucia.

———. 1987. *St. Lucia Model Farms Ltd: Roseau Valley Smallholder Crop Diversification Project, St. Lucia, 1982–1987*. Castries.

———. 1990. *A Review of the Banana Industry of St. Lucia, Prepared for the Government of St. Lucia*. Castries: Banana Review Committee.

———. 1991. *St. Lucia Population Census: 1990*. Castries.

———. 1995–2003. *Crime Statistics* (annual reports). Castries: Royal St. Lucia Police.

———. 2001a. *St. Lucia Banana Industry Strategy Task Force: Final Report*. Castries: Government of St. Lucia Banana Industry Task Force.

———. 2001b. *St. Lucia Population Census: 2000*. Preliminary Results. Castries.

———. 2002. *Survey of Banana Agro-Ecological Zones*. Cul de Sac, St. Lucia: Banana Emergency Recovery Unit, Ministry of Agriculture.

———. 2003. *National Biodiversity Strategy and Action Plan (NBSAP)*. Castries.

Stovall, J. G., and D. E. Hathaway. 2003. "US Interests in the Banana Trade Controversy." In *Banana Wars: The Anatomy of a Trade Dispute*, ed. Timothy E. Josling and Timothy G.Taylor. Cambridge, MA: CABI Publishing.

Tangermann, S. 2003. "The European Common Banana Policy." In *Banana Wars: The Anatomy of a Trade Dispute,* ed. Timothy E. Josling and Timothy G. Taylor. Cambridge, MA: CABI Publishing.

Taylor, J. Gary and Patricia J. Scharlin. 2004. *Smart Alliance: How a Global Corporation and Environmental Activists Transformed a Tarnished Brand.* New Haven: Yale University Press.

Taylor, Tim. 2003. "Evolution of the Banana Multinationals." In *Banana Wars: The Anatomy of a Trade Dispute,* ed. Timothy E. Josling and Timothy G. Taylor. Cambridge, MA: CABI Publishing.

Ten Thousand Villages. 2007. "Fair Trade Sales Increase around the World!" URL: http://www .tenthousandvillages.ca/cgiin/category.cgi?type=store&item=pageZAAAB45&template= fullpage-en&category=news (2 September 2007).

Tesco. 2006. *Tesco Corporate Information.* URL: http://www.tesco.com/corporateinfo/ (23 August 2006).

Thomson, Robert. 1987. *Green Gold: Bananas and Dependency in the Eastern Caribbean.* London: Latin American Bureau.

Tiffin, Pauline. 2002. "A Chocolate Coated Case for Alternative International Business." *Development in Practice* 12 (3–4): 383–397.

Trouillot, Michel-Rolph. 1988. *Peasants and Capital: Dominica in the World Economy.* Baltimore: Johns Hopkins University Press.

ULG. 1975. *The Windward Islands Banana Industry Consultancy Draft Final Report.* London: ULG Consultants, Ltd.

UN (United Nations). 2003. *Caribbean Drug Trends: 2001–2002.* Bridgetown, Barbados: United Nations Office on Drugs and Crime, Caribbean Regional Office. URL: http://www.unodc .org/pdf/barbados/caribbean_drug-trends_2001-2002.pdf

US (United States of America). 2005. "United States 'Disappointed' with EU Banana Tariff Proposal." Washington, D.C.: United States of America Department of State. URL: http:// usinfo.state.gov/xarchives/display.html?p=washfile-english&y=2005&m=December&x=2 0051202182447aawajuk0.133465 (6 October 2007).

Van de Kasteele, Adelien, and Myriam van der Stichele. 2005. "Update on the Banana Chain: The Macro-Economics of the Banana Trade." Paper presented at the International Banana Conference, Brussels, Belgium.

Vincent, Andrew. 1987. *Theories of the State.* Oxford: Basil Blackwell.

Vitalis, David. 1999. "Bananas – The War Will Go On." *The Mirror.* (Castries, St. Lucia), 22 October: 5.

The Voice. 1996. "If Bananas Disappear People Will Have to Produce Marijuana and Ship It North." *The Voice* (Castries, St. Lucia), 15 August: 5.

———. 2002. "Drugs in Our Banana Boxes." *The Voice* (Castries, St. Lucia), 7 December, 114 (8854): 1.

———. 2003a. "St. Lucia is Chief Dealer in Cocaine." *The Voice* (Castries, St. Lucia), 8 April, 115 (8899): 1.

———. 2003b. "SLHTA President Blasts Cruise Sector." *The Voice* (Castries, St. Lucia), 24 May, 115 (8908): 2.

———. 2003c. "Did the PM Apologize to Pres. Bush?" *The Voice* (Castries, St. Lucia), 7 June, 115 (8914): 4.

———. 2003d. "UWP Leader Emancipation Day Statement." *The Voice* (Castries, St. Lucia), 2 August, 115 (8914): 5.

———. 2003e. "PM Anthony to Meet President Bush." *The Voice* (Castries, St. Lucia), 23 September, 115 (8956): 9.

———. 2004a. "Statement by Mr. Ausbert d'Auvergne, Political Leader, on the Banana Industry." *The Voice* (Castries, St. Lucia), 16 March, 116 (9023): 3.

———. 2004b. "No Cut Strike? `I Will Go Along,' Says Josie.'" *The Voice* (Castries, St. Lucia), 23 March, 166 (9026): 1.

Wallerstein, Immanuel. 1980. *The Modern World System I: Capitalist Agriculture and the Origins of the Modern World Economy in the Sixteenth Century.* New York: Academic.

Watts, Michael. 1990. "Peasants Under Contract: Agro-Food Complexes in the Third World." In *The Food Question: Profits versus People,* ed. Henry Bernstein, Ben Crow, Maureen Mackintosh, and Charlotte Martin. London: Earthscan.

Wayne, Rick. 1987. *It'll be Alright in the Morning.* Castries, St. Lucia: Star Publishing Co.

———. 2002. *Foolish Virgins.* Castries, St. Lucia: Star Publishing Co.

Weekes, Tarik. 2004. "Banana Fight-Back: Industry Leaders in Windwards Come Up with Revival Plan." *The Mirror* (Castries, St. Lucia), 18 June, 10 (39): 5.

Williams, Eric E. 1944. *Capitalism and Slavery.* Chapel Hill: University of North Carolina Press.

Wilson, Patrick J. 1995. *Crab Antics: A Caribbean Case Study of the Conflict between Reputation and Respectability.* Prospect Heights, IL: Waveland.

WINFA (Windward Islands Farmers Association). 2003. "Fairtrade in the Windward Islands." St. Vincent (mimeo).

Wittfogel, Karl. 1957. *Oriental Despotism.* New Haven, CT: Yale University Press.

Wolf, Eric R. 1969. *Peasant Wars of the Twentieth Century.* New York: Harper Colophon.

———. 1982. *Europe and the People without History.* Berkeley: University of California Press.

Young, David P. 1993. *All A We A One: A Caribbean Scrapbook.* New York: Friendship Press.

INDEX

ACP (African, Caribbean and Pacific)
    countries, 70–71, 73–74, 78–82,
    85–87, 128n. 9
Adrien, Peter, 27, 29
Afro-Caribbean
    attitudes toward land, 26, 42, 141
    culture and identity, 5, 41, 202
    personal autonomy, 41–42
    residents of St. Lucia, 23
Age
    of banana growers, 43, 65, 141–42,
        144, 152n. 18, 195, 206, 219n.
        11
    of emigrants, 150, 152n. 17
    of Fair Trade vs. conventional
        growers, 196, 209–11
    and language use, 40n. 1
Agency Model of the State, 10, 13–14,
    39, 92
    See also politics
Anthony, Kenny D., 87, 109, 113–14,
    118–19, 122–23, 127
Appadurai, Arjun, 181–82

Banana Act, 56, 60, 92
Barth, Frederic, 102, 110–11
BERU (Banana Emergency Recovery
    Unit), 120–21, 123, 132, 134, 142,
    209, 217, 219n. 10
Banana Growers' Associations (BGAs)
    colonial promotion of, 32
    on other islands, 47–48, 76, 118,
        128n. 7, 133–34, 151n. 1, 202,
        225
    See also St. Lucia Banana Growers'
        Association

Banana industry
    Caribbean vs. Latin American, 71,
        77, 84, 93n. 1, 219n. 10
    colonial policy toward, 32, 74
    and Compton government, 35,
        38–39, 108
    decline of, 4, 39, 55, 57, 87, 90, 123,
        130–31, 137, 140, 156, 158,
        167, 169, 172, 205, 208, 216
    politics, 15, 24, 38–39, 95, 107–9,
        114, 116, 126, 131
    privatization of, 60, 91, 113–14, 117,
        127
    and technological change, 4, 89, 91,
        118, 120ff., 131, 135, 208–9,
        217
    and trade policy, 77ff., 85, 88, 192,
        218
Banana prices, 10, 37, 50, 55–56, 58,
    71–72, 74, 75, 77–82, 87, 88,
    91–92, 95–96, 98–99, 108–9,
    115–17, 126, 130–2, 135, 138,
    140–2
Banana production, 31, 32, 46–47, 49,
    52, 68–71, 74–75, 88, 91, 93n. 6,
    96, 130, 134, 158, 162
    certification, 58, 197
    costs of, 45, 48, 56–58, 60, 77–79, 87,
        95, 126, 131–33, 143–44, 200,
        202, 220, 225
    Fair Trade, 196–197, 202, 206, 212,
        214–16, 225
    intercropping, 50
    loss of autonomy in, 47, 56ff., 131,
        226
    pests, 48, 121